Web Advertising and Marketing by Design

Mary Jo Fahey

PUBLISHED BY
Microsoft Press
A Division of Microsoft Corporation
One Microsoft Way
Redmond, WA 98052-6399

Library of Congress Cataloging-in-Publication Data
Fahey, Mary Jo.
    Web Advertising and Marketing by Design / Mary Jo Fahey.
        p.   cm.
    Includes index.
    ISBN 1-57231-836-8
    1. Internet advertising.   2. Internet marketing.   I. Title.
HF6146.I58F34   1998
    658.8'00285'4678--dc21   98-9350
                                                     CIP

Printed and bound in the United States of America.

1 2 3 4 5 6 7 8 9   WCWC   3 2 1 0 9 8

Distributed to the book trade in Canada by Macmillan of Canada, a division of Canada Publishing Corporation.

A CIP catalogue record for this book is available from the British Library.

Microsoft Press books are available through booksellers and distributors worldwide. For further information about international editions, contact your local Microsoft Corporation office, or contact Microsoft Press International directly at fax (425) 936-7329. Visit our Web site at mspress.microsoft.com.

Credits appear on page x, which constitutes an extension of the copyright page.

Macintosh and TrueType fonts are registered trademarks of Apple Computer, Inc. FrontPage, Microsoft, Microsoft Press, Verdana, Windows, and Windows NT are registered trademarks and Expedia, Mungo Park, Outlook, and Sidewalk are trademarks of Microsoft Corporation. Other product and company names mentioned herein may be the trademarks of their respective owners.

Acquisitions Editor: Kim Fryer
Project Editor: Jenny Moss Benson
Technical Editor: Steve Sagman

Contents

Part 2   **Generating Web Traffic**

Part 4   Direct Marketing

Acknowledgments

This book was made possible due to the shared ideas, designs, software, and creative energy of a large group of people. Many thanks to: Kim Fryer, acquisitions editor; Lucinda Rowley, managing editor; Jenny Benson, project editor; and Bill Teel, publishing support at Microsoft Press; Steve Sagman, technical editor and desktop publisher; and Claire Horne, literary agent at the Moore Literary Agency.

Many thanks also to Travis Anton of BoxTop Software for GIFmation; Carol Braverman, author of *Fractal Design Painter 5*, published by MIS Press, and *The Retouching Handbook:Digital Image Correction with Photoshop*, published by IDG Books Worldwide, for in-depth information about color palettes; Peggy Burton of Burton Communications for her insights on marketing and interactivity; Matt Dominianni of MetaPlay for Argle; Curtis Eberhardt for his GIF animation; Michael Floyd, editor-in-chief of *Web Techniques*, for his advice on how to approach a magazine editor with a story idea; Kathy Forer of the New York VRMLSIG for her work on the VRMLSIG Web site; John A. Junod of Ipswitch for creating WS_FTP Pro; David Karp, Internet programs manager of Ipswitch; Robert Liu of Best Business Solutions for the online Color Editor tool; Joe Maissel of Sound Wire, Inc., for information about electronic payments; Jan Mallis of blitcom for Bliss.com; Jim Manley for his knowledge of marketing on the Internet; Paul Marino of MetaPlay for his animated VRML logo; Mark Pesce of blitcom for Bliss.com; Larry Rosenthal of Cube Productions for his innovative

Starbase C3 site; John Scott, Melissa Scott, and Nick Bodor of alt.coffee for their delightful Internet café in New York City; Alex Shamson of VRmill.com for his artwork and his loyal support of VRML; Dave Teich for the form•z and Electric Image Users' Group and his 3-D GIF animation; Marc Thorner of ThornerGraphics for Pegasus and his in-depth knowledge of motion graphics; and John D. Young, director of creative services at New York's Poppe Tyson, for his thoughtful talks about the real world of interactive advertising.

Additional Credits

Images of Web pages and/or individual files therein appear courtesy of Joseph Maissel of Sound Wire, Inc.; Larry Rosenthal of Cube Productions, Inc. All images, trademarks, and designs related to STARBASE C3 are the property of Cube Productions, Inc., www.cube3.com; John Scott of alt.coffee, Inc.; Michael Floyd of Miller Freeman, Inc. All appropriate credit to *Web Techniques*; ThornerGraphics, Inc. All images © appropriate copyright holders, 1998 ThornerGraphics, Inc.; VRmill, Inc. The entire contents of the VRmill.com Web site, including all documents and designs, are the exclusive property of VRmill, Inc., and Alex Shamson.

Cube 3-D animation still appears courtesy of David Teich, © Dave Teich, Mind of the Machine, mindmachine@mindspring.com. Images and files of alien animation appear courtesy of Curtis Eberhardt. Images of Color Editor appear courtesy of Robert Lui, Best Business Solutions. Images of Web pages, the Argle character, and the MetaPlay logo appear courtesy of Matt Dominianni, MetaPlay. Images of WS_FTP Pro appear courtesy of Ipswitch Inc. WS_FTP ™ Professional by Ipswitch Inc. Information on GIFmation software appears courtesy of Travis Anton of BoxTop Software, Inc. The image of Bliss.com appears courtesy of blitcom. Copyright © 1998, blitcom Llc. All rights reserved.

Introduction

Whether you are planning a Web site to promote a record label, a retail storefront, or your resume, marketing will motivate people to buy what you're selling. The Internet will add fuel to your marketing strategy because it's an inexpensive medium that anyone can tap. This book presents do-it-yourself marketing strategies and shows you how to implement them on the Web with easy-to-use software such as Microsoft FrontPage, Microsoft Word, Microsoft Outlook, and Microsoft Image Composer.

What Is Marketing and Why Is It Important?

Marketing is the broad spectrum of tools used to bring buyers and sellers close, with an underlying objective of influencing sales. Those sales occur in an increasingly competitive market in which the development of new business and the retention of existing business are fundamental focuses. Although the underlying objective of marketing is to influence sales, it's also to develop new business and retain existing customers. To succeed in business today everyone must learn to market and sell.

Marketing on an Interactive Web

For several decades, print, radio, and television have been the three principle mass-market media that businesses have used for reaching consumers. *Mass*-market refers to the very large populations that these media serve. Now, magazine editors have begun calling the Web the fourth mass-market medium.

Advertising is valuable for building a brand. The objective of traditional advertising is to build brand awareness. Advertising communicates information about a product's specific attributes to prospective customers. With an identity, the product is more likely to be purchased by consumers. According to marketers at New York's Poppe Tyson, an interactive advertising agency, most major companies have accepted the Web as a valuable new medium for brand building.

Intervista's 3-D business reporting software. Intervista has created WorldChart business reporting software, which harnesses 3-D graphics and data visualization to create Internet-ready reports with imported Microsoft Excel, Microsoft Money, and Microsoft Investor data. Through a series of templates and wizards, WorldChart converts data into Internet-standard 2-D and 3-D representations. WorldChart is also compatible with Microsoft FrontPage, and this makes it easy for users to transfer their visualization to a Web page. WorldChart is approximately $100 and can be purchased from the Intervista Web site at www.intervista.com/worldchart.

Although the Web may not yet be mature as a marketing medium, it has the potential to offer benefits not found in any other mass-market medium. It's inexpensive, it's often more immediate, and it's interactive.

Unlike newspapers, magazines, or most television programs, Web pages can be updated instantly to offer new information in seconds. Some Web marketers see a relationship between the speed with which consumers get information and the faster purchasing decisions they make. This conclusion is based on research studies that indicate that most Web users visit home pages to gather product information.

Every element on a Web page that consumers activate with a mouse click or a key press offers interactivity. Anyone who has surfed the Web has used text links, button links, e-mail links, and fill-out forms, for example. Businesses gain from the exchange when customers use such links and forms to interact with marketers and even participate in live Internet events. In the short time that television news and newspapers have experimented with the Web, for example, they have discovered a huge response on their Web sites from audiences eager to contribute responses to news events. Although news organizations are not technically marketers, their new Web outlets are valuable to marketers because of the high-traffic nature of news sites.

Electronic commerce, or e-commerce, offers a more sophisticated form of interactivity than links and forms. While online, Web users can buy products, both physical and digital, with an instant and secure transaction that eliminates the need to send a check or phone in a credit card number. The Web offers marketers the opportunity to extend commerce into cyberspace, using direct marketing to sell their products directly to consumers. Electronic commerce is expected to burgeon this year as large, established retailers set up sites on the Web.

The advertising and marketing industries that have grown up with print, radio, and television in the past five decades have only just started to shape the Web. As professional marketers study what Web users want, innovative marketing strategies will evolve and make today's success stories seem small compared to tomorrow's marketing breakthroughs.

A marketing campaign.
An online marketing campaign requires identifying a target market, identifying where the target market can be found on the Internet, and identifying a message and events that you can use to deliver that message to the market. Like any media campaign, an online marketing campaign requires establishing campaign goals and strategic planning to deliver a message several times to the same people. Examples of campaign goals might include an increase in Web traffic and in brand awareness. Marketing vehicles that deliver the message can overlap. For example, you can simultaneously use banner ads, publicity, and traditional direct mail to deliver a message to the same market.

Adapting Marketing Tools to the Web

Although there are innovative new marketing functions already emerging on the Web that have no parallel in the world of conventional marketing communications, this book shows how traditional marketing and communications tools can be adapted to fit the Web. History suggests that adapting traditional practices often eases the transition to new practices. After all, the first automobiles were called horseless carriages, and the first skyscrapers were built to look like stone buildings.

The traditional mix of marketing communications activities is illustrated in the following pie chart. Adapting four of these activities to the Web is the subject of the book's four parts. These parts are numbered within the slices of the pie.

Part 1, "Targeting the Media," covers gaining publicity for your product or service. Part 2, "Generating Web Traffic," covers promoting your site with advertising. Part 3, "Providing Customer Service," covers increasing repeat business and satisfying customers. Part 4, "Direct Marketing," covers selling directly to consumers.

Guerrilla Marketing Online Weapons. *Guerrilla Marketing Online Weapons,* by Jay Conrad Levinson and Charles Rubin, is a helpful guide for businesses wanting to define and refine their Web marketing effort.

***Fast Company* magazine.** *Fast Company* is a publication focused on preparing businesses for the challenges of today's rapid business cycles (www.fastcompany.com).

The Book's Step-by-Step Web Projects

The projects in this book have been created by professional graphic designers, writers, illustrators, and 3-D animators. You can follow the step-by-step numbered procedures in each chapter to re-create each project for yourself.

While Chapter 1 introduces a technique for building a Web site's foundation and planning its navigation, the underlying theme of Chapters 2, 3, and 4 is publishing the elements of a press kit on a Web site. These chapters cover the construction of a fact sheet, a backgrounder, and a press release. Chapter 4 also introduces the concept of sending a pitch letter with a story idea rather than a press release. Mike Floyd, the editor-in-chief of *Web Techniques* magazine, has contributed valuable tips for writers and publicists who want to pitch story ideas to magazines.

Generating Web traffic is the goal of the projects in Chapters 5 and 6. Chapter 5 focuses on how to optimize you Web site's placement in search engine results, and Chapter 6 teaches how to create an animated banner ad. Techniques that cause your site to be found when people search the Web can increase your viewership. When banner ads are placed at high-volume sites on the Web, they can also drive Web traffic to your site. Banner ads are also a strong tool for building brand awareness, an aspect of traditional advertising.

Chapters 7 and 8 demonstrate how you can use the Web to provide customer service—traditionally regarded as a post-purchase marketing function. Customer service includes tangible activities that you can use to retain existing customers, increase a customer's business, or do both. In Chapter 7, the services are an information page and an online registration form that customers can easily use to reserve space at an online, improvisational comedy show. Chapter 8 demonstrates how you can use a newsletter on the Web as a vehicle for providing product information, driving traffic to your site, and reminding customers of your product line.

Chapter 9 introduces direct marketing on the Web with a storefront and catalog. Analysts who watch trends in ad sales on the Web see the present emphasis on consumer product ads as the start of an electronic commerce

Employee Web seminars. Few employees will investigate your firm's Web marketing efforts themselves. Market your Web site in house by sponsoring weekly employee seminars. Buy lunch or breakfast and invite local Internet vendors as guest speakers. Once a month, collect employee feedback about the seminar content and ask for suggestions.

Marketing is a numbers game. The more you market, the more you will get results. Try to keep your marketing effort moving. Plan ahead and write pitch letters to magazine editors at least four times a year. Each time you write pitch letters, try to send at least 12 letters. Never view a lack of response as a failure. Just continue to send your letters. Eventually, you will get results.

wave. The example in Chapter 9 shows how it's possible to sell digital goods without owning a commerce server. Web entrepreneurs Larry Rosenthal and Joe Maissel have worked out the details for selling Larry's 3-D spaceships on the Web using CyberCash and Microsoft Wallet software. Their solution puts storefront sales of digital products within the reach of anyone who wants to sell products on line—including writers, illustrators, 3-D artists, and musicians.

Project List	
Chapter	Project
1	Planning a Web Site (Targeting the Media)
2	Fact Sheet (Targeting the Media)
3	Backgrounder (Targeting the Media)
4	Press Release (Targeting the Media)
5	Optimizing Placement in Search Engine Results (Generating Web Traffic)
6	Animated Banner Ad (Generating Web Traffic)
7	Registration Form (Customer Service)
8	Newsletter (Customer Service)
9	Storefront with a Catalog (Direct Marketing)

Guide to the Software Used in This Book

To demonstrate the ways a range of products can be used to create Web pages, an assortment of Microsoft software and utilities from other companies is used throughout the book. Use the chart on the next page as a guide to selecting a project according to the software products it highlights.

Tip icons used in this book. Margin tips provided in the book's left margin contain advice, resources on the Internet in the form of URLs, and general interest notes that supplement the book's text.

General tips. These provide useful ancillary information.

Technical tips. These provide information about the software programs covered in the chapters.

Writing tips. These include recommendations for working with words, and sources for writers' guides.

Software Used in This Book		
Chapter	Topic	Software
1	Planning a Site's Structure	Image Composer, FrontPage 98, and Internet Explorer
2	Fact Sheet	Word 97, Image Composer, and Internet Explorer
3	Backgrounder	FrontPage 98
4	Press Release	Outlook, FrontPage 98, and the Microsoft Web Publishing Wizard
5	Optimizing Placement in Search Engine Results	Word 97, Internet Explorer, and WS_FTP Pro
6	Animated Banner Ad	GIFmation and Internet Explorer
7	Registration Form	FrontPage 98, WS_FTP Pro, and Internet Explorer
8	Newsletter	Word 97 and BBS Color Editor
9	Storefront with a Catalog	FrontPage 98

Where to Find Art and Text Files

Artists and Web entrepreneurs Larry Rosenthal, Marc Thorner, Joe Maissel, Alex Shamson, Curtis Eberhardt, Paul Marino, Matt Dominianni, and John Scott have generously made available the text and graphics files that you will need to create the projects in this book. You will find references to these files next to the procedures that require them, along with instructions you can use to find them on the following page on the Microsoft Press Web site: mspress. microsoft.com/mspress/products/1576.

PART 1

Targeting the Media

Web site navigation bars are popular mechanisms for simplifying navigation. You can create navigation bars with text links or button graphics. You can also offer users an image map, a graphic that they can click to choose a destination within the site.

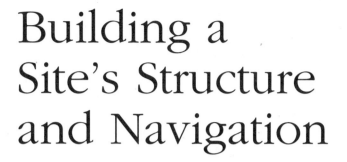

Building a Site's Structure and Navigation

Animated VRML logo. The animated VRML logo for the NYVRMLSIG Web site was created by designer and animator Paul Marino (havoc@interport. net). Paul has won an Emmy for his television graphics and he's an early pioneer in the field of VRML 2.0 animation.

The Web is a system of linked pages that has no beginning and no end. You can't anticipate how a visitor will navigate a Web site so you need to plan links on every page to major content areas.

The subject of this chapter is a prototype, an empty, preliminary site without content that is based on a design for the New York VRML Special Interest Group (www.nyvrmlsig.com) created by graphic designer Kathy Forer (kforer@ interport.net). For this project, you will begin the planning process as Forer did, by sketching a site map on paper. Then you will use Microsoft FrontPage 98 to transfer your ideas to a simple, working prototype that contains only text links.

After the text links are in place and you've used them to test the navigation of the site, you can begin replacing them with button graphics and adding the rest of the content for the pages.

VRML browsing and Internet Explorer. VRML, or Virtual Reality Modeling Language, is an Internet language that describes 3-D space on the Internet. Microsoft Internet Explorer has a built-in VRML browser created by InterVista. The Microsoft VRML 2.0 Viewer is an Internet Explorer 4.0 add-on. Visit www. microsoft.com/ie/ie40/download/addon.htm.

Creating signage for your site. Navigation bars on every page of a Web site make navigating easy. High-profile sites that use this simple strategy include Microsoft, Adobe, and Mercedes-USA.

In this chapter, you will create some simple button graphics with Image Composer, Microsoft's tool for creating Web graphics, which is included with FrontPage 98. As you will see, Image Composer is an ideal tool for creating button graphics because it treats each graphic as a sprite, an individual, discrete element. Sprites remain discrete even when they are combined into compositions, so they can be edited individually at any time.

Building a Site Foundation

Because most of the projects in this part of the book are related to the News area of a Web site, the text-only prototype you build in this chapter can be used again and again. You can save it and use it again each time you need to start building a site.

Making Site Maps

Take the time to sketch a site map on paper, perhaps with an inverted tree, a popular format used to represent the structure of a hypermedia system. The process forces you to organize the content of a site into major areas. The tree that you draw in this chapter will contain five areas, each containing links to additional pages. Your site map will be a helpful tool during the entire life of your project. For example, after the site is built, you can use the site map as a visual aid in meetings with management or as a tool for communicating site changes to team members who work on graphics or copy.

Sketch a Site Map

Draw a NYVRMLSIG site that is divided into five areas: People, Events, Resources, Projects, and News.

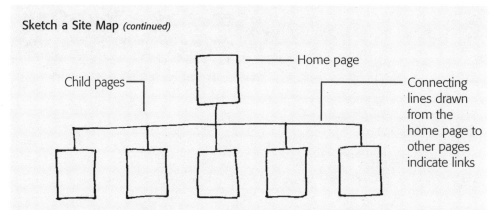

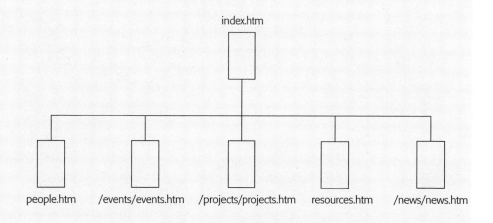

Using designer–writer teams. Writers can assist graphic designers by helping to invent a tightly organized plan for a Web site's content. In an advertising agency, writers typically team up with graphic designers to produce written and visual content.

Creating animation with VRML 2.0. VRML 2.0 animation can be used effectively in banner ads because the file size of a VRML animation is very small. Banner ads are small, rectangular ads that are often 500 pixels wide by 65 pixels tall. Adding GIF animation to a 6–10K banner ad often quadruples the file size. However, animated VRML banner ads are much more compact. A well-known VRML 2.0 Pepsi banner ad demonstrates how much animation can be accomplished in a 6K file. Visit www.outoftheblue.com/html/pepsi.htm. V-Realm Builder from Ligos Software is a favorite VRML 2.0 tool among the members of the New York VRMLSIG. Although VRML can be hand-coded like HTML, V-Realm Builder lets artists use menu commands to add animation and interactivity.

Sketch a Site Map *(continued)*

Home page

Child pages

Connecting lines drawn from the home page to other pages indicate links

Replace Your Sketch with a More Detailed Diagram

Larger sites need folders to manage the many files they require. By adding path names to your site map, you will have the folder information you need when you create links later. You also will have a detailed visual guide describing the exact location of all your Web documents.

index.htm

people.htm   /events/events.htm   /projects/projects.htm   resources.htm   /news/news.htm

Building the Structure

Creating a Text-Only Prototype

A text-only prototype can help you communicate your ideas to a client or a Web team. If you're creating a site for a client, ask your client to approve the prototype before you begin work on the graphics.

Open a New Web

1 Start FrontPage 98.

2 Select Create A New FrontPage Web and click OK.

3 In the New FrontPage Web dialog box, choose Empty Web from the list of wizards and templates.

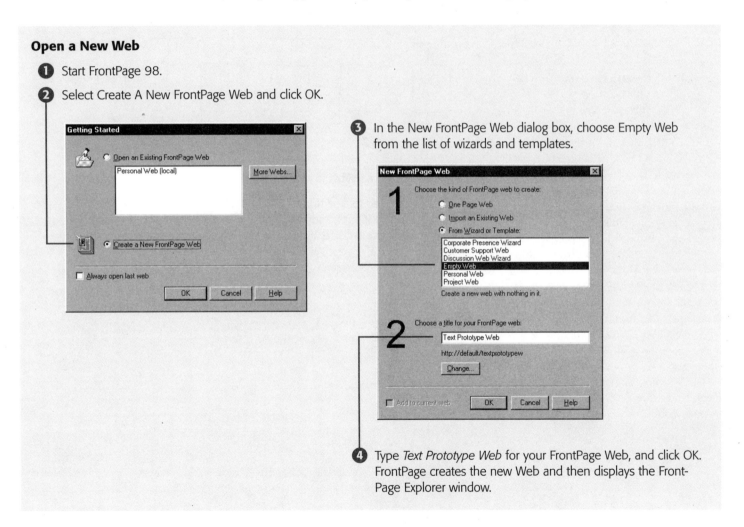

4 Type *Text Prototype Web* for your FrontPage Web, and click OK. FrontPage creates the new Web and then displays the FrontPage Explorer window.

Understanding a Web's folder structure. Note the presence of a Web site file list window beneath the navigation panel in the FrontPage Explorer window. The directory contains a folder labeled "images," which is created each time you make a new Web.

Test the procedure for uploading to your Internet Service Provider's server early in the project to determine if folders are appropriate. For example, the file transfer software built into America Online requires that each file be uploaded to a member's Web server area one at a time. As a result, folders are cumbersome.

Create Pages for Your Site

❶ In the FrontPage Explorer window, click the New Page button.

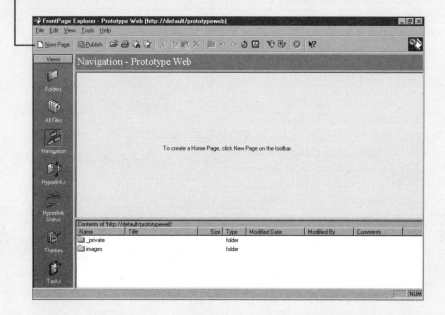

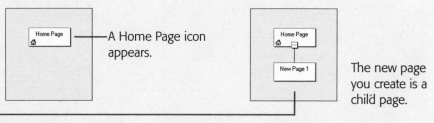

A Home Page icon appears.

The new page you create is a child page.

❷ Click New Page again and click No in the dialog box that asks if you want FrontPage to create navigation bars linking your pages together.

Is your marketing department Web savvy?

In his book, *Corporate Internet Planning Guide: Aligning Internet Strategy With Business Goals*, Richard Gascoyne explains that for an Internet strategy to be successful, marketing must become a firm's top— and possibly even its first—priority.

Easy-to-read Web sites.

Web visitors will do more scanning and glancing than reading from left to right. Review your content carefully to make sure it contains only essential information. Copy should be easy to read for quick consumption. Pages with lengthy content should be designed for optional printing. For example, the news release in Chapter 6, "News Releases and Pitch Letters," is designed with dark type on a light background, which should print successfully.

Create Pages for Your Site *(continued)*

③ Click the default name on the second page, "New Page 1," and then pause and click again. Type *News* to replace the default name.

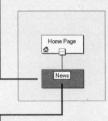

④ Double-click the News page icon to open the page in the FrontPage Editor window.

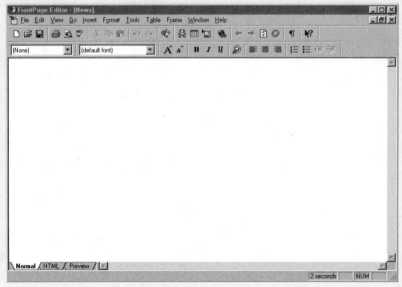

E-mail newsletter on Internet trends. *EduPage* is a useful newsletter that gives capsule summaries of the latest Internet news and trends. Published by EduComp, the newsletter is distributed to readers through e-mail. To subscribe, send an e-mail message to listproc@ educom.unc.edu and type *subscribe edupage* in the body of the message. You can leave the subject line blank.

Dragging pages to rearrange them. You can drag any of your pages to rearrange them. In the example in this chapter, the new pages were created to the right of the News page, making the News page end up on the far left. A rearrangement was necessary so that News could appear at the far right.

Create Pages for Your Site *(continued)*

5 From the File menu, choose Save As to save this page. In the Save As dialog box, "news" will appear in the Title field because you replaced the default name in Navigation view. Type *news* in the URL field, click OK, and then close the FrontPage Editor window.

6 With the Home page selected in the FrontPage Explorer window, click New Page on the toolbar. Name the new page "Projects."

7 Click the Home page so that it is selected, and then create three additional pages and name them "People," "Events," and "Resources."

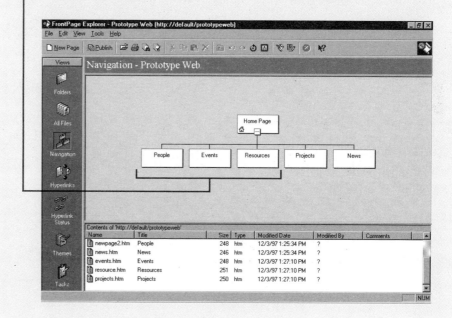

8 Save each page separately.

The Default.htm home page. FrontPage automatically names the home page file "default.htm," which is a convention used on many Web servers. Your Internet Service Provider's server software may require the file name "index.htm" instead. Check with your provider to determine the name that is required. If necessary, you can use the Rename command in FrontPage to change a file name and the program will automatically update all links.

Parents, children, and peers. On a Web site, pages are often described with words such as "parent," "child," and "peer." These definitions help to define the relationships between pages and make it easy to organize branches or hierarchical components of your site. In an inverted tree or hierarchy, a parent resides on a level above a child. Peers reside on the same level.

Adding Navigation to Your Pages

Now that you've created pages for the NYVRLMLSIG Web site, you'll add a text navigation bar to each page. You can use the Navigation Bar command in FrontPage to add a set of navigation bar links to each page of your text-only prototype Web site.

Add Navigation Bars

1 In Navigation view, double-click the Home Page icon.

2 From the Insert menu, choose Navigation Bar.

3 Click Child Level in the Hyperlinks To Include section, click Text in the Orientation And Appearance section, and then click OK. A text navigation bar is added to the page.

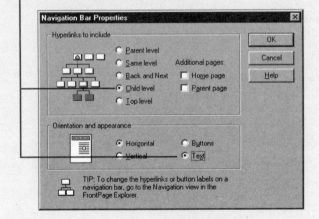

The FrontPage Navigation view. In the FrontPage Explorer, Navigation view shows a graphical representation of your Web site. You can reorganize pages by dragging the page icons in this view. You can also collapse sections of your Web by clicking a minus sign where it appears in the tree structure. To expand the view, click the plus sign in the same location.

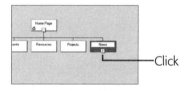

Click

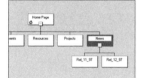

Add Navigation Bars *(continued)*

④ Click the Center button to center the navigation bar, and then save and close the page.

Text navigation bar

⑤ In Navigation view, double-click one of the child pages, and then choose Navigation Bar from the Insert menu.

⑥ Click Same Level and Home Page in the Hyperlinks To Include section, click Text in the Orientation And Appearance section, and then click OK. The navigation bar appears.

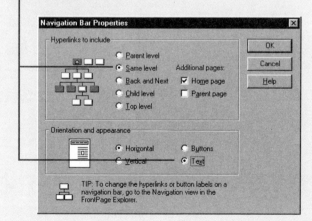

Building a Site's Structure and Navigation   **11**

The FrontPage HTML layer. Although you don't have to learn HTML to use FrontPage, you can view the HTML tags that make up a page by clicking the HTML tab at the lower left corner of the FrontPage Editor window.

Add Navigation Bars *(continued)*

7 Center the navigation bar, and then save and close the page.

8 Open the remaining child pages and add similar navigation bars by repeating these steps.

Testing Navigation Within Your Site

Navigation is a critical aspect of your Web site. You should spend time testing the site's navigation to determine whether the links work properly.

Navigate Your Pages in FrontPage

In the FrontPage Editor window, hold down the Ctrl key on the keyboard and click the links in the navigation bars to test your links. As you navigate your site, you can identify pages in the title bar, and when you link to each of the pages, the link you've clicked changes from an underlined link to plain text.

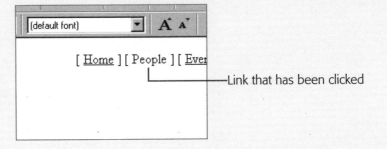

Link that has been clicked

Organizing a focus group to test your site's navigation. Although focus groups have been criticized as unreliable, even their harshest critics admit that they can be helpful when a company wants to explore a topic, obtain suggestions, or provoke opinions. Marketing firms typically run four sessions with eight to ten participants in each focus group. Consider holding focus groups to determine if your finished Web site is easy to navigate and understand.

Testing Your Pages in a Browser Window

The Preview In Browser command in FrontPage lets you choose any browser installed on your computer. The Window Size command in the Preview In Browser dialog box will help you determine how your page will look on an average monitor. This is helpful because many people who use the Web have their screens set to a 640-by-480 resolution.

Preview Your Pages in a Browser

1 From the File menu of the FrontPage Editor, choose Preview In Browser Window.

2 In the Preview In Browser dialog box, click Preview. Your page is displayed in a browser window so that you can test the links on your prototype pages. If your browser is not listed on the Browser list, click Add to add your browser.

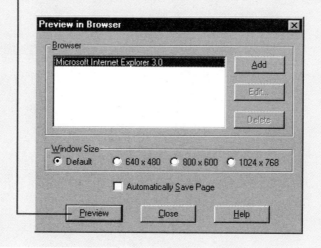

Designing for 14-inch monitors. A 14-inch monitor is still the most popular size. This is the size for which you should plan your navigation buttons. Many designers consider 600 pixels to be a maximum width for a Web page. This pixel width takes into account the screen space used by the browser window itself.

Image Composer's Web palette. Although the True Color palette in Image Composer can support up to 16 million colors, you will need to save your Web graphics with a limited palette to keep file sizes to a minimum. Image Composer's Save For The Web command can optimize the colors in an image for the Web so that the color is consistent in a majority of browsers.

Creating Button Graphics in Image Composer

With text links in place and working, you can now create a set of button graphics to replace them. Although the button graphics will completely replace the text links in this example, you should consider adding graphic buttons while still maintaining a set of text links. This will ensure that visitors can still see links should the button graphics fail to load in their browsers. It will also provide a set of links for visitors who use text browsers. Make your buttons and button text as small as possible while keeping the text readable. When you glance at a page, your eye should not be drawn immediately to the navigation bar. Small type and small buttons will be less distracting. In this example, the text created for the button graphics is 9-point type.

Create a Button

1 Start Image Composer. A workspace containing a central composition space is displayed.

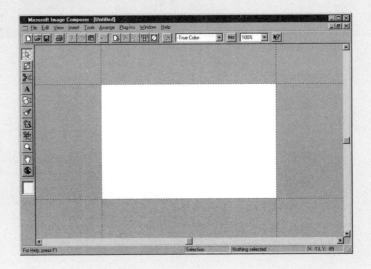

Button size. Make all your navigation buttons the same size, and choose a text size that does not make the buttons look crowded. Try to keep 10 to 12 points of space, about the height of a capital letter on this page, on either side of the button text.

Reversing the text on navigation buttons. Not all typefaces work well with reversed or white type on a black background. Typefaces with fine lines may disappear and small type sizes may have too few pixel elements to appear readable. Notice how the detail in the 9-point Garamond letters disappears (upper figure), while the 9-point Verdana letters are more readable (lower figure).

Create a Button *(continued)*

2 From the File menu, choose Composition Setup.

3 Type *100* for the width and *22* for the height.

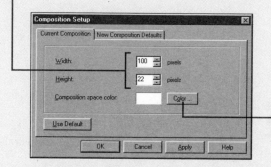

4 Click the Color button.

5 Type *0* (zero) in each of the Red, Green, and Blue fields to set the current color to black. Click OK.

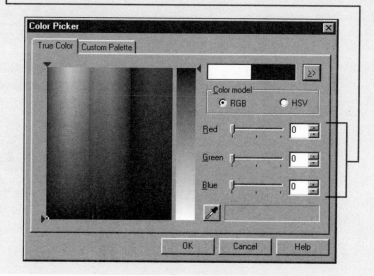

Expect several spelling and proofreading cycles. To make sure your site looks professional, use the spelling checker in FrontPage to correct spelling. In addition to checking spelling, make sure the Web site's text is proofread carefully. Print the pages to review the site's content and expect at least four to eight revision cycles.

Saving an MIC version of your Image Composer file. When you save a file in Image Composer in any format other than the Image Composer file format (.mic), the program will display a warning box to let you know that the image will be flattened and can no longer be edited as individual sprites. Always save your graphics in an Image Composer file so that you can still edit or revise them later.

Create a Button (continued)

6 Click OK in the Composition Setup dialog box. The composition space is reduced to the size of a button.

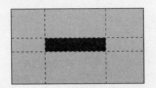

Choose White Type for a Black Background

1 Click the Text tool in the toolbox on the left. The Text palette opens.

2 In the Text dialog box that follows, choose Verdana from the Font menu.

3 Choose 9 points.

4 Choose Bold.

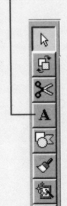

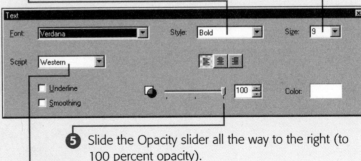

5 Slide the Opacity slider all the way to the right (to 100 percent opacity).

6 Leave Western as the default Script setting.

Checking for broken links. To check all the internal and external links in your Web, use the Verify Hyperlinks command on the Tools menu in Front-Page Explorer. Internal links lead to files on the Web server and external links lead to other sites on the Internet. This command is one of FrontPage's most powerful features. Because the Web changes frequently, you'll want to check external links on a regular basis.

Choose White Type for a Black Background *(continued)*

7 Click the color swatch on the Text palette, not the one on the toolbox.

8 In the Color Picker dialog box, tab to the fields labeled Red, Green, and Blue and type *255* in each field. This sets the current color to white.

Enter the Button Text

1 Click anywhere on the workspace and type *Home* in the bounding box that is displayed. When you finish typing, click anywhere on the workspace. The bounding box is replaced by a set of selection handles.

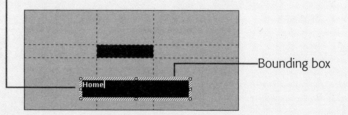

Bounding box

2 Position the mouse pointer at the Ycenter of the word "Home" and drag this sprite on top of the black button. Be careful not to drag on a selection arrow or the word will change shape and the type will be distorted.

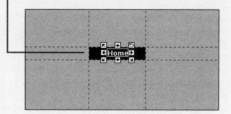

You can also click the Arrange button on the toolbox, click Relative To Composition Space on the Arrange palette, and then click the Align Centers button to align the sprite at the center of the composition space.

Avoiding distracting table borders. Tables have become an important design tool. Most designers leave table borders on while they are creating a page and then turn off the borders when their design is complete. The information inside a table is important, and the borders are often distracting.

Borders

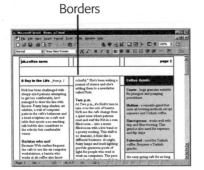

No borders

Save the Button

1 From the File menu, choose Save.

2 In the Save As dialog box, locate a folder for the saved button and name the button "home."

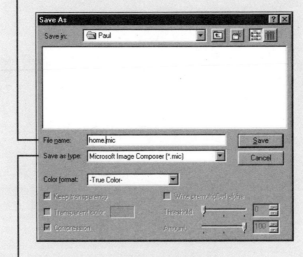

3 Choose Microsoft Image Composer from the Save As Type menu and click Save.

Resave the Button as a CompuServe GIF file

1 Choose Save Copy As from the File menu.

2 Click to remove the check mark in the box labeled Transparent Color.

3 Choose CompuServe GIF (*.GIF) from the Save As Type menu and click Save. The contents of the composition space will be saved as a GIF file.

Editing the Button Graphic to Create Other Buttons

Now that you've saved a button graphic as an Image Composer file, it can be used as a template to create other buttons. The type of file you have created is a sprite graphic, which is easy to edit.

Edit the Home Button

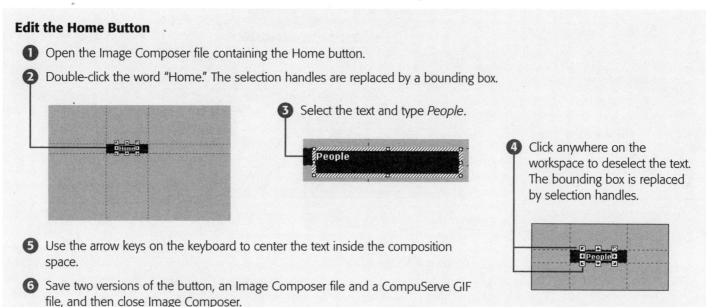

1 Open the Image Composer file containing the Home button.

2 Double-click the word "Home." The selection handles are replaced by a bounding box.

3 Select the text and type *People*.

4 Click anywhere on the workspace to deselect the text. The bounding box is replaced by selection handles.

5 Use the arrow keys on the keyboard to center the text inside the composition space.

6 Save two versions of the button, an Image Composer file and a CompuServe GIF file, and then close Image Composer.

Replacing Text Links with Buttons

In FrontPage, you can use the Shared Borders command to create a bottom page border and then create a table to hold the button graphics. The content of a shared border appears on every page of your site.

Margins in Internet Explorer. The Internet Explorer browser supports the Leftmargin and Topmargin attributes in the HTML Body tag. To specify top and left margins in FrontPage, right-click the background of a page and choose Page Properties from the shortcut menu that is displayed. In the Page Properties dialog box that follows next, click the Margin tab and type your desired top and left margin values in the fields provided.

The dreaded splash screen download. Large splash screens, or rectangular images, are no longer popular on Web home pages. Smaller, efficient graphics that download quickly are the trend among well-designed Web sites.

Open the Text Prototype Web in FrontPage

Restart FrontPage, and on the Getting Started dialog box, select your Text Prototype Web, and then click OK. The Text Prototype Web is displayed.

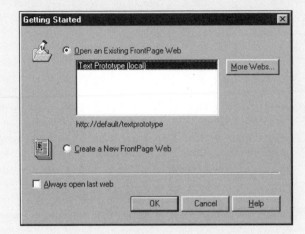

Enable a Shared Border

1 Choose Shared Borders from the Tools menu in the FrontPage Explorer.

2 Click Bottom and click OK.

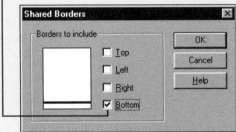
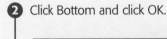

Meta tags. To increase the chances for Web travelers to find your site, pay extra attention to your page title, the page's Meta tags, and the first fifty words of text on the page. Meta tags are part of the HTML that is assembled behind the scenes while you work in FrontPage. These are the elements that get indexed by the Web's search engines, such as Alta-Vista and HotBot. (For more information, see "Building Meta Tags," page 126.)

Submitting your URLs to search engines. Even though search engine spider programs will eventually find your Web site, you should submit your own URL or URLs to get the process started.

Open a Child Page in the FrontPage Editor

1 Open any of the site's child pages in the FrontPage Editor.

In the Editor window, you will notice a dashed line under the text navigation bar with a comment underneath.

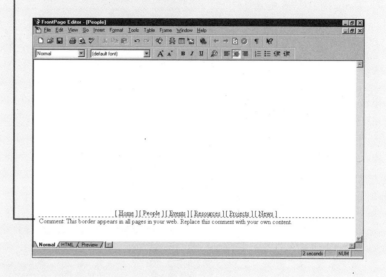

2 Press the Enter key enough times to move the navigation bar and text line to the bottom of the screen.

Create a Table to Hold Navigation Buttons

1 Double-click the comment below the border to select the text.

The Internet and TV. Ever wonder about the relationship between the Internet and TV? According to the research firm Dataquest, 98 percent of U.S. households will own at least one television by the year 2001, and an estimated 6 percent of households will have set-top boxes accessing the Internet. In December 1997, the FCC auctioned licenses for local multipoint distribution systems (LMDS), the wireless equivalent of fiber-optic cable. With a satellite dish the size of a small plate, households will be able to receive signals from local providers that bundle telephone, television, and high-speed Internet access. These services will include local TV, something that national broadcast satellite services, such as DirecTV, cannot offer.

Create a Table to Hold Navigation Buttons *(continued)*

2 Click the Insert Table button on the toolbar and highlight a row of six cells. When you release the mouse button, an empty table appears inside the bottom border replacing the comment text.

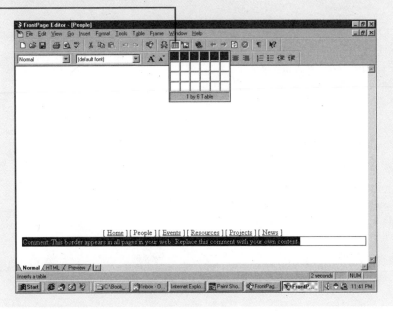

Add Button Graphics to Your Table

1 Click inside the first cell in your table.

2 From the Insert menu, choose Image.

Creating a custom texture with a kaleidoscope filter. The cMulti demo from Andromeda Software contains optical effects software filters from the company's Photography Series 1. Create circular or straight multiple lens kaleidoscope effects by altering the settings on the filter's dialog box. For example, these before and after images show the Basalt.jpg pattern that comes with Image Composer. The Circular Multiple Image filter has been applied as a tiled pattern. For more information on how to download and install the cMulti demo, see "Installing and testing the Andromeda cMulti demo filter plug-in," on the next page.

Before

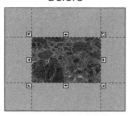

After

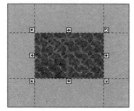

Add Button Graphics to Your Table *(continued)*

3 Click the Select File button.

4 In the Select File dialog box, locate the home.gif button you created and saved in Image Composer and click OK. The button will be inserted in the table cell. Repeat steps 1 through 3 to add other button graphics you've made to other table cells.

Note that when you navigate to pages on your site, every page will have a navigation bar inside the bottom border. Press Enter on these pages several times to move the border to the bottom of the screen.

Installing and testing the Andromeda cMulti demo filter plug-in. Download the cMulti demo from the Andromeda Software Web site at www.andromeda. com/info/GetDemo.html. Unzip the demo and drag the files into the Plug-Ins folder inside your Image Composer software folder. Restart Image Composer. Open the Basalt.jpg image that comes with Image Composer and choose Andromeda/cMulti demo from the Plug-Ins menu. Click the splash screen and experiment with the settings on the Circular Multiple Image dialog box. For example, click Tiles and then click the Next button to cycle through the tiled kaleidoscope patterns. When you have selected a tile that you'd like to try, click OK. Click the splash screen, and the filter will be applied.

Add Hyperlinks to the Button Graphics

1 Click the Home button on any of the child pages.

2 Choose Hyperlink from the Insert menu.

3 Click the default.htm page on the file list, and click OK.

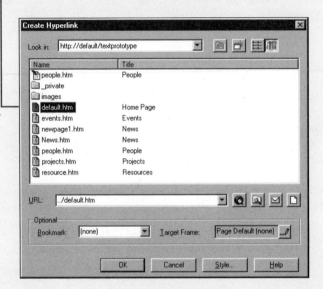

4 On the Save Embedded Files dialog box that appears, click OK so that FrontPage will save the embedded files to the current FrontPage Web.

5 Repeat steps 1 through 4 to add hyperlinks to all your navigation buttons, matching the name on the button to the name of the page.

Installing and testing the Andromeda Screens demo filter plug-in.
Download the Screens demo from the Andromeda Software Web site at www.andromeda.com/info/GetDemo. html. Unzip the demo and drag the files Screens.8bf, Screens.prf, and Screens.hlp into the Plug-Ins folder inside your Image Composer software folder. Restart Image Composer. If you do not see the Screens demo listed in the Plug-Ins menu, you will need to download the Msvcrt10.dll file from www.andromeda.com/info/GetDemo.html directly into your Windows\System folder. You will also need to restart your computer. Unlike the cMulti demo from Andromeda, the Screens demo is a try-before-you-buy trial that does not allow saving or exporting. However, you can test visual effects on screen.

(Optional) Delete the Text Navigation Bars

❶ Select the text navigation bar on each page. Be careful not to select your new buttons.

❷ Press the Delete key on the keyboard.

❸ Save the pages again.

Deleting a FrontPage Web

Although you may instinctively want to drag unwanted Webs to the Recycle Bin, this is not the best way to delete a Web. Because each Web you create is a system of folders, you should use the Delete FrontPage Web command in the FrontPage Explorer window.

Using a Photoshop plug-in filter from Andromeda for a mezzotint effect. Andromeda Software has created a number of plug-ins for Photoshop and Image Composer that you can use to apply special visual effects to graphics. Trial versions are available at www.andromeda.com/info/GetDemo.html. Andromeda's Screens plug-in, shown below, creates mezzotints by converting photographs and other continuous tone images into patterns of dots. ·

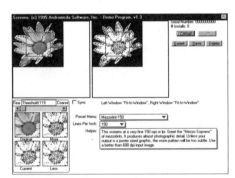

Delete a Web

① Open the Web that you want to delete.

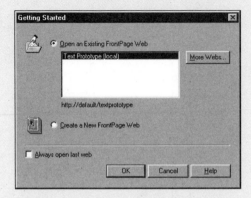

② Choose Delete The FrontPage Web from the File menu in the FrontPage Explorer window.

③ A warning dialog box notifies you that deleting is a permanent action. Click OK. FrontPage will return to the Getting Started dialog box, which is convenient if you'd like to start another Web.

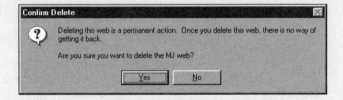

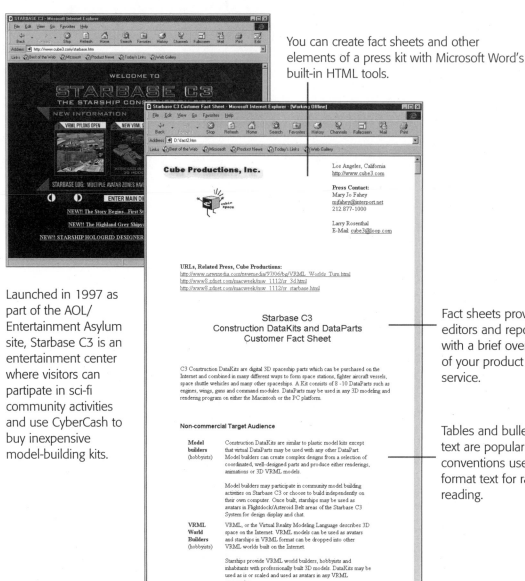

You can create fact sheets and other elements of a press kit with Microsoft Word's built-in HTML tools.

Launched in 1997 as part of the AOL/ Entertainment Asylum site, Starbase C3 is an entertainment center where visitors can partipate in sci-fi community activities and use CyberCash to buy inexpensive model-building kits.

Fact sheets provide editors and reporters with a brief overview of your product or service.

Tables and bulleted text are popular conventions used to format text for rapid reading.

A Fact Sheet

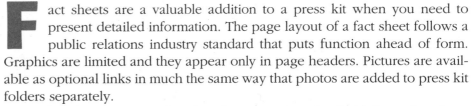

F act sheets are a valuable addition to a press kit when you need to present detailed information. The page layout of a fact sheet follows a public relations industry standard that puts function ahead of form. Graphics are limited and they appear only in page headers. Pictures are available as optional links in much the same way that photos are added to press kit folders separately.

In this chapter's example, a fact sheet organizes detailed information about digital spaceship-modeling kits sold by Cube Productions, Inc., over the Internet (www.cube3.com/starbase). To prepare the fact sheet, you will use Microsoft Image Composer and Microsoft Word to create both the logo art and the Web page.

The Fact Sheet Page Design

The page elements you'll use for the fact sheet layout are:

> Large indents that adhere to the established design principle that limiting line length improves readability.

> Light background with dark text for reporters and editors who may want to print pages.

> Ample white space between paragraphs.

> Logo art, page header text, and definitions, which require side-by-side formatting held in place with tables.

> Bulleted lists, referred to as unordered lists in HTML (ordered lists are numbered), that organize lists of spaceship parts.

E-mail aliases. Internet Service Providers are sometimes willing to provide up to five e-mail aliases with one Internet account. If you have a small company and you'd like to provide more than one person with an e-mail address, give them e-mail aliases. Although all of the mail will be delivered to a single mail box, e-mail aliases are often very useful. Many companies use aliases for non-specific e-mail address links on a company Web site. Webmaster@cube3.com and editor@web-techniques.com are examples.

Fact Sheet

Sample Layouts

Even though traditional public relations press kit pages include few graphics, you can still explore many different layout options with pages that contain mostly text. Designers often find it helpful to create miniature page sketches, called thumbnails, to work out their page design ideas. They draw thumbnails on paper or create them in page layout programs.

Although HTML page design is more limiting than print page design, it follows many of the same conventions. For example, the customer fact sheet and the Triad System fact sheet, shown in the following graphic, make exten-sive use of tables and bulleted lists.

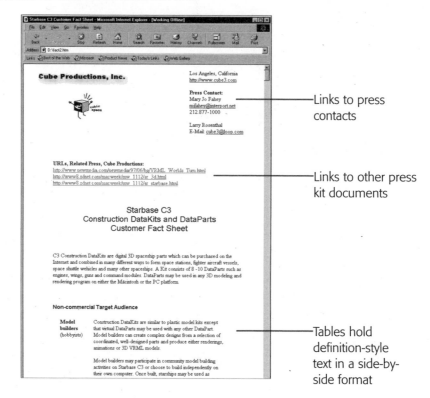

Links to press contacts

Links to other press kit documents

Tables hold definition-style text in a side-by-side format

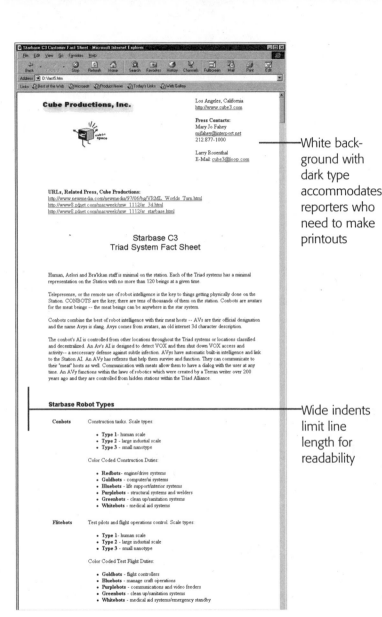

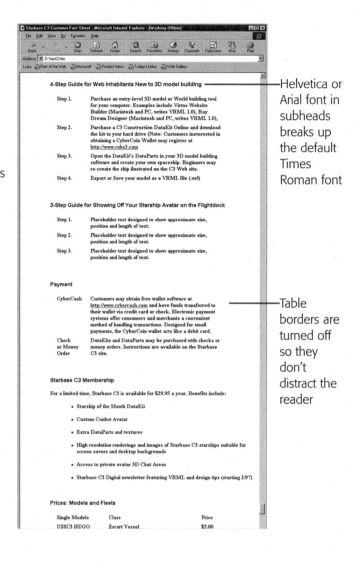

White background with dark type accommodates reporters who need to make printouts

Wide indents limit line length for readability

Helvetica or Arial font in subheads breaks up the default Times Roman font

Table borders are turned off so they don't distract the reader

Fact Sheet

Public computer rental facilities. If you don't own your own computer, you can still use the Internet. A growing number of public computer rental facilities rent computer time on the Internet by the hour or by the minute. Internet cafés and Kinko's copy centers are examples. Even if you own your own computer, consider renting a computer for 15 or 20 minutes to check how your site looks on another computer platform or another computer model. Global Computing's site at www. globalcomputing.com/cafes.html lists cyber cafés in the United States and The Cyber Cafés of Europe at www. xs4all.nl/ ~bertb/index.html is a European resource list. By March 1998, all Kinko's stores will have Internet connectivity. Call Kinko's customer service to find a center in your area: 1-800-2KINKOS.

Creating the Fact Sheet

For the fact sheet project in this chapter, you'll prepare logo art in Image Composer, create a new HTML document in Word 97, use Word's Table tool to create a page header for the fact sheet, add hyperlinks to the page header, and complete the fact sheet with tables. You will also format the lists on the page.

Getting Organized

If you've selected Word 97 to create Web pages, you'll need to:

> Create one or more folders on your system to store HTML documents, art files, and other files that you plan to transfer to a Web server. Ideally, the folder structure on your hard disk will be identical to the folder structure on the Web server, so your hyperlinks will work the same way as they do on the server.

> Prepare images for your Web pages in advance using Image Composer or some other image editor, and save the art files as GIF or JPEG files.

> Locate software to copy your files to a Web server. For example, you can use the free Microsoft Web Publishing Wizard to copy files to a local Internet Service Provider or to a Web server on your local area network.

Preparing a Logo in Image Composer

Image Composer treats images as objects referred to as sprites. You can use its collection of built-in tools, art effects, and filters to alter these sprites.

In this example, you will use Image Composer to create text for a company logo and add a drop shadow effect.

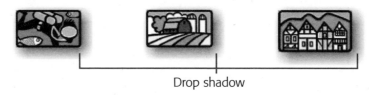

Drop shadow

Geek speak. The Internet has been nerd heaven for more than 20 years. Although Web browsers have recently put a friendly face on the Internet, geeky terms still make most people wrinkle their brow, particularly when they are used as words. Here are a few examples and definitions (to prepare for a meeting with a client whose 15-year old son runs the company Web server):

FTP—File Transfer Protocol is used to transfer files from one computer to another. FTP links embedded on Web pages allow users to download files using a browser.

Telnet—An application that allows users to emulate a virtual terminal for communicating with a wide variety of remote computers. The user's computer, which initiates the connection, is referred to as the local computer, and the machine being connected to, which accepts the connection, is referred to as the remote, or host, computer.

Open a New Document

Start Image Composer. A workspace containing a central composition space is displayed.

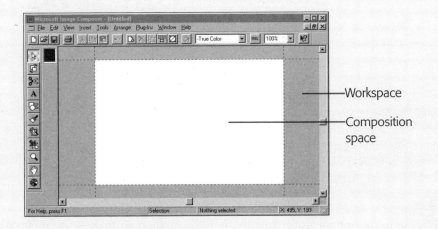

Workspace

Composition space

Create a Custom-Sized Document

① Choose Composition Setup from the File menu.

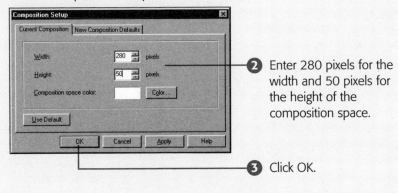

② Enter 280 pixels for the width and 50 pixels for the height of the composition space.

③ Click OK.

Mirrored servers. If money is no object, consider mirroring your Web site. As the name implies, a mirror is a duplicate that ensures your Web presence is never interrupted. Larger Internet Service Providers (ISPs) offer mirrored service but their prices will be higher than regular commercial service.

Chat@Talk City. Live World Productions, Inc., has introduced a free software program called Chat@Talk City, which allows individuals or businesses to create text-based chat for a Web site without actually hosting chat on a server. Since June 1997, over 10,000 chat rooms have opened (www.talkcity.com). Apply for a new chat room at www.talkcity.com/irc/apply.html.

Create a Custom-Sized Document *(continued)*

The adjusted composition space is displayed.

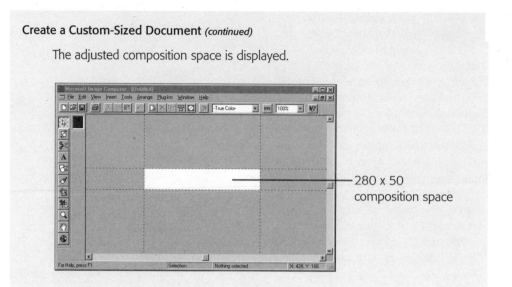

280 x 50 composition space

Creating a Text Sprite with a Soft Drop Shadow

Creating a text sprite and adding a drop shadow effect is a good way to get acquainted with Image Composer.

Preselect Text Formatting

① Click the Text tool. The Text palette appears.

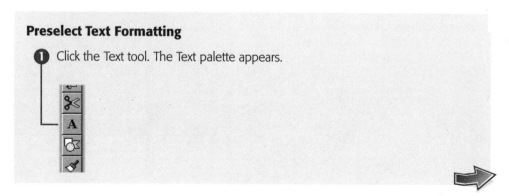

Tiled browser backgrounds. Tiny bitmap files can be tiled as a texture on a browser background with the addition of an attribute to the HTML Body tag:

<Body Background = "filename.gif">

The pattern will be repeated over and over in the browser background as you add content to your Web page. A particularly popular tiled background is a very wide 600-pixel bitmap that is only 10 or 20 pixels tall. This stripe usually consists of two colored rectangles, a shorter, 2- to 3-inch rectangle on the left and an 8- to 10-inch rectangle on the right. With so few colors, this bitmap can be a very small file. Because of its width, it creates a colored border along the left edge of the screen when it tiles. The CyberCash home page at www. cybercash.com uses this popular left border.

Preselect Text Formatting *(continued)*

2 From the Font list, choose Arial Black.

3 From the Size list, choose 16.

4 Make sure the Opacity Slider is all the way to the right, at 100 percent opacity.

5 Leave the Script set to Western (default) and the Style set to Regular (default).

Select a Text Color

1 Double-click the color swatch at the lower-right corner of the Text palette.

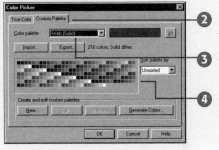

2 In the Color Picker dialog box, click the Custom Palette tab.

3 Choose Web (Solid) from the Color Palette drop-down list.

4 Click a dark violet shade and then click OK.

Married vs. unmarried subheads. Designers like to see subheads "married" to the related text that follows. In Word and Microsoft FrontPage, you can press Shift+Enter rather than Enter at the end of a subhead line to create a <BR> tag. This adds a line break without additional paragraph space below so that the subhead looks married to the text underneath it.

 Uploading pages to the Web. Microsoft's Web Publishing Wizard software simplifies the task of copying your completed Web pages to a Web server. The Web Publishing Wizard is part of FrontPage 98. For a free download, you can also visit www. microsoft.com/ windows/software/webpost/.

Add Text

1 With the Text tool selected, click inside the composition space. A text bounding box and a blinking insertion point appear.

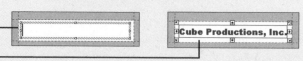

2 Enter text for your logo, such as *Cube Productions, Inc.* You may need to stop typing, use the mouse pointer to stretch the text bounding box out to the right, and then continue typing.

Add a Soft Drop Shadow

1 Click the Effects button on the Toolbox.

2 On the Effects palette, select Drop Shadow.

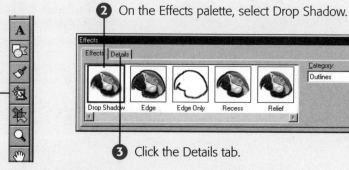

3 Click the Details tab.

4 Click the lower-right light source control to indicate the position of the shadow.

5 Drag the Distance slider to 10, and make sure the Opacity slider is all the way to the right.

6 Move the Softness slider slightly to the left of center.

A bitmap solution for lack of kerning in HTML.
Kerning, or the adjustment of letterspacing to obtain consistent visual space between letters, is an important process when type is set for a printed page. Unfortunately, kerning is not available in HTML. As a workaround, designers often create bitmapped type in an image editor such as Image Composer for headings, in which the lack of kerning is most obvious.

In the examples below, from the BoxTop Software site, notice the letterspacing between the "P" and "h" in "PhotoGIF" and between the "T" and "r" in "Try."

The tighter letterspace represents appropriate kerning, something that you cannot achieve in HTML, shown below.

**Try It Today
PhotoGIF Series**

Add a Soft Drop Shadow *(continued)*

7 Double-click the color swatch on the Effects palette.

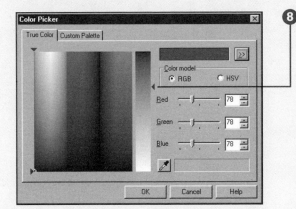

8 In the Color Picker dialog box, click the True Color tab and then click a medium to dark gray on the black-to-white scale. Click OK.

9 Click Apply in the Effects dialog box.

A soft drop shadow appears to the lower right of the text, the position you chose on the Effects palette.

You control the relative lightness or darkness of the shadow with your selection of a shade of gray.

TrueType fonts for your collection. To add to your font collection, visit www.microsoft.com/truetype/fontpack/ default.htm. Microsoft offers free True-Type fonts, which are available as a downloadable fontpack. You can install these fonts and use them in Image Composer to create bitmap fonts. Image Composer also comes with a collection of TrueType fonts that you can use.

Crop the Image to Create a Small File for Downloading

1 Position the mouse pointer on the text and drag the text to the upper-left corner of the composition space.

2 Choose Composition Setup from the File menu.

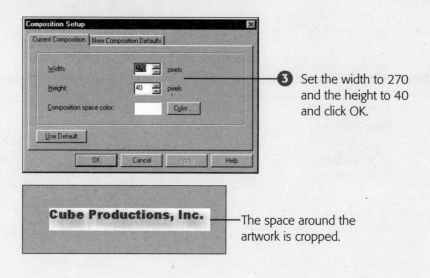

3 Set the width to 270 and the height to 40 and click OK.

The space around the artwork is cropped.

Use the Save For The Web Wizard to Save the Image

❶ Select Save For The Web from the File menu.

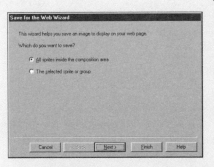 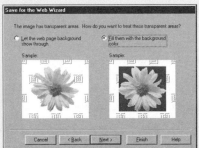

❷ Select All Sprites Inside The Composition Area and click Next.

❸ On the next page of the wizard, select Fill Them With The Background Color and click Next.

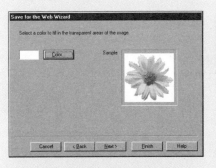 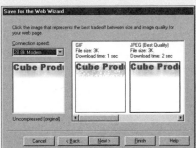

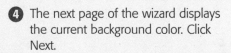

❹ The next page of the wizard displays the current background color. Click Next.

❺ On the page that follows, select JPEG (Best Quality) and click Next.

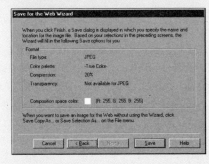 

❻ On the final page, review the save options and click Save.

❼ In the Save Copy As dialog box, select a folder in which to save the image, name the file "Cube_shadow," and click Save.

Image Composer tips.
For tips and tricks on using Image Composer, visit www.microsoft.com/imagecomposer/ usingic/ictips.htm or obtain *The Official Microsoft Image Composer Book* by Will Tait and Steve Sagman, published by Microsoft Press.

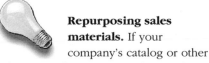

Repurposing sales materials. If your company's catalog or other sales materials exist in Word, consider publishing the pages on the Web by saving the Word files in HTML format.

Creating an HTML Document in Word 97

Now that you've created an image, you're ready to create an HTML document. Microsoft Office 97 provides easy-to-use Web page creation tools within a familiar application. You can create a document as though you were preparing it for print, but then save it as an HTML file.

You'll start your page by creating a page header template that you can use for other documents in your press kit.

Open a New Document

1 Start Word. A new, untitled document is displayed.

2 From the View menu, choose Normal.

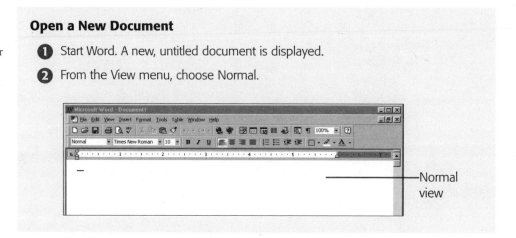

Normal view

Using Tables As a Design Tool

Tables have emerged as an important HTML design tool because they provide a way to position elements side by side with lots of control. You can use tables to place images, text, and other multimedia elements on a page. For the fact sheet, you'll use a table to position page elements in the page header.

Hyperlinks on press kit pages. If photographs or other multimedia elements would enhance your presentation, don't simply place them on your pages. Provide links to them instead. In a conventional press kit, photographs are never added to a press kit document, but 8 x 10 photos may be inserted into a press kit folder. Links to photographs are roughly equivalent to separate photos. For images, consider offering a choice of high-resolution or low-resolution images for Web publications. Musicians and videographers should consider offering links to short music or video clips.

 The Web's 216 browser-safe colors. Image Composer's Web palette consists of 216 browser-safe shades that will look best in any browser.

Create a Table to Hold the Page Header

1 Click the Insert Table button.

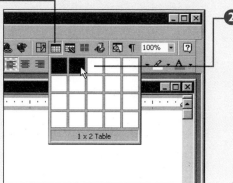

2 Drag across two cells.

An empty table appears on the page.

Insert Art and Text in the Table Cells

1 Click the left table cell, and then, from the Insert menu, choose Picture/From File.

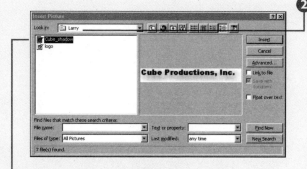

2 In the Insert Picture dialog box, locate the Cube_shadow text line on your system. If a graphic is in a format other than GIF or JPEG, Word will convert the file to a GIF image when you insert it into a document. Word also copies the graphic to the folder that contains the HTML file.

3 Choose Cube_shadow and click Insert.

Free artwork for your Web site. The Microsoft Internet Explorer Multimedia Gallery contains free backgrounds, banners, navigation controls, images, and sounds to add to your Web site. Visit www.microsoft.com/gallery/files/images/default.htm.

Insert Art and Text in the Table Cells *(continued)*

The art will appear in the left-hand cell where you positioned the cursor.

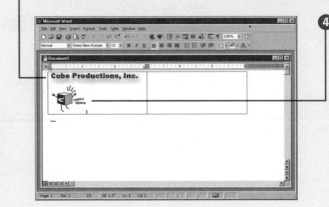

❹ With the cursor in the same position, press Enter. Repeat steps 1 through 3 to add the logo graphic.

The logo graphic is available on this book's Web page at mspress.microsoft. com/mspress/ products/1576.

Add Text to Complete the Page Header

Word will automatically format URLs and e-mail addresses as hyperlinks if Word's automatic formatting is turned on.

❶ Select AutoCorrect from the Tools menu.

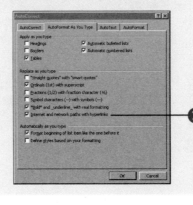

❷ On the AutoFormat tab of the AutoCorrect dialog box, add a check mark to the box labeled Internet And Network Paths With Hyperlinks, and click OK.

Creating a silhouette.
You can create a silhouette by using a transparent GIF image made in an image editor that is capable of assigning transparency to the background color of an image.

For best results, the shade you make transparent should be close to the background color of the Web page and it should not be present in the image.

If the shade you choose to be transparent is close to the background color of the Web page, you'll eliminate fringe around the edge of the image. To save an image as a transparent GIF file in Image Composer, choose Let The Web Page Background Show Through in the Save For The Web Wizard dialog box.

—Silhouette

Add Text to Complete the Page Header *(continued)*

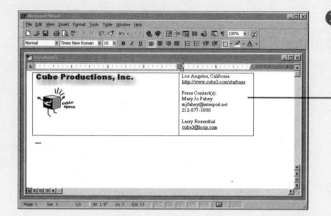

❸ Click the right cell and enter the company, address, phone number, e-mail address, URL, and press contact. Press Shift+Enter at the end of each line to add a line break.

❹ Drag the middle table cell border so that it lines up as shown in the following figure.

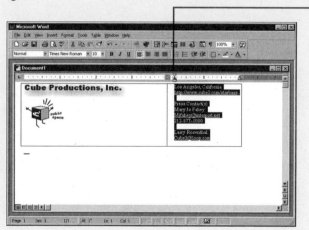

You can also drag the indent marker to add space between the text and the table cell border.

Image files and file extensions. Images that you plan to use on a Web page need a GIF or JPG file name extension. Image Composer will automatically put the appropriate extension on a file name when you select a file type. When you save the file, be careful not to type over this part of the file name.

HTML editors. Software that puts a friendly face on the steps used to create HTML belongs to a new application group called HTML editors. Word 97 may be described as a word processor, a text editor, and an HTML editor.

Saving the File As a Word Document

In this step, you'll save the file that you've created as a Word document and give it the name "Page Header." Each time you create a new press kit document, you can start with this header document. After you've added unique content to a document, you can save it again as a Word file.

Save Your File

1 Select Save from the File menu.

2 In the Save As dialog box, select a folder in which to save the document, name it "Page_header," and click Save.

Removing the Table Border

Tables have become a popular design tool, but they're rarely visible—because table borders are distracting, most designers remove them.

Remove the Table Border

1 Click anywhere in the table.

2 Choose Select Table from the Table menu.

3 From the Format menu, choose Borders And Shadows.

Explore views in Word.
Although you'll want to use Normal view for most of your work, Word's Page Layout view offers a formatted view of the page. Although the type may be too small for page composition, reducing the zoom level in Page Layout view lets you see how elements are positioned on a page.

The HTML beneath the page. Word 97 creates HTML when you use the Save As HTML command on the File menu. If you've saved your document as a Web page in this manner, you can view the HTML by selecting HTML Source from the View menu of Internet Explorer. Although you don't need to learn HTML tags, the source HTML page provides a helpful reference for designers who want to learn tagging.

Remove the Table Border (continued)

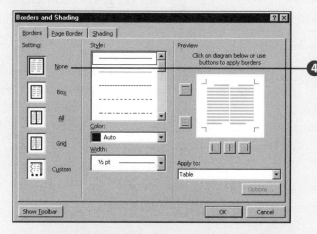

④ In the Borders And Shading dialog box, click None and then click OK.

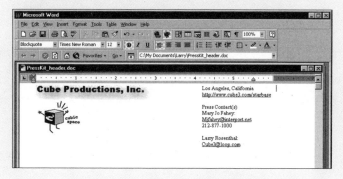

The table border disappears.

GIF or JPEG—Which is best? Use the GIF file format for line art. This 8-bit file format uses LZW compression, a lossless compression/decompression scheme that doesn't throw away any information when it compresses. Because an 8-bit palette is limited to 256 colors, the GIF format often gives photographs a posterized, paint-by-number appearance. Although this patchy look is sometimes used deliberately to create an art effect, it's considered undesirable for most pictures.

The JPEG compression algorithm (invented by the Joint Photographic Expert Group) is a 24-bit file format that has more than 16 million colors available.

GIF87 vs. GIF89a. The GIF file format, owned by CompuServe, consists of more than one file type. GIF87 is the original 8-bit format, which uses LZW lossless compression and decompression. GIF89a is the format that stores interlacing, which builds images progressively, and which provides transparency.

Adding Press Kit Hyperlinks to the Page Header

Because you're creating a virtual press kit for your Web site, a visitor won't have a folder to flip through. As a result, a short list of related press kit URLs in the header will guide visitors to other important press kit documents. In this example, the list contains a link to a news hub.

When AutoFormatting is on, Word underlines hyperlinks automatically when you type URLs or e-mail addresses. You can add a few more hyperlinks to your page header, but this time you'll need to use Word's Hyperlink tool.

Add Text for Related URLs

1 Press Enter and then type

Related Press Kit URLS, Cube Productions
Cube Productions News Hub
Bring Your Own Design, Shop and Play at the Starbase Site, Eric Taub, MacWeek

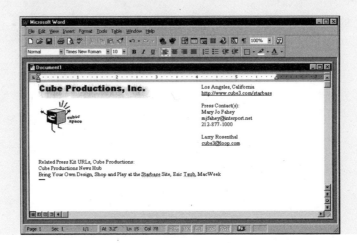

Photos look better as JPEGs. Photos look better when saved as JPEG files rather than GIF files, particularly those with gradations or skin tones. Never open and then resave an image as a JPEG because the compression scheme is a lossy algorithm. Whenever you save a JPEG file, some of its information is thrown away, so the image progressively deteriorates.

Photograph courtesy of Microsoft corporate photographer, Michael Moore. From Microsoft Gallery at www.microsoft.com/gallery/files/images/default.btm.

Add Hyperlinks

1 Select the text that you would like to link to another document on your Web server.

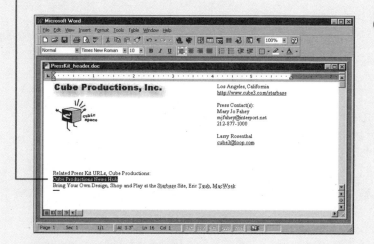

2 Select Hyperlink from the Edit menu. The Insert Hyperlink dialog box appears.

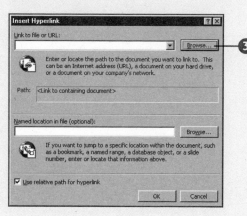

3 Click the Browse button to the right of the field labeled Link To File Or URL

Using an em dash. In writing, phrases are sometimes emphasized with a dash. For years, a double dash on a typewriter created this emphasis. In typography, an em dash does the same thing. In HTML, a long dash does exist (it's created with the HTML code &#95) and Word will convert a long dash to this HTML code properly.

HTML's soft return. In word processing and page layout software, a line break is referred to as a soft return. In Word, an Enter is converted to a <p> tag in HTML, which adds additional space between paragraphs. To break a line without additional paragraph spacing, press Shift+Enter to add a <br> tag in HTML.

Add Hyperlinks *(continued)*

❹ In the Link To File dialog box, locate the file you've created as a news hub. In this example, it's News_dest.htm. Click OK. The path to this file will be added to the Link To File Or URL field.

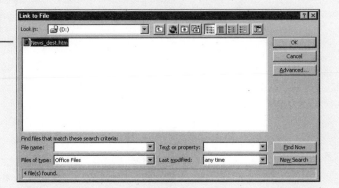

Optional field describing the path to a location for your Web document (see the chart on page 50 for more information).

❺ Click OK. The link text will change to bright blue and it will be underlined.

Absolute vs. relative links. A hyperlink links a document on a Web site to another document on the Web site or to an other document on the Internet. Links to documents that are external to a Web site need absolute links with paths that describe the exact URL or address, including transfer protocol, computer or network name, directory, and file name (for example, http://mspress.microsoft.com/mspress/products/1576).

Use relative links when linking one document to another or to a graphic file within your Web site. Choose the Use Relative Link check box on the Hyperlink dialog box in Word 97. Relative links are partial URLs with paths that describe the location of the linked files relative to one another. Relative links are recommended for new pages that you plan to move from your hard disk to a Web server.

Add Hyperlinks *(continued)*

6 Select the text that you would like to link to a document on the Internet.

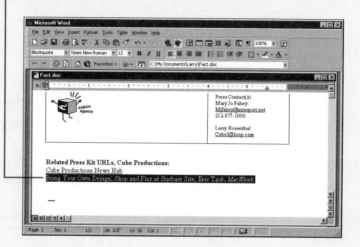

7 Select Hyperlink from the Edit menu.

8 In the Insert Hyperlink dialog box, type a URL in the field labeled Link To File Or URL.

The chart below describes the variations in URLs that you can type into the fields in the Insert Hyperlink dialog box. Absolute links are required for links to documents on the Internet, and relative links are preferable for links to documents on your own Web server.

Link to File or URL Field (for Absolute Links)		
To link to:	Type	Notes
A document on the Internet	http://*URL*	The Hypertext Transfer Protocol (HTTP) is used by Web servers to send HTML documents over the Internet. Example: http://www.microsoft.com
A file on the Internet	ftp://*URL*	File Transfer Protocol is used to transfer files from one computer to another. Example: ftp://ftp.microsoft.com/deskapps/Q122/3/31.txt
A file on the local hard disk	file://*URL*	A file URL refers to a file on a local disk. This URL is used when there is a Web site on a network intranet. Example: file://localdrive/dir/file.htm

Link to File or URL Field (for Relative Links)		
To link to:	Type	Notes
An e-mail address	mailto:*e-mail address*	A Mailto link is used to send e-mail. When a Mailto link is clicked, a browser opens an e-mail form with the e-mail address filled in. Example: mailto:*your e-mail@your domain*

Named Location in a File Field (for Relative Links)		
To link to:	Type	Notes
A document on a local Web server	*Filename.ext*	When you enter a file name, Word creates a relative link.

Both Fields (for Absolute or Relative Links)		
To link to:	Type	Notes
A location in the same document	*bookmark name*	To create a bookmark in a document, select the text that you'd like to bookmark, select Bookmark from the Insert menu, type a bookmark name, and click Add.
A location in another document	*A document URL and a bookmark name*	Follow the steps above, but add the bookmark in the destination document to which you will link.

Create a news hub. The Cube Productions news hub is a table of contents for all the site's press kit documents, including backgrounders, press clips, press releases, photos, and fact sheets. At the top of press kit documents, a link to the news hub helps visitors navigate.

Hyphens. There are few clearly defined rules on the subject of hyphens. Hyphens are used to join closely associated nouns, adjectives, and numbers, and they're also used for dividing words at the end of a line. Closely associated nouns and adjectives are referred to as compounds—two or more distinct words treated as a unit. *Two-year-old* and *mother-in-law* are examples. Many compounds have evolved from two words to hyphenated words to single words. For example, the word *free-lance* is now *freelance*. There is also a great deal of variation between the British and American use of the hyphen. In general, because there are so few rules, hyphen usage is considered to be a matter of spelling. If in doubt, consult an up-to-date dictionary.

Adjusting the Page Indent

To shorten the lines of text on the page and make them more readable, you can add a wide left indent. By adding such an indent to the text you've just completed, you'll create a guide for the rest of the fact sheet.

Page indents don't line up the same way in HTML and Word. The indent in Word will be larger than the HTML version.

Select the Text and Increase the Page Indent

1 Select the text.

2 Drag the indent marker to the half-inch mark on the ruler.

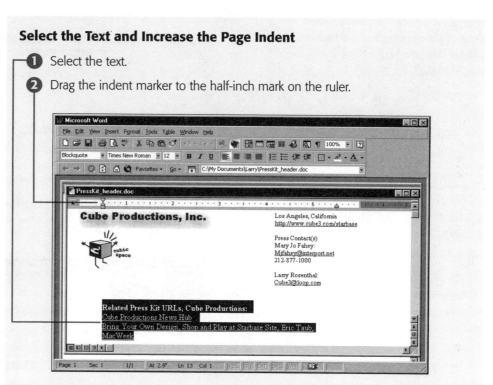

The nondiscriminatory language debate. Traditional usage rules dictate the use of masculine singular pronouns in situations where a writer is forced to make a reference to one sex or the other. To avoid sexist writing, you can use plural pronouns in most references, regardless of whether the previous pronoun is singular, but the best solution is to rewrite the sentence to avoid the whole issue.

For example:

The photographer asked everyone to remain because each one had arranged to have his photo taken.

is often written:

The photographer asked everyone to remain because they had arranged to have their photos taken.

but is best rewritten to:

The photographer asked everyone to remain so he could take a photo of each person.

Saving the Page as HTML

When you save a page as HTML, Word creates the HTML tags needed for the Web. You'll notice a slight change in the appearance of the page.

Save Your File

1 Select Save As HTML from the File menu.

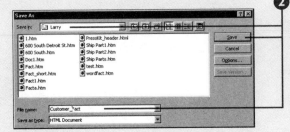

2 In the Save As dialog box, locate a folder in which to save the file, enter a file name, and then click Save. Word will add an .htm extension to the document file name.

View Your Document in Internet Explorer

1 Select Web Page Preview from the File menu.

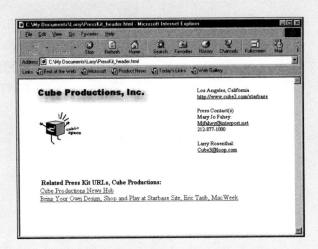

2 Word starts Internet Explorer and displays your document in the browser window.

New CyberCash and Microsoft Wallets. Cube Productions' new Starbase C3 Design Center inside the AOL Asylum site on the Web and at www.cube3.com/starbase offers inexpensive model-building kits that can be purchased with CyberCash Wallet, a client software program that allows you to buy hard goods or digital goods on the Internet. Microsoft Wallet, which is distributed with Internet Explorer 4.0 and future versions of Windows, is compatible with the CyberCash server and allows Windows users to purchase products from CyberCash merchants.

Using the Page Header Template to Create a Fact Sheet

The next text you add to the document will be a headline followed by the fact sheet text. You should work in the Word document first, and then save the file as an HTML document. For the fact sheet text, you'll use tables to hold text in place in much the same way as you used them in the page header. You first add text to the Word document as a list, and then add bullets after you've saved your document as HTML.

Add Headline Text To Your Page Header File

1 In Word, click to place the cursor at the end of the press kit URLs.

2 Press Enter twice and type
Starbase C3
Construction DataKits and DataParts
Customer Fact Sheet

Press Shift+Enter at the end of each line to add a line break.

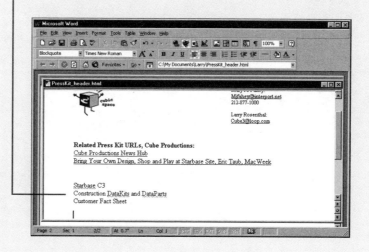

For speed-conscious Web travelers. Some people who browse the Web may turn off the display of graphics to speed downloading, or they may use a text browser such as Lynx to browse the Web. To accommodate these viewers, you should add alternate text that will be displayed rather than images. After a document has been saved as an HTML file in Word, alternate text can be added to an image. To add alternate text, select an image and select Picture from the Format menu. In the dialog box that follows, select the Settings tab and type the alternate text in the Picture place-holder box. If you haven't saved the document as an HTML file, you will not see a Settings tab.

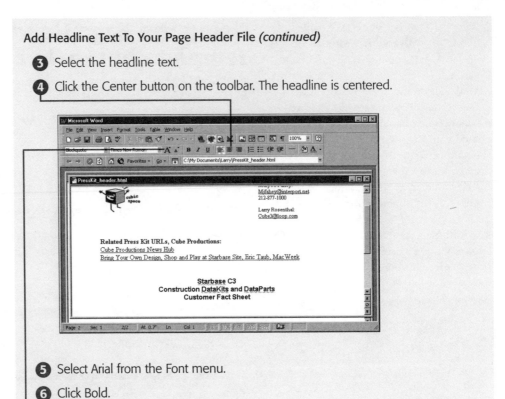

Add Headline Text To Your Page Header File *(continued)*

3 Select the headline text.

4 Click the Center button on the toolbar. The headline is centered.

5 Select Arial from the Font menu.

6 Click Bold.

7 Click the Font Size button to increase the font size.

Formatting Lists

In this fact sheet example, you'll add a list to display products. HTML provides bulleted lists and numbered lists, which are both useful for fact sheets. Word also offers a selection of graphical images that you can use in place of standard bullets.

Converting to HTML.
When you save a Word document in HTML, Word displays the page in a way that is similar to the way it will appear in a Web browser. Formatting that is not supported by HTML is removed.

Bored with plain bullets?
In HTML, bullets are created with an Unordered List tag. The distance between the bullet and the text cannot be controlled. Word 97 offers a selection of graphical images that you can substitute for the bullet characters. Graphical characters that perform the same function as bullets are sometimes called dingbats.

Create a Bulleted List

1 Type the text as shown.

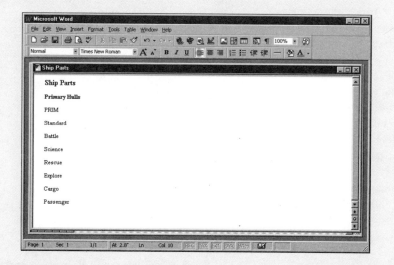

2 Select the text after "Primary Hulls" and then choose Bullets And Numbering from the Format menu.

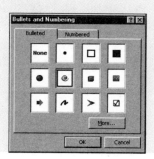

3 The Bullets And Numbering dialog box will display a selection of graphical bullets. Select a standard bullet symbol or a graphical image and click OK.

Dividing words. The rules of word division require that certain words never be divided. For example, proper names such as "New York" and number word groups such as "page 80" should stay together. To adhere to word division rules, replace a standard space with a nonbreaking space using Word's Symbol palette on the Insert menu.

Writer's guides and writing handbooks are useful source books for writers, editors, and managers who are composing pages for the Web. These books offer rules and guidelines summarizing punctuation, grammar, and usage. Of these, Strunk and White's *The Elements of Style* is the most famous. Others include:

> Theodore Bernstein's *The Careful Writer: A Modern Guide to English Usage*

> Margaret Bryant's *Current American Usage: How Americans Say It and Write It*

> Bergen and Cornelia Evans' *A Dictionary of Contemporary American Usage*

> The University of Chicago Press' *A Manual of Style.*

Create a Bulleted List *(continued)*

4 Select the list and then drag the left paragraph indent marker one half-inch away from the edge of the page. The text is indented.

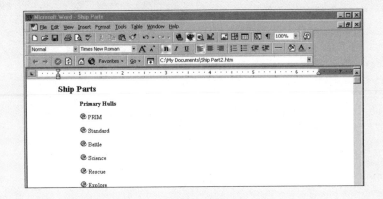

Additional Formatting for Fact Sheets

The formatting you use on a fact sheet will depend on the content. Limit line length in paragraph text with paragraph indents. Use ample white space between paragraphs and use tables to control side-by-side elements.

Copyright and the Web.
Much of the material on the Web is protected by copyrights. To use anything you find on the Web in your own site, you must have a license to copy and use the work. Some exceptions:

> If the material is in the public domain

> If your use is fair use (see below)

> If the material is factual or an idea

Copyright without permission is fair when a copy is used for criticism, comment, news, reporting, teaching (including multiple copies for class-rooms), scholarship, or research.

Saving a document in the native Word file format. Because some Word formatting features are not supported in HTML, save a document in Word's own format and then use Save As HTML to save an HTML version. By maintaining an original in Word's own File Format, you will preserve any formatting that may be lost when you save a copy of the document as an HTML file.

Enter Title Text, Paragraph Text, and Table Text

Add the following characteristics:

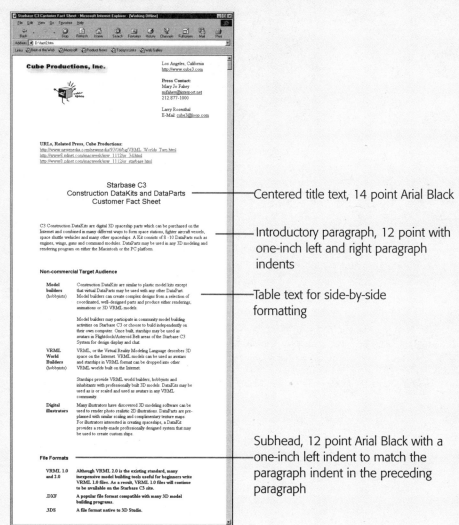

Centered title text, 14 point Arial Black

Introductory paragraph, 12 point with one-inch left and right paragraph indents

Table text for side-by-side formatting

Subhead, 12 point Arial Black with a one-inch left indent to match the paragraph indent in the preceding paragraph

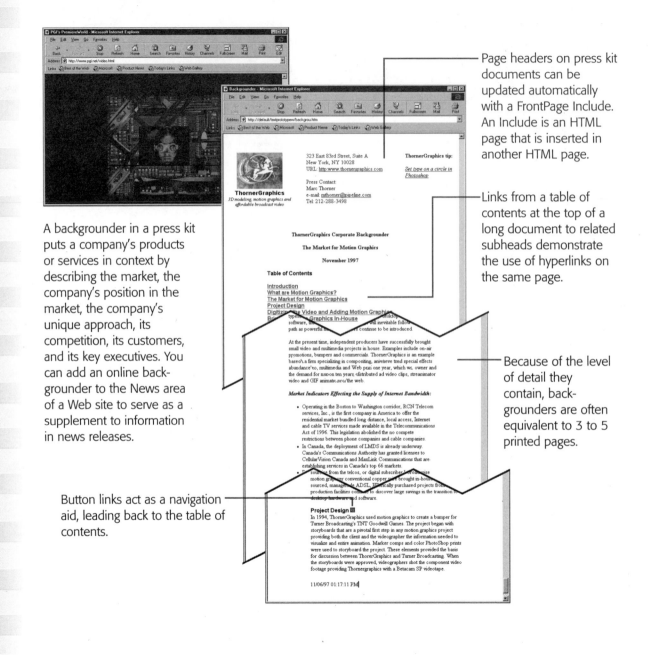

Page headers on press kit documents can be updated automatically with a FrontPage Include. An Include is an HTML page that is inserted in another HTML page.

Links from a table of contents at the top of a long document to related subheads demonstrate the use of hyperlinks on the same page.

A backgrounder in a press kit puts a company's products or services in context by describing the market, the company's position in the market, the company's unique approach, its competition, its customers, and its key executives. You can add an online back-grounder to the News area of a Web site to serve as a supplement to information in news releases.

Because of the level of detail they contain, back-grounders are often equivalent to 3 to 5 printed pages.

Button links act as a navigation aid, leading back to the table of contents.

3 A Backgrounder

A company backgrounder may be the longest document among those in your press kit because of the breadth of information it provides about your company's products or services. To re-create this type of longer Web document, you'll use Microsoft FrontPage. You'll create hyperlink jumps as navigational shortcuts within the backgrounder and you'll use a FrontPage Include to update the graphic tip inside the document's header on a weekly basis. A FrontPage Include is a separate HTML page that is incorporated into the page as it is viewed in a browser.

Importance of a company backgrounder. In today's competitive market, you must distinguish your company from others offering similar products or services. A backgrounder is an appropriate place to define the unique attributes of your business, such as your product's pricing, the kind or level of customer service you offer, profiles of your customers, and information about any competitive variables you can think of.

Overview of the Backgrounder Project

ThornerGraphics (thornergraphics@worldnet.att.net) is a New York–based creative firm specializing in 3-D models and motion graphics. The backgrounder it offers in its online press kit describes the market for motion graphics and the company's position in that market.

You'll start the ThornerGraphics backgrounder by importing a Microsoft Word document into FrontPage 98. Then you'll remove the Word formatting, check the spelling of the text, and add formatting to the new FrontPage document. Because the backgrounder is a long document, you'll create links from the table of contents text to the subheads. After the backgrounder is complete, you can create a page header as a separate HTML document. You will add this separate HTML document to the top of each backgrounder page as a FrontPage Include. Running a site-wide Replace in the FrontPage Explorer window, you will also replace all instances of *ThornerGraphics* with *ThornerGraphics, Inc.*

GIF Wizard at Raspberry Hill. The GIF Wizard at the Raspberry Hill Web site is an online bit-depth reduction tool that you can use to optimize the colors in a static or animated GIF file, reducing the file size of the GIF by as much as 90 percent.

Noncommercial users can go to useast.gifwizard.com/cgi-bin/nph-gifwiz?task=frontpage for a free guest login. Click Login As Guest. If you have an image on the Web, type the URL in the field labeled URL. If your image is on your local hard disk, click the link that directs you to an alternate page. Click Browse and then locate the GIF image on your hard disk and click Open. Click Start GIF Wizard. The page that's returned will contain an optimized version of your original image. In Microsoft Internet Explorer, click the right mouse button and choose Save Image File to save the image to your system.

Backgrounder Page Design

The page characteristics that you will give the backgrounder are:

> Document subheads that are married to the paragraphs below them with line breaks rather than paragraph breaks.

> Items in a table of contents that jump to bookmarked subheads or named locations.

> A page header composed of a FrontPage Include.

> Wide page margins, which limit line length for readability.

> Dark text on a light background for editors and reporters who will print the pages.

> Ample white space between paragraphs, which provides relief to the reader.

> Logo art and page header text that require side-by-side formatting held in place with tables.

> A bulleted list, which is used to organize a list of market indicators.

A Sample Layout Using Includes

Includes, also called client-side includes, are component sections of HTML pages that are picked up by a browser when the main page is loaded. They are efficient shortcuts that you can use when building Web pages, and they are supported by both Internet Explorer and Netscape Navigator.

You may also want to add a time stamp to pages that contain time-sensitive information. After the time stamp is in place, FrontPage will update the "last modified" date whenever you make changes to the page.

Music marketing on the Internet. Music companies have been aggressive in using the Web as a marketing medium because college students make up a large segment of the music market and many dorm rooms are wired to the Internet. Examples include Geffen Records at geffen.com, Polygram–US Online at www.polygram.com, and Sony at www.sony.com.

Page header added as a FrontPage Include, which contains a frequently updated tip. Changing the Include automatically updates any page headers that have been created with the Include.

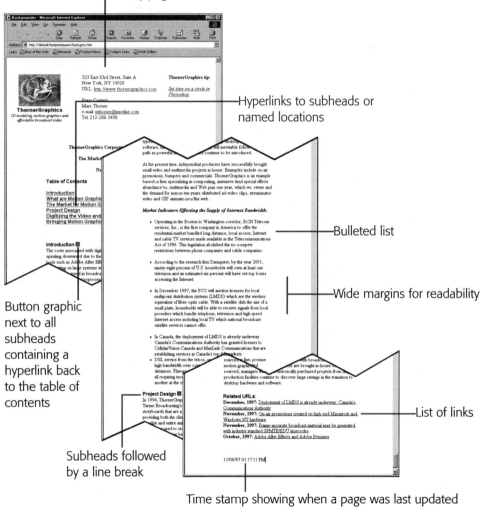

Hyperlinks to subheads or named locations

Bulleted list

Wide margins for readability

List of links

Button graphic next to all subheads containing a hyperlink back to the table of contents

Subheads followed by a line break

Time stamp showing when a page was last updated

Aligning the navigation bar with an invisible page axis. Chapter 2 describes how adding navigation bars is a popular way to simplify navigation.

When you create a page, visualize vertical left and right axes along each side of the navigation bar. Try to line up other page elements along these axes. Your page content should not extend to the edge of the browser window.

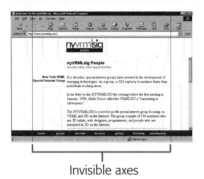

Invisible axes

Getting Organized

Before you begin working in FrontPage, you'll need to:

> Review Chapter 2 to learn how to build a text prototype of your Web site before you develop its content in depth. Build an organized structure in advance and add content to your prototype as you develop it.

> Prepare images for your Web pages in advance using Image Composer and save the art files in GIF or JPEG format.

> Consider importing an existing Web site into FrontPage using the Import Web wizard, which appears when you choose Import An Existing Web from the New FrontPage Web dialog box. Web sites can be imported from a local computer, a Web server on an intranet, or a Web server on the Internet.

Adding a Word Document to Your FrontPage Web

Although you can type the text for a Web page into the FrontPage Editor window, Web page content is often written by copywriters who use Word as a word processor, so you will often need to transfer the text from Word to FrontPage.

You will begin the ThornerGraphics backgrounder by importing a Word document into a site that has a structure similar to the site illustrated in Chapter 2. You will add text that was developed in Word to a new backgrounder page in the News area of the Web site. The News page acts as a grouped area or index page and contains table of contents links to a backgrounder, news releases, fact sheets, and press clips.

Using the Private folder in a FrontPage Web. The Private folder in a FrontPage Web site is a convenient place to archive pages that need to be put away for several months. For example, if you use your Web site to recruit college graduates, you might publish a schedule of college interviews twice a year. When the interviews are concluded, you can put the event page in the Private folder. The next time college interviews are scheduled, you can reuse the page.

Add a Backgrounder Page to Your FrontPage Web Site

1 Start FrontPage and open the Text Prototype Web that you created in Chapter 2.

2 Click the Navigation view icon.

3 In the FrontPage Explorer window, click the News page icon and click the New Page button on the toolbar. A new page icon labeled New Page 1 appears beneath the News page.

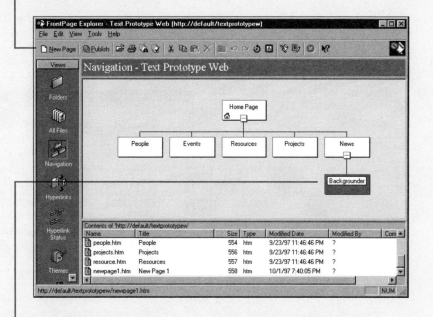

4 Click the default label on the New Page 1 icon, rename this page to "Backgrounder," and press Enter.

Backgrounder

Downloading the text file for this project. The ThornerGraphics document is available on this book's Web page. You can find it at mspress.microsoft.com/mspress/products/1576.

Save the Backgrounder Page

1 Double-click the Backgrounder page icon to open the page in the FrontPage Editor window.

2 Choose Save As from the File menu to save this page, and enter the name "Backgrounder.htm."

Import a Word Document into the Backgrounder Page

1 With the Backgrounder page open in the FrontPage Editor window, choose File from the Insert menu.

2 In the Select File dialog box, locate the ThornerGraphics document and click Open. The Word document will be displayed, showing the formatting created in Word.

A source for marketing reference materials. In New York City, the Professional Practice Center at the Public Relations Society of America is a valuable source for books that describe how to write publicity pieces. The Center is also a source for publicity directories and other marketing reference materials. PRSA members can use the library for free. Nonmembers pay a fee. The Center is at 33 Irving Place, NY, NY 10003. For information, call (212) 995-2230.

For those outside the New York City area, the PRSA has a fax on demand service at 1-800-778-7066. Outside of the United States, call 402-449-2270. Other information about the PRSA is available on the organization's Web site at www. prsa.org.

Import a Word Document into the Backgrounder Page *(continued)*

Formatting added in Word is visible in FrontPage.

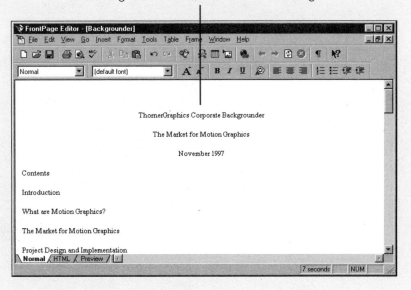

Removing Word Formatting from the Imported Text

Remove formatting from the ThornerGraphics imported Word document so that formatting added in the FrontPage Editor will work properly.

Select the Text and Remove its Formatting

1 Choose Select All from the Edit menu.

2 Choose Remove Formatting from the Format menu.

The FrontPage spelling checker. The FrontPage spelling checker displays any misspelled words it finds in the FrontPage Editor window. Portions of the page created with an Include must have their spelling checked independently.

Checking the Spelling of Your Document

FrontPage 98 uses the Microsoft Office spelling checker (including the Microsoft Custom Dictionary) as well as the Microsoft Office Thesaurus.

Run the FrontPage Spelling Checker

① Choose Spelling from the Tools menu.

② In the Spelling dialog box, click one of the following options:

Ignore to ignore the highlighted word if it is spelled correctly.

Ignore All to ignore all instances of the highlighted word.

Change to replace the highlighted word with the word you've clicked on the Suggestions list or with the word you've typed into the Change To field.

Change All to change all instances of the word.

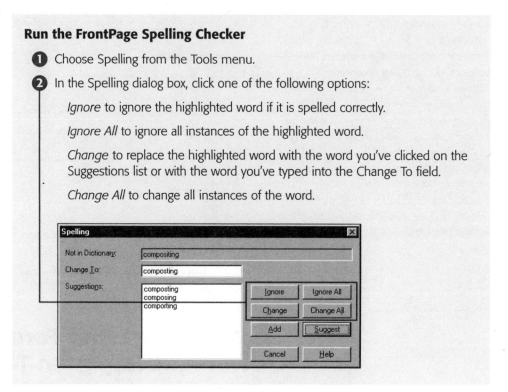

Adding Formatting Suitable for a Backgrounder

You can now apply formatting that would be suitable for the backgrounder, such as wide margins and bulleted lists.

Marketing electronically. The platform-independent nature of the Web means that businesses no longer need to develop applications for several different computing platforms. This offers an overwhelming competitive advantage when information is marketed electronically to a variety of different customers at different locations.

View the Format Marks in Your Document

With the Backgrounder page open in the FrontPage Editor window, click the Show/Hide ¶ button on the toolbar. Page formatting elements such as paragraph marks and line breaks will be displayed.

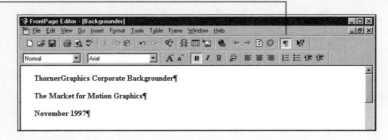

Format the Title, Subhead, and Date

1. Select the title, subhead, and date text.

2. Click the Center button to center the title, subhead, and date.

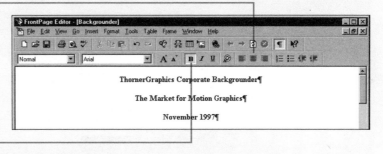

3. Click the Bold button to make the selected text bold.

Backgrounder

Pantone matching. If your client asks you to use a corporate color on a Web site, what do you do? The color in your client's logo or letterhead is most likely a Pantone color that you can look up in Photoshop. Graphic designers assign Pantone colors to the artwork they create and printers use matching inks. (If your client does not know the exact Pantone number, you'll need to call the client's graphic designer or printer.)

Format the Table of Contents

1 Select the table of contents text.

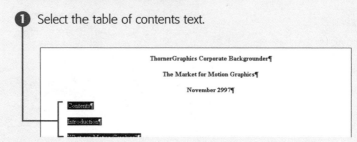

2 Choose Arial from the Font list on the Format toolbar.

3 Assign the subheads the Arial font also.

Add Large Page Indents to Limit Line Length

1 Select all the backgrounder text beginning with the words "Table of Contents."

2 Click the Increase Indent button twice. Large paragraph indents are added to the body of the backgrounder to make the lines more readable.

3 Click anywhere in the document to deselect the text.

Converting a Pantone color to a hexidecimal triplet. To specify a Pantone color on an HTML page, you'll need to know the hexadecimal triplet that is the equivalent of the color. A hexadecimal triplet is three pairs of digits. Each pair is the hexadecimal equivalent of one of the three numbers that make up an RGB (red, green, blue) color.

To learn the hexadecimal triplet for a Pantone color, open Photoshop and click the Foreground color chip at the base of the Photoshop toolbar. In the dialog box, click Custom. Use the list of Pantone colors to find your client's color. Copy down the numeric values for the R, G, and B fields and exit Photoshop. Visit the Color Editor for CGI at www.bbsinc.com/bbs-cgi-bin/colorEditor.cgi, scroll down the page and put an *x* in the check box labeled Input RGB Value. Type the numeric RGB numbers into the fields provided and click Test It Now. The page will display the color you are testing and the hexadecimal triplet you'll need for the Web will be displayed near the top of the page in an HTML Body tag.

Replace Paragraph Marks with Line Breaks

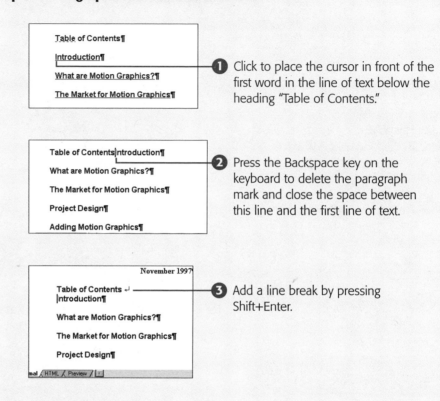

1 Click to place the cursor in front of the first word in the line of text below the heading "Table of Contents."

2 Press the Backspace key on the keyboard to delete the paragraph mark and close the space between this line and the first line of text.

3 Add a line break by pressing Shift+Enter.

4 Repeat these steps to replace each of the paragraph marks in the table of contents text with line breaks.

Direct marketing on the Web. If you've never seen a Web site that sells products, visit Amazon.com at www.amazon.com. The Amazon home page boasts savings of up to 40 percent. Use the store's powerful search engine to browse the 2.5 million titles by keyword, by subject, by author, or by title.

Glenn Fleishman, catalog manager at Amazon, is well known for being a pioneer in Internet marketing. In July 1994, Fleishman started the now-defunct Internet Marketing discussion list. The list archive still exists at www.i-m.com.

Format a Bulleted List

1 Select the text to be formatted with bullets.

2 Choose Bullets And Numbering from the Format menu.

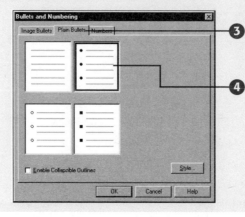

3 In the Bullets And Numbering dialog box, click the Plain Bullets tab.

4 Select a bullet style on the Plain Bullets tab and click OK.

If you want regular, round bullets, you can just select the text and click the Bulleted List button on the Format toolbar.

Remove the Word Processed Bullets from the Text

1 Click to place the cursor to the right of one of the bullets that is left over from the Word document.

> • Operating in the Boston to Washington corridor, RCN Telecom services, Inc., is the first company in America to offer the reside market bundled long distance, local access, Internet and cable services made available in the Telecommunications Act of 1996 This legislation abolished the no compete restrictions between companies and cable companies. ¶
> • According to the research firm Dataquest, by the year 2001, ninety-eight percent of U.S. households will own at least one television and an estimated six-percent will have set-top boxes accessing the Internet.¶
> • In December 1997, the FCC will auction licenses for local mult distribution systems (LMDS) which are the wireless equivalent fiber-optic cable. With a satellite dish the size of a small plate,

2 Press the Delete key on the keyboard to remove the bullet character.

3 Repeat steps 1 and 2 to remove the remaining bullets.

Web users' views about ads on the Internet.

According to an independent study by the Internet Advertising Bureau, 55 percent of Web users who were asked for their views about online advertising were positive about Web ads. Sixty-three percent of those surveyed viewed Web advertisers as forward-thinking.

Adjust Paragraph Spacing Between List Items

1 If the paragraph leading between list items is too tight, click to place the cursor to the left of a paragraph mark at the end of a paragraph.

- Operating in the Boston to Washington corridor, RCN T services, Inc., is the first company in America to offer the market bundled long distance, local access, Internet and services made available in the Telecommunications Act of This legislation abolished the no compete restrictions bet companies and cable companies. ¶
- According to the research firm Dataquest, by the year 20 ninety-eight percent of U.S. households will own at least television and an estimated six-percent will have set-top accessing the Internet. ¶

2 Add a line break by pressing Shift+Enter. A line break and a paragraph mark are displayed.

- Operating in the Boston to Washington corridor, RCN Telec services, Inc., is the first company in America to offer the res market bundled long distance, local access, Internet and cabl services made available in the Telecommunications Act of 19 This legislation abolished the no compete restrictions betwee companies and cable companies. ↵
  ¶
- According to the research firm Dataquest, by the year 2001, ninety-eight percent of U.S. households will own at least one television and an estimated six-percent will have set-top boxe accessing the Internet. ¶

3 Repeat steps 1 and 2 to adjust the leading between the remaining list items.

4 Click Show/Hide ¶ on the Format toolbar to remove the marks. The paragraph marks and line break marks disappear from view.

Button graphics containing hyperlinks.

In the ThornerGraphics sample, an arrow graphic from the FrontPage Clip Art Gallery was inserted to the right of each subhead in the backgrounder. The words "Table of Contents" were defined as a bookmark and a hyperlink to the table of contents bookmark was added to each of the button graphics. This helps viewers navigate to the top of the page.

The clip art folder that comes with Microsoft FrontPage contains a button graphic named WB01728_.gif located in the clip1 folder (C:\Program Files\ Microsoft FrontPage\clipart\clip1). Before you insert the button graphic, use Image Composer to reduce the size of the graphic by 50 percent. Open the button in Image Composer, choose Composition Setup from the File menu, and reduce the height and width on the Composition Setup dialog box from 21 to 10. Resave the graphic.

Creating Bookmarks for Hyperlink Jumps

In the ThornerGraphics document, you can add bookmarks to each subhead so that you can create hyperlinks in the table of contents that jump to the bookmarks. Bookmarks are named locations on a page that can be the target of hyperlinks.

Plan Named Locations in Your Document

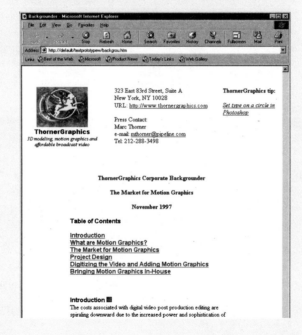

① Check to see if the table of contents items match your subheads.

② Identify one or two words in each subhead to be designated as named locations. These words will be your bookmarks. The matching table of contents items will contain hyperlinks that jump to the bookmarks.

Web-related ad spending. According to a Cowles/Simba Information report, Web-related ad spending is due to reach $2.57 billion in the year 2000. This figure is still only a fraction of what is spent on print and broadcast media. Web ads are heavily weighted in the computer category, although consumer product advertisers such as Procter & Gamble, Kellogg's, and Sears have launched aggressive Web ad campaigns.

Create Bookmarks

1 Select the first named location in a page subhead.

2 From the Edit menu, choose Bookmark.

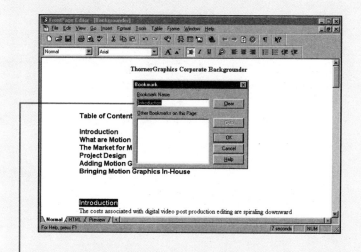

3 In the Bookmark dialog box, the named location appears in the field labeled Bookmark Name. Click OK. FrontPage displays a dotted underline beneath the bookmark or named location.

4 Repeat steps 1 through 3 to create bookmarks for the remaining subheads.

Adding Hyperlinks to Bookmarks

After the bookmarks are created, you can add hyperlinks to the table of contents text so that visitors can jump to subheads instead of scrolling down through the document manually. You can create hyperlinks to bookmarks on the same page, to bookmarks on another page in the Web site, or to bookmarks on any page on the Web.

Backgrounder

Standard formats for press kit documents.
Every marketing and public relations textbook advises you never to deviate from the standard formats developed for press kit components. Resist the temptation to add elaborate formatting to your press kit components. News releases, backgrounders, and fact sheets are intended to be source materials for editors and reporters rather than finished, published pieces.

Create a Hyperlink

1 Select the text that requires a hyperlink.

Table of Contents

Introduction
What are Motion Graphics?
The Market for Motion Graphics
Project Design
Digitizing the Video and Adding Motion Graphics
Bringing Motion Graphics In-House

2 From the Insert menu, choose Hyperlink.

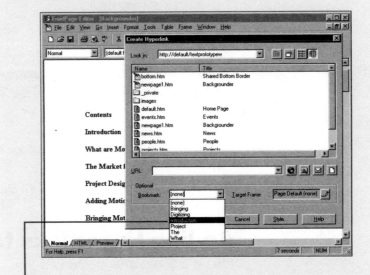

3 In the Create Hyperlink dialog box, choose the bookmark from the Bookmark drop-down menu that matches the table of contents entry you've chosen.

4 Repeat steps 1 through 3 to add hyperlinks to the remaining entries. FrontPage displays hyperlinks as underlined text.

Changing a file name in your Web. If you need to change the file name of the home page from default.htm to index.htm to accommodate your ISP's server, select the file in the All Files view or in the file list beneath the Navigation pane in Navigation view. Choose Rename from the Edit menu, retype the file name, and press Enter. FrontPage will manage the change and all related changes in the HTML for your Web.

Adding a Time Stamp to a Page

The FrontPage Timestamp function stamps the time from your computer's clock wherever you position the cursor. Many Web sites precede timestamp text with the phrase, "This site was last updated on..." This gives visitors an idea of how often content changes.

Add a Time Stamp

1 Position the cursor at the end of the backgrounder.

2 Choose Timestamp from the Insert menu.

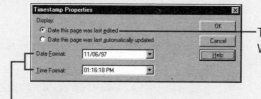

The button labeled Date This Page Was Last Edited is selected.

3 Select date and time formats and click OK.

Planning a FrontPage Include

In the ThornerGraphics backgrounder, the page header that contains a graphics tip is a FrontPage Include. You can use Includes for sections of pages that change frequently. When changes are needed, you can edit the Include, and the change you make will be reflected on all other press kit headers that include the Include. Once you understand how FrontPage Includes work, you'll be able to invent many applications for Includes, such as the ideas in the table on the next page.

Changing your HTML.
If you need to make a change in the HTML for a page, you'll need to click the HTML tab in the FrontPage Editor and change the HTML tags by hand. The FrontPage Replace command will search only the text content of the pages in your Web site, not the HTML.

Uses for Includes	
Content	Include Applications
Press kit documents	List of links in a page header that gets repeated on several documents
Fact sheets	Prices or data that appear on more than one page

Creating Content for a FrontPage Include

You should create the HTML document for the FrontPage Include inside the Private folder in your Web. This will prevent viewers from accessing it directly.

Create a New Page Within the Private Folder

1 Double-click the Private folder (it's named "_Private") on the file list window beneath the Navigation pane in the FrontPage Explorer window.

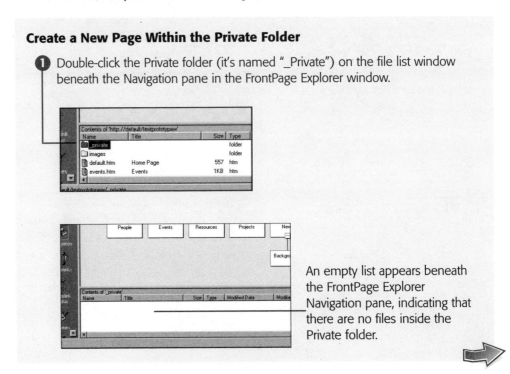

An empty list appears beneath the FrontPage Explorer Navigation pane, indicating that there are no files inside the Private folder.

Mass e-mail is spamming. Sending commercial, off-topic, or mass e-mail messages to newsgroups is considered intrusive and has been nicknamed spamming. Blacklists, watchdog groups, and lawsuits have been the result. Surprisingly, a few large mailing list firms have started to offer e-mail lists to their customers and they're not shy about setting up exhibit space at direct marketing shows worldwide. Most forms of mass e-mail messages are considered an invasion of privacy, so you should avoid this form of marketing.

Create a New Page Within the Private Folder *(continued)*

② Click the New Page button on the FrontPage Explorer toolbar. A document named "Default.htm" appears on the file list.

③ Rename this new document "Newshead.htm," and then double-click it to open the page. The page opens in the FrontPage Editor.

Turning Off the Include's Shared Border

If you've used the Text Prototype Web in Chapter 2 as your foundation Web site for the backgrounder project, the page you created for the Include may have a shared border. In Chapter 2, you created a shared border to build a navigation bar on every page. Because an Include is a small HTML page that gets inserted into the backgrounder, you will want to turn off the shared border on the Include page.

Turn Off Shared Borders

❶ Choose Shared Border from the Tools menu of the FrontPage Editor.

❷ In the Page Borders dialog box, click the button labeled Set For This Page Only.

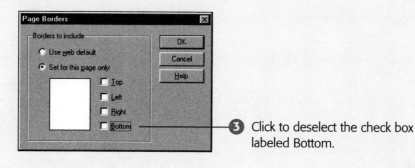

❸ Click to deselect the check box labeled Bottom.

The importance of a site map. Chapter 2 describes the importance of developing a site map at the start of your project. As you update the site and add pages, keep updating the site map. You'll discover that it will be an important tool for communicating changes to your Web team, which might consist of a manager or client, one or more graphic designers, a writer or marketing specialist, and a technical specialist. Keep the site map in a central place for everyone to refer to or send every team member an up-to-date printout as the site changes.

The HTML page you'll create for the Include will contain enough text and graphics for a ThornerGraphics letterhead. The Include will become the entire top of the backgrounder page or the top of any other document that uses the Include. Once you've created a New Page inside the Private folder, create a three-celled table, add the logo to the left cell, type contact information into the middle cell, and enter a tip about graphics into the cell on the right.

Adding Include Content to a Web Page

After you finish creating content for the FrontPage Include, you are ready to add it to your principal Web document.

Add the Page Header Include to the Backgrounder Page

1 Double-click the Backgrounder page in the FrontPage Explorer. The page will be displayed in the FrontPage Editor.

2 Position the cursor at the top of the document. You may need to press Enter to make room at the top of the document.

3 From the Insert menu, choose FrontPage Component.

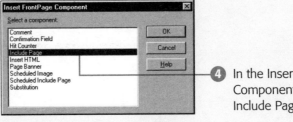

4 In the Insert FrontPage Component dialog box, choose Include Page and click OK.

Press clips on the Web. If you have press clippings, investigate whether the articles have been published by other sources on the Web. If so, some of the press clips on your News page could be links to online articles.

Add the Page Header Include to the Backgrounder Page *(continued)*

5 In the Include Page Component Properties dialog box, click the Browse button.

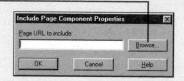

6 In the Current Web dialog box, open the Private folder by double-clicking it.

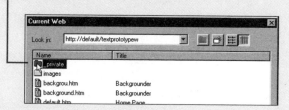

7 Select the newshead.htm page and click OK. The Page URL of the Include will be displayed in the Include Page Component Properties dialog box.

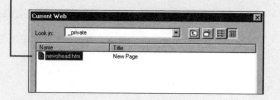

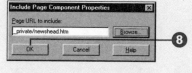

8 Click OK to close the Include Page Component Properties dialog box.

Backgrounder

Focusing on the uniqueness of your customer. *Breakthrough Thinking,* by Gerald Nadler and Shozo Hibino, explains that focusing on the uniqueness of a customer takes your eye beyond the bottom line to the product or service that predicts future success.

Using the FrontPage Replace Command

The FrontPage Replace command is one of the program's most powerful features. You can start it from the FrontPage Explorer to find and replace text on an individual Web page or from the FrontPage Editor to find and replace text on all the pages in a Web site. In this example, you will replace "ThornerGraphics" with "ThornerGraphics, Inc." on all the pages of the Web site.

Run the Replace Command from the FrontPage Explorer

1 Choose Replace from the Tools menu in the FrontPage Explorer window for a site-wide Find and Replace.

2 Enter the text to replace, ThornerGraphics, in the field labeled Find What.

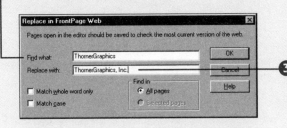

3 Enter the new text, ThornerGraphics, Inc., in the field labeled Replace With and click OK.

FrontPage displays a report of the number of instances changed and a list of pages where the changes were made.

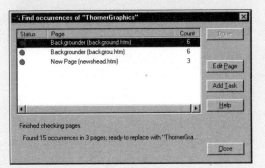

4 Click Close to close this dialog box.

Written words on the Web. The visual layout of a Web site is important, but so is the content. As Jay Conrad Levinson and Charles Rubin explain in *Guerrilla Marketing Online Weapons*, "the written word is the main method of communication in the online world." Refining the web's visual layout should not mean eliminating most of its written communication.

Run the Replace Command from the FrontPage Editor

1 If you need to replace text on only one page, open the page in the FrontPage Editor and choose Replace from the Edit menu.

2 In the Replace dialog box, click Find Next, Replace, or Replace All to start the search.

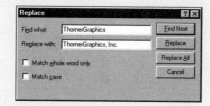

3 Click Cancel to close the dialog box.

Sound Wire, a Web music store founded in 1994, has recently made a transition from vinyl and music CDs to all-digital music sold to customers who use CyberCash Wallets.

FOR IMMEDIATE RELEASE

SOUND WIRE LAUNCHES DIGITAL COMMERCE SITE FOR ONLINE DELIVERY OF MUSIC

Drop Media, a Sound Wire Subsidiary, Will Broker CyberCash Payment System

to Other Merchants on the Internet

NEW YORK - November 1, 1997 - Designed for discriminating audiophiles who wish to acquire music digitally, the new Sound Wire Web site is an early example of how digital products will be sold through micropayments.

Beginning November 1, 1997, Sound Wire will launch an all-digital music retail site with songs from artist/songwriters Spike Preggin, Anders Parker, Jud Ehrbar, Chris Harford and Sean Thompson.

Two's Compliment
Two's Compliment is Sound Wire's new label that will publish and distribute sound digitally over the Internet. In a city considered to be the center of the music industry, Sound Wire will distinguish itself as an all-digital music publisher and retailer using micropayment technology to sell songs.

Music Formats for Digital Audiophiles
The Sound Wire site's playlist gives visitors an option to listen via RealAudio streams or to purchase MP2 files for approximately $1.50 each. Given that a customer has sufficient funds in his/her CyberCash or Microsoft wallet, songs may be downloaded when a purchase is electronically approved.

Sound Wire's CyberCash Broker Business
Sound Wire's CyberCash broker business is analogous to all-digital consignment Sales.
Sound Wire founder Joe Maissel is a Microsoft Certified Systems engineer who formerly worked for Apple Computer and he's also comfortable with the UNIX operating system. Realizing merchant systems may be technically overwhelming to digital illustrators and digital 3D modelers, Joe has developed Drop Media, a Sound Wire subsidiary that brokers CyberCash micropayment technology to small companies interested in selling digital products on the Internet.

CyberCash Wallet and Microsoft Wallet are Compatible
Recently, CyberCash, the company who created CyberCoin wallet client software, has provided their CyberCoin Payment Module for Microsoft's new wallet software. The Microsoft wallet, which will be distributed with Internet Explorer 4.0 and future versions of Windows is available now as a plug-in to Internet Explorer 4.0 and Netscape Navigator 3.0. The wallet software is available at http://www.microsoft.com/commerce/wallet/local/plginst.html. The CyberCoin wallet from CyberCash is available at http://www.cybercash.com. Either wallet may be used to purchase products from CyberCash merchants.

About Sound Wire
Headquartered in New York, Sound Wire is a music publisher, distributor and retailer specializing in digital music and electronic commerce. Founded by owner Joe Maissel, Soundware first opened a music store on the web in 1995 and has recently made the transition from vinyl and CDs to all-digital music. Sound Wire is located on the Web at http://www.soundwire.com

###

Press Contact:
Mary Jo Fahey
mjfahey@interport.net

The news release is a 500– to 1000–word document that contains an announcement about the company, a product, an idea, a promotion, or an event.

You can use FrontPage 98 to create an HTML news release for the News section of your Web site.

A News Release and Pitch Letter

Editors and writing samples. Some editors put more emphasis than others on writing samples. If your work has never been published, look for publications with tips or notes. These are safe areas for editors to try out new writers. Small regional weekly newspapers are also good starting points. Some have columns on new media or the Internet.

News releases and pitch letters are the fundamental instruments that publicists use to suggest story ideas to magazine and newspaper editors. Although many publicists now send news releases through e-mail, some editors report that they routinely delete these messages because, as one editor has said, "the noise level is overwhelming." Although the chapter does not suggest abandoning the e-mail news release format, it does suggest an alternative: mailing a carefully researched pitch letter to an editor instead. It also shows how to place news releases on your site that are organized by date.

The Sound Wire sample in this chapter also demonstrates how to research contacts at magazines and gather editorial calendars so you can develop an e-mail distribution list in Microsoft Outlook and create a pitch letter that is designed to match a publication's editorial calendar.

The subject of the Sound Wire pitch letter and news release is the company's newsworthy, real-life story about the launch of an all-digital music commerce site at www.soundwire.com.

Sample Layouts

The following sample layouts show the characteristics of a pitch letter, a news release, and a news page on which you can organize the news releases.

E-Mail Pitch Letter

The Sound Wire pitch letter proposing a story idea has minimal formatting because it's an ASCII document that you'll send out through e-mail. If you've never written a pitch letter, follow the step-by-step Sound Wire exercise and use it as a model to craft your own pitch letter.

Opening summary introduces your story idea

Suggested topics in the form of bullets. Begin this section with "Topics may include:"

Optional section suggests a round-up or story that compares two or more competitors

Titles of other articles you've written. If the articles are on the Web, include the URLs

The difference between a news release and a pitch letter. A news release suggests to an editor that a story idea be assigned to a staff or freelance writer. A pitch letter suggests that you write the story. Increase your chances of success by investigating a publication's editorial calendar and look for an upcoming issue that complements your topic. Editorial calendars are often available at a publication's Web site.

HTML News Release

The online news release uses an HTML format that mimics the public relations news release that a company might send out on paper.

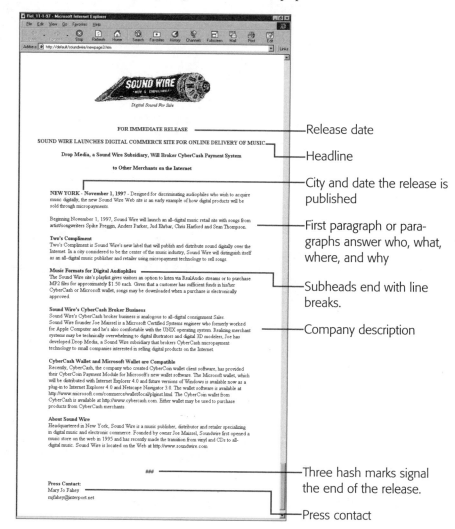

— Release date

— Headline

— City and date the release is published

— First paragraph or paragraphs answer who, what, where, and why

— Subheads end with line breaks.

— Company description

— Three hash marks signal the end of the release.

— Press contact

Robot indexing at search engines. Robot software programs used by search engines constantly search the Web for new or updated pages. Although search engines will eventually find your Web site by following links, submit your URL to the Internet's top search engines to speed up the process. For more information about search engines and submitting your URL, see Chapter 5, "Optimizing Placement in Search Results."

HTML News Page

The HTML news page uses a list to organize news releases in reverse date order so the most recent news is at the top of the list.

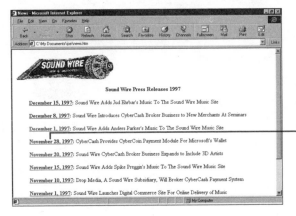

List news releases in reverse chronological order with the most recent first.

Make the release date a hyperlink to the press release.

Getting Organized

This chapter requires more preparation than any other chapter. For example, before you write your pitch letter, you need to gather e-mail addresses, editorial calendars, and author guidelines from the Web and save this information on your system. Then you can enter this editorial information in Microsoft Outlook, which allows you to attach to a contact record the editorial calendar and author guidelines as journal entries. In this chapter, you'll also learn how to create a contact record, create categories for your contact records, find a record, and automate a news release mass mailing.

Before you use Microsoft FrontPage to create the Web pages, you'll need to:

> Review Chapter 2 to learn how to build a text prototype of a Web site prior to developing its in-depth content. Add content to the prototype as you develop it. With this approach, you build an organized, underlying structure in advance.

Feature article vs. round-up. A feature article is a full-length descriptive article covering one company or one product. Although this is a prestigious position for your story, a round-up is the next-best alternative. A round-up is the nickname for a story that rounds up competitive products or services and stitches together smaller features on each one. Your company or project may fit into a larger story or theme.

> Develop a contact list of editors' e-mail addresses.

> Thoroughly research each publication site to investigate how the publication prefers to receive news releases. Look for links such as "How to contact us," "About us," or "Masthead."

Planning a Pitch Letter

A pitch letter is a one-page, mini-proposal that presents a story idea to an editor. It consists of two to three paragraphs and a list of bulleted topics for a suggested article. If you've thought about submitting an article for a publication, never write the entire article before you send the editor a pitch letter. If an editor is interested in your story, the editor will want to discuss the content with you first and provide directions about topics that should be added, deleted, or emphasized. Your article idea may be more appealing to an editor if you suggest a round-up article covering two or three firms offering a similar product or service. Round-ups are a popular format in computer magazines. Readers like comparison shopping pieces and the format lends itself to sidebars containing details such as product features, benefits, prices, URLs, and contact information.

Your Contact List

The title of the editor who assigns stories varies from publication to publication, but this is important information that you'll need to research and record in your notes or your Outlook database. At *Web Techniques*, for example, the editor-in-chief assigns stories. At *Web Review*, the all-digital sister publication to *Web Techniques*, the managing editor makes story assignments.

Is an E-Mail Pitch Letter Acceptable?

The Sound Wire pitch letter that you'll create in Microsoft Outlook is an example of a letter that could be sent to editors@web-techniques.com. Michael Floyd, the editor-in-chief of *Web Techniques* magazine, encourages developers

Your marketing effort in newsgroups. Like mailing lists, newsgroups consist of shared messages. Instead of reading e-mail, newsgroup participants view newsgroup messages in a newsreader program. Web browser software comes bundled with newsreader software.

Never post an ad to a newsgroup. Newsgroup participants adhere to strict rules of conduct, and newbies who break the rules get a rush of nasty messages, or "flames." Marketing in a newsgroup should be limited to your company name and contact information within the signature at the end of your messages.

Contributing to an online discussion in a newsgroup helps your marketing effort on the Internet. If you contribute valuable information, no one will mind if your signature contains a company name and contact information. Refer to DejaNews at www.dejanews.com to find a newsgroup that matches your business interests. Also review the news.newusers. questions newsgroup to get acquainted with newsgroup etiquette.

to submit story ideas for hands-on, how-to articles. When asked whether he prefers to be contacted about article ideas via e-mail or paper mail, he relates the story of a writer who contacted him with e-mail, paper mail, and phone calls. The writer first sent a short e-mail message containing a story idea, and followed it with a paper proposal, and then a phone call. Floyd liked the fact that the writer used all three methods.

Creating a Pitch Letter

This chapter shows a sample pitch letter that you can use as a model or template for your own letters. In the first two paragraphs of a pitch letter, summarize why you think your story is right for the publication. Tell how your article fits within a particular issue on the publication's editorial calendar. Suggest a 1500-word feature, and then use the following language exactly: "The article might include the following topics:" Follow with six or eight topics in bulleted text. This approach signals to an editor that you understand that the pitch letter offers only story suggestions. Finish the letter with a list of other articles you've written, and offer to send writing samples through regular mail. Also list the URLs of articles that you've written and that are on the Web. Send your e-mail pitch letter and don't expect a response the next day. Most editors will take at least two weeks to reply, but sometimes you may get a response a month or two later.

Using the Web to Research Editorial Information

Magazines and newspapers often use their Web sites to make editorial calendars available to writers and advertisers. Editorial calendars provide information about themes planned for particular months. For example, the theme for the November 1998 issue of *Web Techniques* is electronic commerce. If you suggest a story idea that fits within a theme and the editor agrees that it fits, you've increased your changes for a "hit." You can use a search engine such as Yahoo to find a publication's Web site, and then search the site for information that you'd want to add to your Outlook Contacts database.

FTP utility. John A. Junod's Windows Sockets FTP client application, WS_FTP Pro, is a shareware Windows FTP utility that can be used to transfer files to and from your Web server. It's available at www.ipswitch.com.

Call your Internet Service Provider. You'll need to contact your ISP to investigate the name of the Web server, the directory path, and the default name of your home page. FrontPage names your home page "default.htm." You may need to change the name to "index.htm" or "home.htm."

If your ISP is not familiar with the Microsoft Web Publishing Wizard, ask your ISP's representative to give you instructions for using a shareware FTP utility such as WS_FTP Pro.

For the Sound Wire publicity project, you'd first want to target Internet magazines, so the *Web Techniques* magazine site is a good example of the kind of site you'd like to find. It's a highly organized magazine site complete with an editorial calendar, author guidelines, and an e-mail link to the editor.

Save an Editorial Calendar

1 Visit the *Web Techniques* site at www.webtechniques.com.

2 On the magazine's home page, click the Meet Staff button. The staff Web page is displayed.

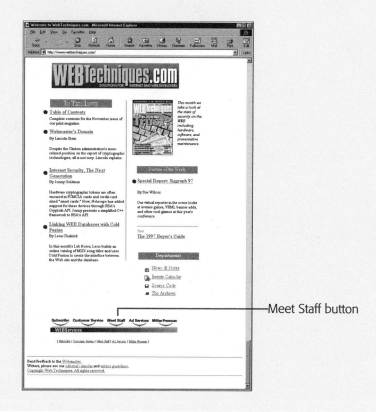

Meet Staff button

Press release index page.
A press release index page, or news page as it is called in this chapter, has become a popular convention among high-profile companies. Examples include Yahoo (www.yahoo.com) and Marriott International (www.marriott.com).

Save an Editorial Calendar *(continued)*

3 Click the e-mail link to the magazine's editor, usually the managing editor, and copy the address from the mail form that is displayed. If the e-mail address is listed in the text on the page, record the address.

4 Click the link to the magazine's editorial calendar. The editorial calendar is displayed.

5 From the File menu, choose Save As.

6 In the Save HTML Document dialog box, choose Text File from the Save As Type drop-down list, locate a folder for saving the editorial calendar text file, name it "webtechniques_edcalendar," and click Save.

Save an Editorial Calendar *(continued)*

7 Click the link to Author Guidelines. The author guidelines page is displayed.

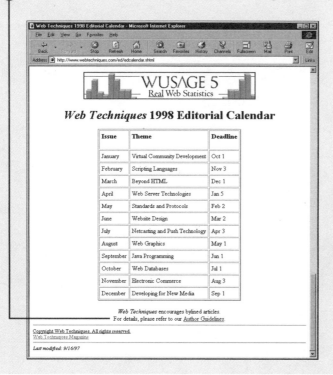

8 Repeat steps 5 and 6 to save the author guidelines to your hard disk, but name the file "webtechniques_authorguide."

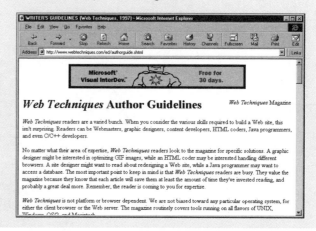

Developing an E-Mail Distribution List

Microsoft Outlook is an all-in-one tool for publicists who need to manage information and compose and send e-mail. You can use it to record detailed information about your industry contacts. Although the editor at *Web Techniques* is the contact used in this example, you'll want to develop a database of contacts at several publications.

About Microsoft Outlook.
Microsoft Outlook is a desktop information management program and e-mail client that helps you manage messages, appointments, contacts, and tasks. It also tracks activities, opens and views documents, and shares information with others using Outlook on a network.

The Outlook interface is organized into views, which represent separate folders for e-mail, calendar entries, contacts, tasks, and journal items.

Open Outlook

Start Outlook. The Outlook window opens.

Name of
current view

Outlook Bar

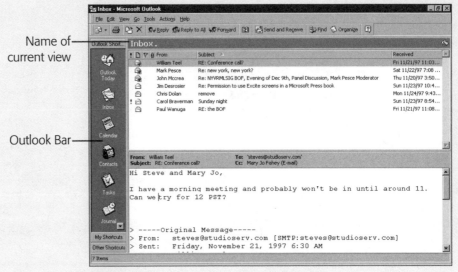

Create a Contact Record

❶ If Contacts view is not open in Outlook, click the Contacts icon on the Outlook Bar. Contacts view is displayed.

❷ Click the New Contact button. An empty Contacts record opens.

Outlook's Tip of the Day.
If you've installed the Office Assistant, Outlook's Tip of the Day is an easy way to learn more about the program. Click the Office Assistant button on the Outlook toolbar, click Options, and click the check box labeled Show Tip Of The Day At Startup.

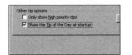

Create a Contact Record *(continued)*

3 Type a contact name in the field labeled Full Name. Press Tab on the keyboard to move the blinking insertion point from field to field and type as much information as you have about the contact.

4 Click the Save And Close button.

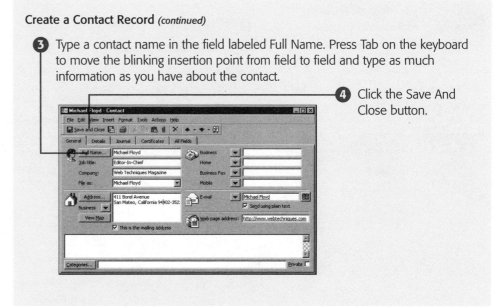

Adding Editorial Information to a Contact Record

The *Web Techniques* editorial calendar and author guidelines that you saved to your hard disk can be added to a Contacts record as a journal entry, an attachment in the form of a text file. A journal entry is normal a record of an activity, but here you are using the Journal feature in Outlook to attach a document to a Contacts record. Gathering the *Web Techniques* editorial calendar is just practice. You'll want to gather editorial calendars and author guidelines from many publications. When you're ready to pitch your idea to an editor, look through all the editorial calendars you've stored and match your article idea with a publication that has planned an entire issue around a similar topic.

Viewing two windows simultaneously in Outlook. If you'd like to see contacts while you're looking at the Inbox, right-click the Contacts icon on the Outlook Bar and choose Open In New Window from the shortcut menu.

Create a Journal Entry

1 Double-click the Contact that you just entered.

2 Click the Journal tab on the Contact dialog box. Outlook displays a summary screen of journal entries for this contact.

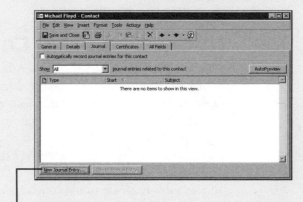

3 Click the New Journal Entry button in the lower-left corner.

Plain text in an e-mail message. The default text style for an e-mail message in Outlook is HTML. If most of your recipients need to see plain text in e-mail messages rather than HTML, choose Options from the Tools menu, click the Mail Format tab, choose Plain Text from the menu labeled Send In This Format, and click OK.

Create a Journal Entry *(continued)*

4 From the Entry Type drop-down list, choose Note.

5 From the Insert menu, choose File.

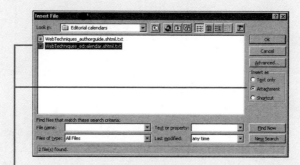

6 On the Insert File dialog box, choose the editorial calendar text file, make sure the Insert As Attachment button is selected, and then click OK.

Journal attachments in Outlook 98. Journal attachments become part of a Contacts record and can be viewed at any time. If you manage a large client list, you may forget what you've attached to your contact records. Create custom categories such as Editorial Calendar, Author Guidelines, and Calendar of Events. These categories will help you search for all contact records with editorial calendars, and so on.

Create a Journal Entry *(continued)*

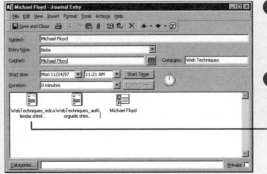

7 Repeat steps 4, 5, and 6, but add the author guidelines file as an attachment instead.

8 Double-click the editorial calendar icon to test it. A dialog box opens to warn that the attachment may contain a virus.

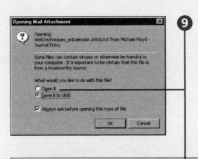

9 Select Open It and then click OK. The editorial calendar is displayed in Internet Explorer. Close the attachment, and then click Save And Close on the Outlook toolbar to close the Contact dialog box.

The Find command in Outlook 98. If you need to manage a large contact list, you'll occasionally need to use the Find command to find and correct entries. If you get a "Returned Mail: User Unknown" message indicating that an e-mail address has changed, click Outlook's Find button on the toolbar to search for the Contact record that has the incorrect e-mail address.

Trade publications. Standard Rate and Data Services publishes a multi-volume set of directories that list advertising rates of business publications, newspapers, spot radio, spot TV, direct mail lists, and outdoor and consumer magazines. These directories contain a complete list, and they can also be used to research contact information. Use the business publication directory to research the names of trade publications in your field. Most public libraries have a copy of the SRDS volumes in the business reference section.

Composing and Sending an E-Mail Pitch Letter

A pitch letter should be tailored to a particular editor's needs. Follow the creation of this sample pitch letter to *Web Techniques* magazine and use it to generate ideas for your own letter.

Compose an E-Mail Letter

1 Click the Inbox icon on the Outlook Bar. The Inbox view appears.

2 Click the New Mail Message button. An Untitled Message dialog box appears.

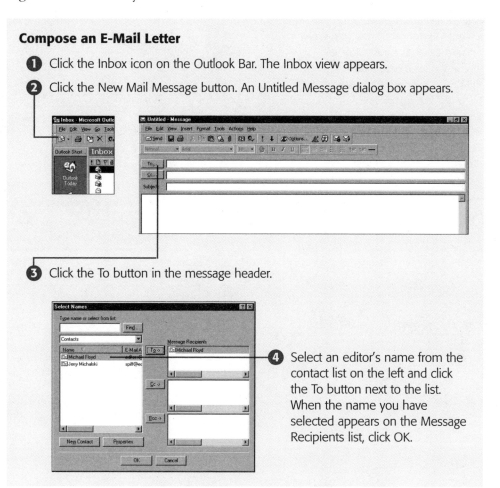

3 Click the To button in the message header.

4 Select an editor's name from the contact list on the left and click the To button next to the list. When the name you have selected appears on the Message Recipients list, click OK.

Setting up an e-mail signature in Outlook 98.
An e-mail signature is text that is automatically appended to an outgoing e-mail message. Most signatures contain content information such as your name, job title, and phone number. You can create multiple signatures and select a signature to insert after you have created an e-mail message.

To add an e-mail signature, open a mail message and select Signature/More from the Insert menu. If you do not have a signature stored, you'll see a dialog box that asks you if you'd like to create a signature. Click Yes. The Create New Signature wizard appears. Follow the directions in the wizard to create your signature.

```
-- Travis Anton
BoxTop Software, Inc.
http://www.boxtopsoft.com
```

Compose an E-Mail Letter *(continued)*

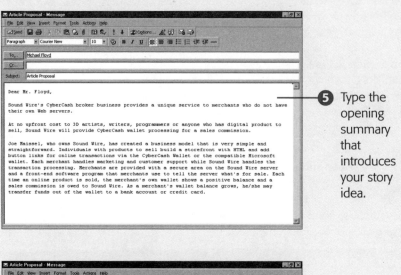

5 Type the opening summary that introduces your story idea.

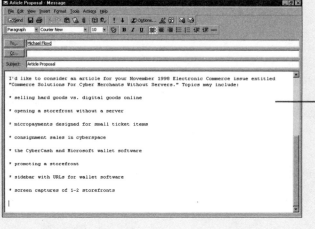

6 Below the opening summary, enter bulleted items with suggested topics.

Creating a filter in Outlook 98. You can create a filter in Outlook 98 to handle incoming mail in a variety of ways. A filter can automatically move mail from a particular person or organization to a predefined folder. To create a filter, follow these steps:

❶ Choose Rules Wizard from the Tools menu.

❷ Click New.

❸ In the Rules Wizard dialog box, Choose Move New Messages From Someone from the field labeled Which Type Of Rule Do You Want To Create?

❹ Click Specified in the Rule Description area below, and then click New on the next dialog box and enter a name for the new folder.

❺ When you click OK, Outlook may ask if you'd like a shortcut added to your Outlook Bar. Click Yes if you'd like the shortcut.

❻ Back on the Rule Wizard dialog box, click People Or Distribution List, and then select a person or group from the Address list or type a new name.

❼ Click OK, and then click Finish.

Compose an E-Mail Letter *(continued)*

❼ Below the suggested topics, enter the titles of other articles you have written and include the URLs if the articles exist on the Web.

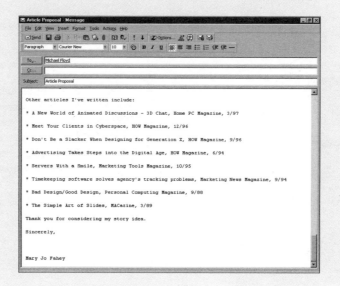

Automating a Mass Mailing

In this example, you will send an invitation to a Sound Wire electronic commerce seminar to Internet magazine editors. The two preferred tools for sending mass mail are a distribution list and the BCC field in the message header. This chapter shows both methods. When you use a distribution list, all recipients see the names, but not the e-mail addresses, of all other recipients. In Outlook, distribution lists are available in the Personal Address Book. The acronym BCC in an e-mail message stands for Blind Courtesy Copy. When addresses are placed in this field, recipients are shielded from seeing who else received the message.

Calendar of events.
Calendars contain short, one-line notices about your company's upcoming activities. They're effective for getting your name or project in front of the public. Build a custom category in Outlook 98 and call it "Calendar of Events." This will help you record which publications have calendars so that you can use the Calendar of Events category as a search criterion when you run the Find command.

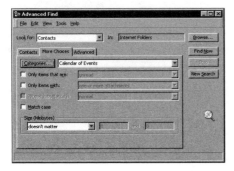

Create a Distribution List

1 In Outlook's Contacts view, hold down the Ctrl key as you click each contact to add to the distribution list.

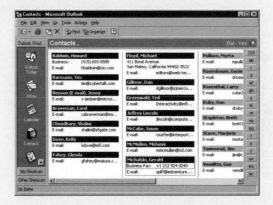

2 From the Edit menu, choose Copy To Folder.

3 Click the Inbox icon and click the New button.

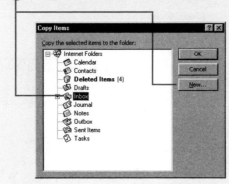

Create a Distribution List *(continued)*

4 Type *Feb_Mailing* in the Name field, choose Contact Items from the Folder Contains drop-down list, and click OK.

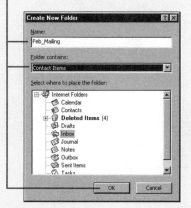

5 Click No in the dialog box that asks if you would like a shortcut added to your Outlook Bar.

6 In the Copy Items dialog box, click OK.

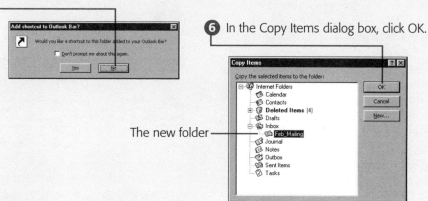

The new folder

7 Select additional contacts to copy.

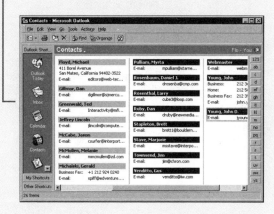

8 From the Edit menu, choose Copy To Folder.

9 With the Feb_Mailing folder icon selected in the Copy Items dialog box, click OK.

Hierarchical tile format for high-resolution images on the Web. Live Picture Corporation's RealSpace imaging technology is an interesting new active streaming protocol that has been defined by Live Picture, Hewlett Packard, and Kodak. Endorsed by both Microsoft and Netscape, the technology allows users to zoom in on an image without loss of detail. A large image is stored on a Web server and the server sends picture data to client software programs across the Internet. Transmission is fast and easy over the HTTP protocol, and the RealSpace technology is designed for both 2-D and 3-D browsing. Users see a high-resolution image as they zoom in because only tiles necessary to fill the viewing area are sent.

Send an E-Mail Message to a Distribution List

❶ Click the Inbox icon on the Outlook Bar. The Inbox view appears.

❷ Click the New Message button. An Untitled Message dialog box opens.

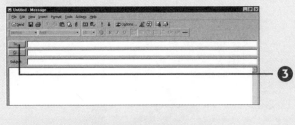

❸ Click the To button in the message header. The Select Names dialog box opens.

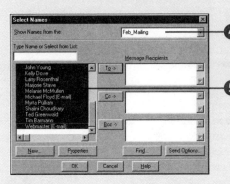

❹ From the Show Names From The drop-down list, select Feb_Mailing.

❺ Hold down the Shift key, scroll to the bottom of the list of names, and click the last name. The entire list will be selected.

Send an E-mail Message to a Distribution List *(continued)*

6 Click the To button. The selected names are copied to the Message Recipients field.

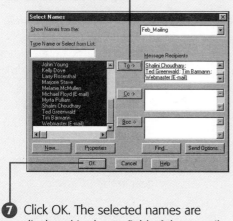

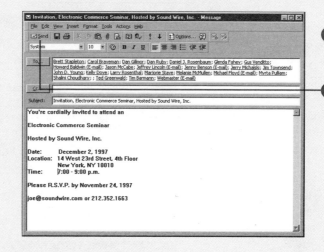

8 Type the text of the invitation.

9 Click Send.

7 Click OK. The selected names are displayed in the To field of the e-mail message.

Send an E-mail Message to BCC Recipients

1 Click the New Mail Message button to start another new e-mail message.

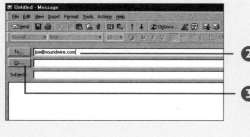

2 In the field labeled To, type your own e-mail address.

3 Click the Cc button. The Select Names dialog box opens.

Free e-mail with banner ads. Free e-mail is a rapidly growing marketing tool. The e-mail is free but banner ads are included. Users don't seem to mind the ads because the demand for free e-mail is skyrocketing. Free e-mail providers include Hotmail, Juno, Lycos, Yahoo, and Excite.

Banks using the net. nFront's nHome banking offers regional banks the opportunity to market banking services beyond their geographic location. Users can open new accounts, view account balances, view account history, transfer funds, pay bills, view personal information on file at the bank, generate reports, and download statements into Microsoft Money and Quicken. For more information, visit www.nfront.com.

Send an E-mail Message to BCC Recipients *(continued)*

4 From the Show Names From The drop-down list, select Feb_Mailing.

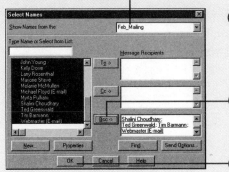

5 Hold down the Shift key, scroll to the bottom of the list, and click the last name on the list to select all the names on the list.

6 Click the BCC button to copy the names to the Message Recipients field.

7 Click OK. The selected names appear in the BCC field.

8 Type the text of the invitation.

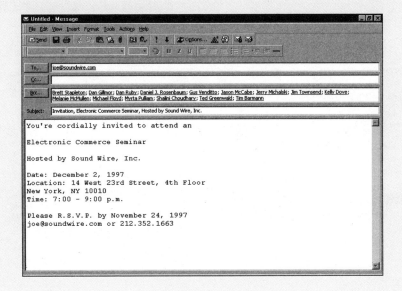

Lifestyle marketing.
Marketers are inventing innovative ways to reach customers. Instead of ad messages on banners, marketers are providing lifestyle services that sell a product or brand indirectly. Examples include nHome banking, a 24-hour home banking service and free e-mail, which is particularly valuable for mobile professionals. If you're moving around, you can take advantage of Internet computers in cafés and libraries to use advertiser-supported e-mail that's accessible via the Web. It's password-protected and you can send and receive e-mail attachments.

Creating Custom Categories for Contact Records

After you've built a contact database, you will want to be able to extract publications that have calendars of events or pull out all records that have editorial calendars for the upcoming year. You can create a custom category such as Calendar of Events or Editorial Calendar and add it to contact records where it applies. Later, you can search for this category to find all related records.

Create Custom Categories

1 Double-click a Contact record to open it.

2 Click the Categories button. The Categories list is displayed.

Mailbots provide a solution for quick e-mail response. Mailbots are autoreply programs that respond to incoming e-mail messages. Although mailbots are used to send a canned message, they can help a marketer respond quickly to incoming e-mail from a Web site. A real reply may follow when several messages have collected in the queue. Check with your ISP about an autoreply. This type of message is usually generated with a CGI script that runs on a Web server.

Create Custom Categories *(continued)*

3 Click the Master Category List button to open the Master Categories list.

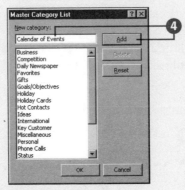

4 In the New Category field, type *Calendar of Events* and click Add.

5 In the same field, type *Editorial Calendar* and click Add.

6 Click OK. The Available Categories list is displayed and the new categories you have created are added to it.

7 Click to put a check mark to the left of Editorial Calendar, and click OK. Editorial Calendar appears in the Categories field on the Contact dialog box.

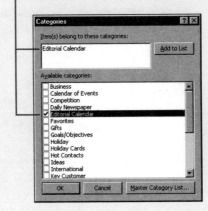

Retail giants open storefronts. The growth of the Internet population and a growing comfort with Internet security have prompted Macy's, Sears, and The Gap to open storefronts on the Internet (www.macys.com, www.gap.com, and www.sears.com.) For more information about opening your own storefront, see Chapter 9, "A Storefront with a Catalog."

Create Custom Categories (continued)

8 Open other Contact entries to add new categories where they apply.

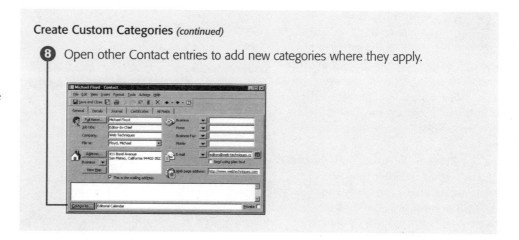

Find Contact Records

If you'd like to contact all publications with a Calendar of Events section, you can find all Contacts records that have a Calendar of Events category. You can use the Find command to search for these records.

Use the Find Command

1 Click the Find button on the Outlook toolbar. The Find dialog box opens.

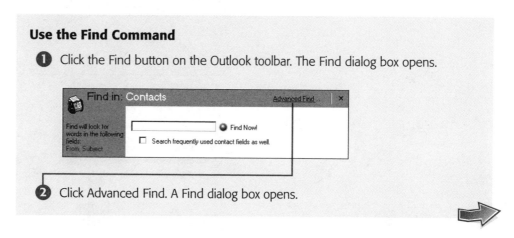

2 Click Advanced Find. A Find dialog box opens.

Cookie control. Internet Explorer and Netscape Navigator both support the use of "cookies" containing user information that's stored on your own hard disk. This cookie information gets fed back to a Web server, and it's a method advertisers use to track Web users' activities and preferences.

Unfortunately for advertisers, the use of cookies has raised privacy issues. Microsoft and Netscape have both decided to support a plan to help users block cookies. New browser software will provide a feature for users to create a profile of cookies that they'll accept.

Create Custom Categories *(continued)*

3 Click the More Choices tab.

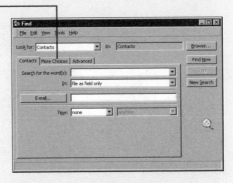

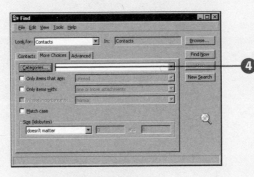

4 On the More Choices tab, click the Categories button.

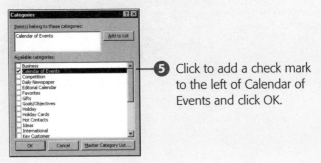

5 Click to add a check mark to the left of Calendar of Events and click OK.

Using the word "hit." In public relations, a "hit" is an expression used by a publicist when an article gets accepted by a publication. On the Internet, a "hit" refers to server access by a user.

Web analysis and Microsoft BackOffice. In March 1997, Microsoft acquired Intersé, makers of Market Focus 3, a Web analysis software product. Market Focus 3 has been added to the Microsoft BackOffice product line. The software can check the number of times visitors come to a site, and new visitors can be differentiated from repeat visitors.

Create Custom Categories *(continued)*

6 Click the Find Now button. Outlook lists the Contacts records that have a Calendar of Events category.

Contacts that have a Calendar of Events category

Creating a News Release for Your Site

Posting press releases to your own Web site is a growing trend that provides a valuable source of information for Web visitors. In this example, you'll create a Sound Wire press release and make the document easy to find by giving it a file name that contains the release date.

Submit your upcoming event via a Web form. Your professional association's Web site may have a form for submitting an event announcement. For example, the New York New Media Association maintains a Web page that has a form you can use to submit the details of an upcoming event (www.nynma.com).

Create a Web Page

1 Start FrontPage.

2 Click your FrontPage Web's News page.

3 Click the New Page button on the FrontPage Explorer toolbar. A New Page icon appears beneath the News page.

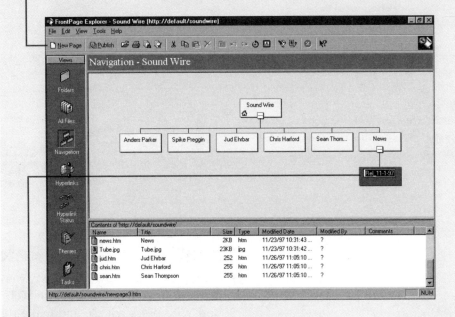

4 Click the default name and type *Rel_11_97*.

5 Double-click the Rel_11_97 page icon to open the page in the FrontPage Editor.

The Sound Wire logo.
You can download the Sound Wire logo from this book's Web page at mspress.microsoft.com/mspress/products/1576.

Audit Bureau of Verification Services, Inc. (ABVS). The Audit Bureau of Circulation is a self-regulatory auditing organization responsible to advertisers, ad agencies, and the media they use for the verification of circulation data. The Audit Bureau of Verification Services is a subsidiary that provides verification of nontraditional media, such as Web site activity or trade show attendance and demographics. Visit www.accessabvs.com.

Add the Logo and Title Text

1 Choose Image from the Insert menu. The Image dialog box appears.

2 Click the File button to the right of the URL field, locate the Sound Wire logo, and click OK.

3 Click the Center button on the FrontPage Editor toolbar, and then press Shift+Enter to add a line break.

4 Type *Digital Sound For Sale,* select it, and click the Italic button.

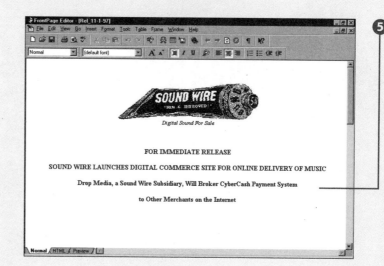

5 Press Enter and then type the rest of the title text.

Searching for an available domain name.

InterNIC is an organization that registers and maintains a database of domain names used on the Internet. InterNIC is the result of a cooperative agreement between the National Science Foundation, AT&T, and Network Solutions, Inc. The main page on the InterNIC Web site lets you search for available domain names. Visit www. internic.com.

Add the Remaining Text

❶ Enter the text shown in the figure below. You can also download the text from this book's Web page at mspress.microsoft.com/mspress/products/1576.

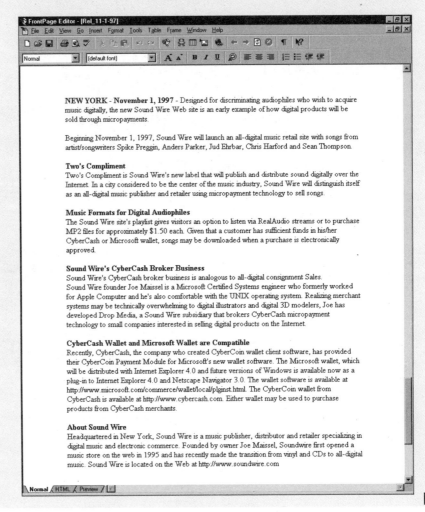

Freelinks. Freelinks is a service to help you promote a Web site. Visitors who use the Freelinks site benefit from the collection of links to promotional sites that are gathered together in one place. Visit www.freelinks.com and follow the links to essential indices, location-specific indices, general indices, and topic-specific indices. Each subcategory contains links to forms.

Add the Remaining Text (continued)

2 Click the Increase Indent button to increase the page indent.

3 Press Enter after each paragraph and press Shift+Enter to add a line break after each subhead.

4 Make each subhead bold.

5 Continue to add the rest of the press release text.

Complete the Page

1 After you complete the text, press Enter twice and type three hash marks.

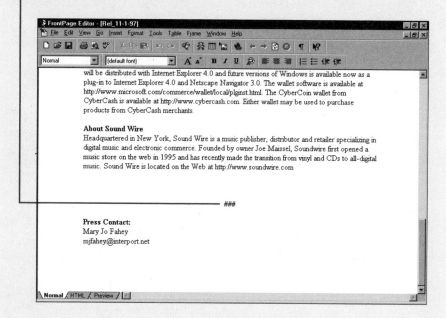

2 Center the hash marks by clicking the Center button.

3 Press Enter, click Left Justify, and enter your press contact information.

Submit-It. Use the Submit-It Web page to announce your Web site to search engines and directories. The site offers submission services for a fee and it also offers a free online tool that supports 18 search engines (www.submit-it.com).

The LinkExchange Advertising Network.
LinkExchange offers free and paid advertising space for banner ads. Free placement requires participants to display advertising banners on their site in exchange for a similar agreement from other LinkExchange members (www.linkexchange.com).

Publishing the Web Site

You can publish your site at any time by using the Microsoft Web Publishing Wizard that appears when you click the Publish button.

Publish Your Site

1 Click the Publish button on the FrontPage Explorer toolbar. The first time you publish a site, the Microsoft Web Publishing Wizard is displayed.

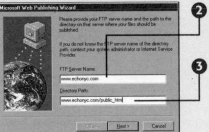

2 In the field labeled FTP Server Name, type the URL for your Web server; for example, *www.echonyc.com*

3 In the field labeled Directory Path, type *public_html* or the complete path to your Web directory as directed by your ISP. Click Next.

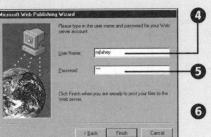

4 On the second page of the wizard, type your user name in the field labeled User Name.

5 In the field labeled Password, type your password.

6 Click Finish.

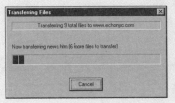

A dialog box with a progress indicator is displayed as your files are uploaded to the Web server.

PART 2

Generating Web Traffic

Add descriptive text to your site title.

Position descriptive text ahead of table text on a page because text inside tables may not be read by search engine robots in the order intended.

Using Meta and Noframe HTML tags is a solution for frameset documents, which are ignored by search engine robots. Alt attributes placed inside Img (image) tags provide text for search engine robots to index.

Optimizing Placement in Search Results

Submitting your URLs to search engines. This chapter does not cover submitting your URLs to the Web's search engines. Submit your main URL and the URLs of your site's primary sections. Use the chart on page 120 to locate the major search engines and follow the links to the URL submission page.

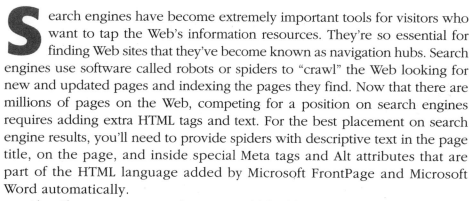

Search engines have become extremely important tools for visitors who want to tap the Web's information resources. They're so essential for finding Web sites that they've become known as navigation hubs. Search engines use software called robots or spiders to "crawl" the Web looking for new and updated pages and indexing the pages they find. Now that there are millions of pages on the Web, competing for a position on search engines requires adding extra HTML tags and text. For the best placement on search engine results, you'll need to provide spiders with descriptive text in the page title, on the page, and inside special Meta tags and Alt attributes that are part of the HTML language added by Microsoft FrontPage and Microsoft Word automatically.

Alex Shamson promotes his 3-D world building and training services on his site at www.vrmill.com. Although his site contains plenty of text and links, it also contains frameset documents that prevent search engines from indexing Web site pages. Frameset documents combine separate HTML documents into single Web pages. To make the text on Alex's Web page searchable by robots, you will use Word to add text to the site that the search engines can index.

HTM extension in Word.
When you resave an HTML document as Text Only, be sure to add an .htm extension to the file name because Word will not add it for you.

Attracting Search Engine Spiders

Although there are no guarantees that the techniques in this chapter will give you top placement on pages that display the results of searches, they are sure to help improve your results dramatically.

The page titles at your Web site should contain descriptive keywords offering clues about your company and the site's content. For example, titles might contain a company name, a city name, and terms that describe your business.

The first 200 words on the home page are important also, but many home pages have mostly graphics and very little text. To compensate, you can add descriptive text inside a Meta tag and in an Alt attribute.

Meta tags provide the place for a descriptive sentence and a collection of keywords that you think will help people find your site. You insert Meta tags at the top of your site's home page, inside the <Head>...</Head> tag. You can also insert them on other key pages of your site to provide search engines with information about the site. The description tag contains a descriptive statement that can be used in place of the summary, and a keyword tag provides keywords related to your site.

Frames present the biggest obstacle to search engine indexing because search engine spiders ignore the links in the frameset document that holds the frame documents together. The Noframe tag, designed for viewers with older browsers, offers a workaround solution that is slightly tricky and assumes some knowledge of frame documents. If you're unfamiliar with frame documents, be sure to read "Before You Start: Basic HTML and Frame Concepts," later in this chapter.

The Alt attribute allows you to add descriptive text to each image on Web pages. This text substitutes for images in text-only browsers or in regular browsers when the display of graphics is turned off. Although the Alt attribute is designed for people who use text browsers, search engines also pick up this text.

In addition to enhancing your pages, you'll want to add your URL to the Web's top search engines by completing the submission form at each search engine site. In addition, you should make sure the home page and key pages on your site contain links because pages without links are not indexed.

WS_FTP95 PRO. The WS_FTP95 PRO FTP software covered in this chapter will provide you with a method for moving files across the Internet that is very different from the way the Microsoft Web Publishing Wizard works. The WS_FTP95 PRO client is well known among Internet Service Providers (ISPs) and their support personnel. In contrast, many ISPs are not familiar with wizard programs.

The Web's Top Search Engines

Although the search engines are now positioning themselves as navigation hubs, assisting Web travelers in reaching destinations on the Internet, they are also partnering with online retailers because they see electronic commerce as a way to enhance their positions in an increasingly competitive market.

The sudden migration to Web partnership deals is also the result of trends in ad spending. Although search engines took in 55 percent of the money spent on Web advertising in 1997, the rate of increase in ad spending has slowed. The resulting increased competition for Web advertisers is making electronic commerce look more attractive. Analysts have noted that consumer advertising is a top ad-spending category on the Web and they attribute it to e-commerce.

The future of search technology is changing rapidly, and changes will undoubtedly create trends concerning where business places listings—or ads.

To help you understand the current state of the search engine business, the chart on the following page describes:

> The Web's largest search engines and their Web addresses

> Recent electronic commerce deals made by search engines

> Whether each search engine indexes Meta tags

> Whether each search engine indexes the Alt attribute text in Img (image) tags

Search Engines				
Search Engine	Marketing News	URL	Indexes Meta Tags	Indexes Alt Attributes
AltaVista	Run by Digital Equipment Corporation. Partnered with Yahoo, and has a commerce relationship with Amazon.com.	www.altavista.digital.com	Yes	Yes
Excite	Created Excite Entertainment with links to the National Enquirer and N2K's Music Boulevard.	www.excite.com	No	No
HotBot	Wired magazine's search engine. Formed relationships with Barnes & Noble, Virtual Vineyards, and Microsoft Expedia.	www.hotbot.com	Yes	No
Infoseek Ultra	Added new spider that filters out millions of dead and duplicate sites.	ultra.infoseek.com	Yes	Yes
Lycos	Formed a commerce agreement with Barnes & Noble.	www.lycos.com	Yes	Yes
Northern Light	Newcomer with articles not available on other search engines. Formed alliance with Collier's Encyclopedia.	www.nlsearch.com	Yes	Yes
Yahoo	A directory with over 500,000 listings. Formed a commerce agreement with CDNow and Amazon.com.	www.yahoo.com	No	No
Yukon	Code name for Microsoft's new search engine, available in 1998	N/A	N/A	N/A

Getting Special Listings

In addition to getting listed at each of the search engines, a Web site marketer will want to investigate announce sites, special-interest sites, and directories. Built by humans rather than robots, these sites are collections of links that direct traffic on the Web. There are hundreds of these sites. To learn more about them, read Don Seller's *Getting Hits: The Definitive Guide to Promoting*

Using image maps on a home page. Opening screens that contain image maps are popular on Web site home pages. Clickable hot spots with embedded links are often mapped on images such as navigation bars, doorways, and geographical maps. Unfortunately, image map links do not provide text for search engines to index.

Your Website (published by Peachpit Press in 1997), an excellent book containing a spectrum of Web promotion resources.

Before You Start: Basic HTML and Frame Concepts

You'll need to hand-code the HTML changes in this chapter. Because the tags you'll be adding are workaround solutions for attracting search engines, they are often not present as menu items in HTML editors. Because frames and framesets are more complicated that standard Web pages, follow the steps for altering frame documents in this chapter and you'll attain power user status.

HTML Concepts

> HTML tags usually have a beginning and ending tag with text in between that is represented by an ellipsis (...) in the examples below:

<Body>...</Body>
<Frameset>...</Frameset>

Notice that the ending tag is like the first tag, but it is preceded by a forward slash. It's often useful to think of the beginning tag as an on switch and the ending tag as an off switch. There are a few exceptions, though. Tags such as the Horizontal Rule <HR> tag and the Paragraph <P> tag do not require an ending tag.

> Tag attributes or parameters added inside the brackets alter the effect of a tag. Example:

<Body Bgcolor="#FFFFFF">

Bgcolor is an optional attribute that you can add to the Body tag to change the browser background color. In HTML, colors are specified with 6-digit codes, or hexadecimal triplets, describing the red, green, and blue information numerically. #FFFFFF is a hexadecimal triplet that changes the background color to white.

> HTML documents are made up of a head and a body:

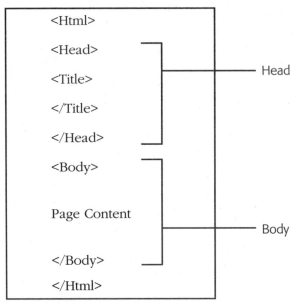

The HTML document and the head and body areas have their own beginning and ending tags.

> Most of the tags you add in this chapter belong inside the <Head>... </Head> portion of the HTML document.

> HTML documents should be saved as plain text, and they need an .htm or .html extension.

Using splash screens.
Splash screens are bitmap images positioned on a home page. Although a single illustration may create a dramatic introduction to your site, it offers very little content for search engines to index.

Frame Concepts

> A frame document with two frames actually consists of three HTML documents:

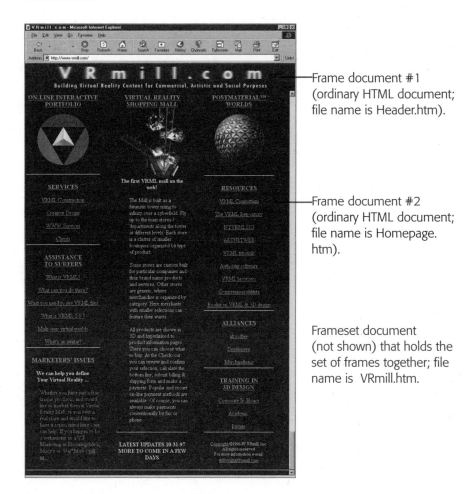

Frame document #1 (ordinary HTML document; file name is Header.htm).

Frame document #2 (ordinary HTML document; file name is Homepage. htm).

Frameset document (not shown) that holds the set of frames together; file name is VRmill.htm.

Robots and your site.
Search engines can detect
how frequently your site
changes. If your site changes infre-
quently, consider resubmitting the URLs
of your site.

Northern Light. Northern
Light is the newest search
engine on the Web. It's
become most known for its ability to let
you search publications that are not
readily available on the Web. (www.
nlsearch.com)

> Frameset HTML documents do not have a <BODY> tag, but the other HTML frame documents do. You'll add changes to each of the HTML documents to attract search engine spiders.

Adding Descriptive Keywords to Your Title

In this example, you'll work on the frameset document, which contains the Frameset tag. You want to make the title more descriptive because the existing title, VRmill.com, offers no clues about Alex Shamson's company or its services.

You can use Word 97 to add the descriptive text to this title.

Make a Change In a Title

1 Start Word 97.

2 Choose Open from the File menu.

4 Locate and select VRmill.htm, and click Open. The frameset document text opens in a Word window. (You can find VRmill.htm at this address: mspress. microsoft.com/mspress/products/1576.)

3 Choose Extract Text From File from the Files Of Type drop-down list.

Spamming spiders.
Adding repetitive keywords in Meta tags and submitting the same page over and over is considered spamming. Another trick spammers use is to make text the same color as the background on the introductory page. The text is indexed but it is invisible. Keywords such as "sex," "naked women," and "genitalia" are examples of words spammers use in Meta tags and invisible text. Spammers know that these words and other sex-related terms are the most frequently used in keywords searches on search engines.

To combat spamming, search engines have installed filters to look for repetitive words. Spammers beware: spiders will ignore documents with repeated keywords.

Make a Change In a Title (continued)

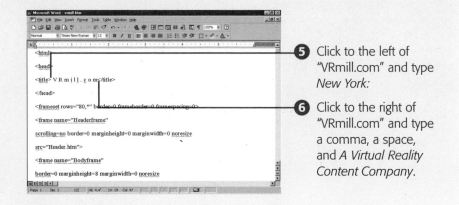

⑤ Click to the left of "VRmill.com" and type *New York:*

⑥ Click to the right of "VRmill.com" and type a comma, a space, and *A Virtual Reality Content Company*.

Save the File

❶ Choose Save As from the File menu. The Save As dialog box opens.

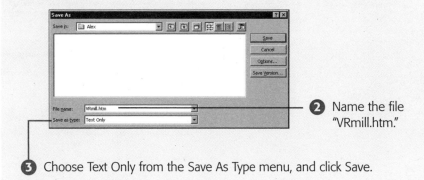

❷ Name the file "VRmill.htm."

❸ Choose Text Only from the Save As Type menu, and click Save.

HotBot. HotBot reindexes its pages every two weeks. Its advanced querying capabilities allow users to limit a search to pages that have changed within a specific period of time, or to specific domains, or to specific geographic locations.

Building Meta Tags

In this example, you will also work on the frameset document. You will insert Meta tags between the <Head> and </Head> tags. Before you create Meta tags for the site, you'll need to create a full-sentence description to insert in the description Meta tag and a group of keywords to insert in the keyword Meta tag.

Insert Meta Tags

1 Click to the right of the </Title> tag and press the Enter key twice.

2 Type *<META name="description" content="Building Virtual Reality For Commercial, Artistic and Social Purposes.">*

<META name="keywords" content="VRML, Training, Virtual Reality, 3D Design, VRML Design, Industrial Designer, New York, Virtual Worlds">

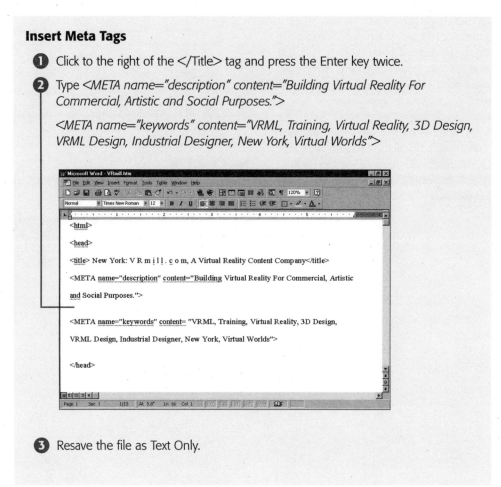

3 Resave the file as Text Only.

Searching for a concept.
Excite's complex search capabilities include the ability to search for a concept as opposed to single keywords. Use quotation marks and terms such as "and" and "or" to narrow your search. In this example, a set of quotation marks around "Discount Brokers" links the words during a search and finds links to pages on which these words are used together. Without the quotation marks, the search engine will find pages with references to the word "discount," such as "discounted airfare." It will also find pages with reference to the word "broker," such as "mortgage broker." "Discount brokers and Mutual funds" will find links to brokers who trade mutual funds. "Discount brokers or Mutual funds" will find less-focused results, including links to both discount brokers and pages about mutual funds.

Downloading the files for this project. You can download the files needed for this procedur from this book's Web page at the following address: mspress. microsoft.com/mspress/products/1576.

Inserting a Noframe Tag

In this example, you will also work on the frameset document. The Noframe tag is designed to instruct a frames-capable browser to ignore all information between the beginning and ending Noframe tags (<Noframe> and </Noframe>). Web authors who use this tag often create a text message warning a visitor with a frames-challenged browser that a frames-capable browser is needed to see the site.

Alex Shamson uses frames to display an ever-present site title. The site title is contained in frame document #1. The contents of his first page are contained within frame document #2. You will paste the HTML text for this page into a set of Noframe tags in the frameset document so that search engines will index it. A visitor who has a frames-capable browser will see the frames. A visitor who does not have a frames-capable browser will see the Noframe solution.

You will copy only what lies between the <Body> tags, including the beginning and ending <Body> tags themselves. When you copy the HTML text from the Homepage.htm document, you won't need the beginning and ending <Html> tags or the beginning and ending <Head> tags.

Copy the Contents of Frame Document #2

❶ Start Word if it's not already running.

❷ Choose Open from the File menu.

❸ Choose Extract Text From File from the Files Of Type drop-down list.

❹ Select Homepage.htm and click Open. Alex Shamson's frame document #2 opens in a Word window.

Deleting URLs from an index. Each of the search engines maintains a form that you can use to instruct a search engine to delete a dead URL. To delete such a URL, visit the search engine and look for a link to a Delete URL form.

Downloading the files for this procedure. You can download the files needed for this procedure from this book's Web page at the following address: mspress.microsoft.com/mspress/products/1576.

Copy the Contents of Frame Document #2 *(continued)*

5 Select the beginning <Body> tag and all the HTML text, including the ending </Body> tag.

6 Choose Copy from the Edit menu.

7 Close this document.

Paste the HTML Text into the Frameset Document

1 Choose Open from the File menu.

2 Choose Extract Text From File from the Files Of Type drop-down list.

3 Select VRmill.htm and click Open. Alex Shamson's frameset document opens in a Word window.

Avoiding search engine indexing problems. Frames, image maps, and dynamically generated pages are all problematic for search engine indexing. Text inside an image map is created in an image editor and made of pixels. Although this method of creating text can yield fonts that are not available in HTML, the text that results cannot be indexed. Dynamically generated pages are created on the fly in response to user queries that often originate in a search form. Unlike static Web pages, generated pages are produced from information stored in database software residing on a Web sever. As a result, the information inside the database cannot be indexed.

Saving the VRmill.htm file as text only. HTML documents must be saved as text only. Other file formats add unwanted formatting inside the file you are saving. To ensure that you will resave the VRmill.htm document as a text-only file, make sure the file extension is .htm. By doing so, you will be forced to pay attention to the file format when you save the file.

Paste the HTML Text into the Frameset Document *(continued)*

4 Scroll down the document until you see the </Frameset> tag.

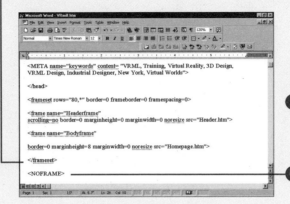

5 Click the line beneath the </Frameset> tag, and then press Enter twice.

6 Type *<NOFRAME>* and press Enter.

7 Paste what you've just copied. When you finish pasting the text, the cursor is located at the end of the pasted text.

8 Press the Enter key and type *</NOFRAME>*.

9 Resave this document as a Text Only file.

Yahoo: A directory.
Because of its size, Yahoo is often included in lists of the Web's top search engines. Unlike search engines that constantly search the Web to create catalogs of Web pages, Yahoo's directories are created by humans. Site listings must be submitted and assigned to categories.

Testing Your Document

Now that you've created a frameset document that can be seen by frames-capable browsers, frames-challenged browsers, and search engines, how do you know if it can seen in every browser if all you have is a new browser that can see frames?

Testing the document in a frames-capable browser reveals a frames document. To test the frameset document in a frames-challenged browser, use DJ Delore's Web Page Backwards Compatibility Viewer (www.delore.com/web/wpbcv.html). DJ Delore is a programmer in Rochester, New Hampshire (dj@delore.com), who has written a CGI script to test for Web page tags such as Frames, Font, Body, Center, Java applets, JavaScript, and Marquees. You can select each test for these characteristics from a list DJ provides on his site.

First, you will test the new frameset document in Internet Explorer, and then you'll use John A. Junod's WS_FTP95 PRO program to copy the frame documents to a Web server. Once the frameset document is on the Web, you can test the page in DJ Delore's backwards compatibility tester.

Test Your Page in Microsoft Internet Explorer

1 Start Microsoft Internet Explorer.

2 Choose Open from the File menu. An Open dialog box is displayed.

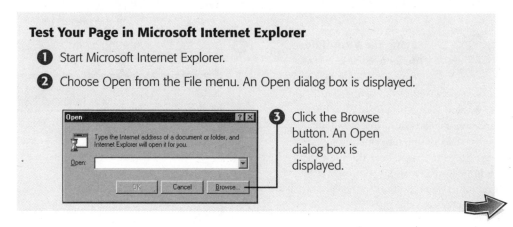

3 Click the Browse button. An Open dialog box is displayed.

Yahoo and other search engines. A query on Yahoo will return a page with links to popular search engines. These links will be located at the bottom of the page. Because Yahoo sends queries to these search engines, you won't need to retype your query.

Can I prevent robots from scanning my site? Robots that index the Web are sometimes not welcome. There have been cases of robots swamping server logs with repeated requests for the same files. In other cases, robots have indexed duplicate or temporary information. To prevent a robot from indexing your site, use a Meta tag designed for robots:

    <metaname="robots" content=
    "noindex, nofollow">

Test Your Page in Microsoft Internet Explorer *(continued)*

④ Locate the VRmill.htm document on your system and click Open.

An Open dialog box is displayed. The path to the document you have selected appears in the field labeled Open. Click OK.

⑤ The VRmill.htm document is displayed in an Internet Explorer window.

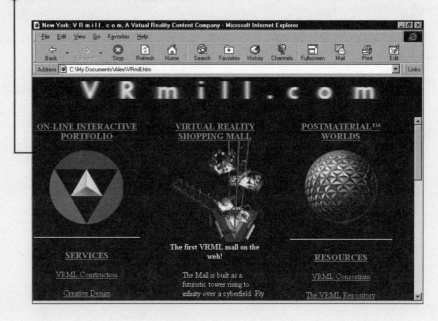

Internet areas that can block robots. Firewalls, intranets, and password-protected areas of the Web cannot be scanned by search engine robots.

A *firewall* is a security mechanism that filters traffic in and out of a company intranet.

An *intranet* is a term used to describe a TCP/IP-based network within an organization that carries HTML content.

Password protection is a security mechanism that protects pages published on the public Internet. Users may request pages, but a password is required for the page to load.

Publish the Frames Document On The Web

1 Start John A. Junod's WS_FTP Pro. The Session Properties dialog box opens.

2 Type a profile name in the field labeled Profile Name, and type the name of your Web server in the field labeled Host Name/Address. In the field labeled Host Type, leave Automatic Detect selected.

3 Type your User ID in the field labeled User ID, and type your password in the field labeled Password and click OK. A dialog box with two windows opens. The window on the left shows the files on your system and the window on the right shows the files on the Web server.

4 Double-click the Public_html folder inside the right window.

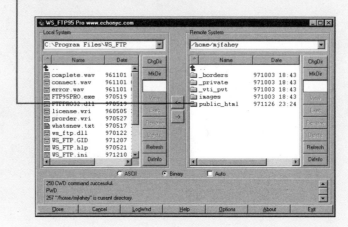

After you open the Public_html folder, you can also click the MkDir button to create a subfolder inside the Public_html folder.

Beyond your site's front door. Your home page is considered your Web site's front door. Otherwise known as the root or index page, the home page is the principal page that will be indexed by search engine robots. Because many robots do not "drill down" to index every page on a site, submit the URLs to your site's subsidiary pages also.

Downloading the files for this project. You can download the files needed for the project in this chapter from this book's Web page at the following address: mspress.microsoft.com/mspress/products/1576.

Publish the Frames Document On The Web *(continued)*

5 Click the up arrow to move up the directory tree on your system.

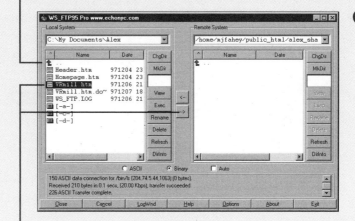

6 Locate the folder on your system that contains the frames documents.

7 Highlight the frame document and click the right arrow button between the document windows. This copies the file from your hard disk to the Web server.

8 Copy the files VRmill.htm, Homepage.htm, Header.htm, StaticLogo.jpg, Bluworld.jpg, and Mallplug.jpg.

9 After the files have been copied to the Web server, click Exit.

Inserting an Alt Attribute in an Image Tag

In this example, you will work on the Homepage.htm document, which has three bitmap images held in place with Img (image) tags.

Avoiding problematic characters in URLs.

Search engines choke on the =, $, and ? characters. Avoid using them in your URL.

Insert an Alt Attribute

1 Open the VRmill.htm document in Word.

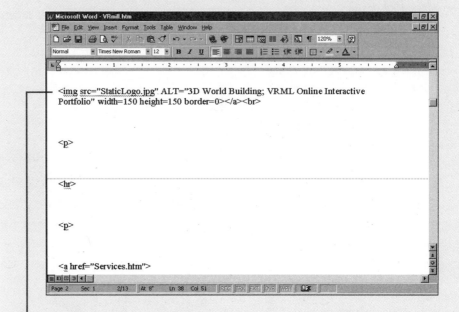

2 Scroll through the document and locate the first <img> tag.

3 Click to the right of "StaticLogo.jpg," enter a space, and type *ALT="3D World Building; VRML Online Interactive Portfolio"*

4 Repeat these steps to enter Alt attribute text in the document's other <img> tags.

Curtis Eberhardt, an animator, graphic designer, and new media artist, created the moving alien ship and viewfinder in this ad.

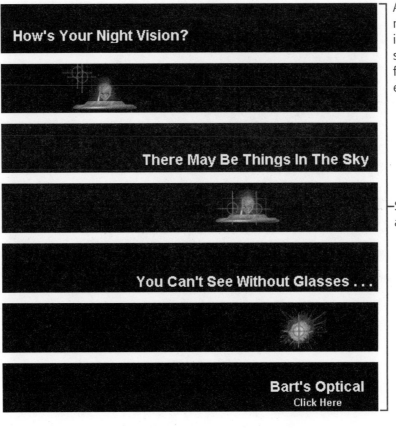

Animated banner ads attract more attention than single image ads. GIF animation, a series of frames saved as one file, is a popular format that's easy to create.

Sample frames from the animation

An Animated Banner Ad

Banner ads are rectangular graphics containing links to an advertiser's home page. By placing ads on other high-traffic sites, advertisers can drive viewers to their own sites by getting them to click the ads. Although record-breaking banner ad response rates can be as high as 30 percent, the average response rate is 2 percent, similar to direct mail.

Curtis Eberhardt (curtis@new-kewl.com) is a graphic designer, new media artist, and 2-D and 3-D animator. The fictitious 7-inch banner ad he created for Bart's Optical (shown reduced on the opposite page) is a GIF animation he assembled using GIFmation from BoxTop Software (www.boxtopsoft.com).

GIF animation software tools, such as GIFmation, stitch together a series of images that you have created in an image editing program. The result is a GIF file that resembles flipbook animation when viewed in a browser.

Placing Your Ad

Ad networks, such as DoubleClick and Softbank Interactive Marketing, offer advertisers a single media buy, multiple ad placements handled by one company, in targeted categories such as sports, business, travel, technology, and art and entertainment. Ad networks inventory ad space by signing up member sites that need greater access to advertisers. As a result, ad networks can help advertisers place targeted ads simultaneously over a wide variety of Web sites.

For small companies with little cash to spend on advertising, barter exchange with networks such as the Internet Link Exchange offers a low-cost alternative.

Planning effective banner ad copy. When you plan a banner ad, use as little copy as possible and include a call to action such as "Click here" or "Click here for savings." Questions, bright colors, and animated text have all proven to be effective in banner ad copy.

Click here for a free* month of MSN™ Premier from Microsoft.

MSN Premier

Calculating cost per thousand impressions (CPM). In traditional advertising, CPM is calculated by dividing the price by the number of impressions divided by 1000. Many Web publishers price ad space on their server(s) or ad networks using the same model. For example, the CPM for a Web site that charges $5000 per month and reaches 500,000 Web viewers would be $10.

$5000 ÷ (500,000 ÷ 1000) = $10

Click-through pricing model. In 1996, Procter & Gamble initiated a click-through pricing model with Yahoo that demonstrated the Web's measur-ability. Instead of CPM-based pricing, Procter & Gamble paid for clicks on ads on Yahoo.

Members of the Internet Link Exchange can either purchase space or barter. To barter, members receive an ad placement on a network of 100,000 sites for every two ads displayed on their site.

Understanding Banner Ad Pricing: Impressions vs. Click Through

A click-through occurs when a user clicks a banner ad containing a link to an advertiser's home page. Because few users click on banner ads—the average click-through rate is only 2 percent—many Internet sites sell advertising impressions rather than click-throughs. Impressions are the number of times viewers see ads on the Web or in the traditional media. CPM, or cost per thousand impressions, is an advertising unit that describes the cost of reaching an audience with an advertising medium.

Testing Banner Ads

Because the Web is a measurable medium, banner ads can be rigorously tested and retested before a full campaign is launched. Advertisers who are interested in Web traffic can check the Web server log on the server where the ad is placed. The server log contains a record of mouse clicks and visitor domain names. Even if an ad is not clicked, visitor domains are measurable and may be used to substantiate impressions. Testing ensures that an ad will draw a maximum click-through rate for advertisers.

Getting Organized

Most banner ads use simple 2-D animation created with still images that have been combined into a single GIF file with GIF animation software.

You can also create 3-D GIF animations from animation stills generated with 3-D animation software.

Color characteristics of images. Web graphics have critical performance issues that relate to file size. Because the Web is a medium that is dependent on modem speed, Web graphics should have the smallest possible file size. The objective for a Web artist is the same objective for game developers: combine what looks like the largest number of colors in the smallest possible file size. Reducing the number of colors in your images, or bit-depth reduction, has an impact on file size. Fewer colors or smaller bit depths make smaller files. Bit depth is defined as the number of bits used to make up a color pixel.

Bit Depth	Number of Colors
2 bits	4 colors
3 bits	8 colors
4 bits	16 colors
5 bits	32 colors
6 bits	64 colors
7 bits	128 colors
8 bits	256 colors
16 bits	65,536 colors
24 bits	16 million colors

For most Web graphics, 8-bit color is unnecessary. Experiment with your images and check the appearance at lower bit depths such as 6 bits, 5 bits, or even 4 bits.

To visualize the motion of an animation composed of multiple frames, you can create a storyboard. You can either sketch individual images on paper or print out animation stills from an image editing program. The storyboard will be a helpful map to follow as you assemble the frames.

The placement of the ad will determine its dimensions and may also determine its file size. Because there are currently over 250 banner ad sizes on the Web, you may need to create your ad in many different sizes. Placing multiple ads on many different sites sometimes requires as many as 50 different sizes. Although the Internet Advertising Bureau has proposed eight standard banner ad sizes, the number of ad sizes is actually increasing.

Preparing Artwork in Advance

You will need to prepare images in advance before you use a GIF animation program to combine them into a single GIF file. When you save the images in the image editing software, use a numbering scheme such as "01_filename," "02_filename," and so on, to make it easy to track their sequence.

The GIFmation program demonstrated in this chapter can import a large number of image file formats. GIFmation can also reduce the number of colors in an image as it is imported to keep the file size to a minimum. This is important because many artists work with 24-bit color (16 million colors) when they create images. GIFmation's 8-bit super palette analyzes the color in a group of images, selects a set of colors from the group, and creates an optimal palette. You can also use the program's bit-depth reduction command to manually reduce the color palette of an image. Ideally, it's best to keep reducing the color palette using a trial and error method until the image begins to deteriorate. That threshold will be different for every image.

GIFmation from BoxTop Software

A free, 30-day trial copy of GIFmation is available from BoxTop Software at www.boxtopsoft.com. Unregistered versions of GIFmation will not save more than three frames, but you can register immediately and obtain a trial registration number by e-mail that will activate the full Save command.

GIFmation's file format support. In computer graphics, a software's value is often related to how many different file formats it supports. Although the GIF file format is the document format in GIFmation, the program can import JPEG, PICT, TIFF, PhotoCD, ScitexCT, Photoshop, and Raw RGB files.

 Mind of the Machine. Dave Teich (mindmachine @mindspring.com), a multimedia designer and animator, has created a 3-D GIF animation on his Web site at www. mindofthemachine.com. 3-D GIF animations have a movielike quality, but their physical dimensions must be kept small because many frames are required to smooth the animation.

Teich's work has appeared in broadcast commercials, in CD-ROM and web-based interactive productions, and on the covers of national and international magazines.

GIFmation offers the most extensive feature set of all the animation tools. Significant capabilities include automatic and manual color optimization for the smallest possible file size, browser compatibility checking, preview control, cropping and scaling, palette control, transparency manipulation, multiple image file format support, and customizable preference settings.

Creating a New Animation Document

Curtis Eberhardt's 19-frame animation, which you will recreate in this chapter, is 500 by 65 pixels and 29K. Only the first frame is a full 500 by 65 pixels. The remaining frames are cropped portions of images to keep the file size as small as possible.

Open a Document Window in GIFmation

1 Start GIFmation.

2 Click the New button on the toolbar. A document window is displayed.

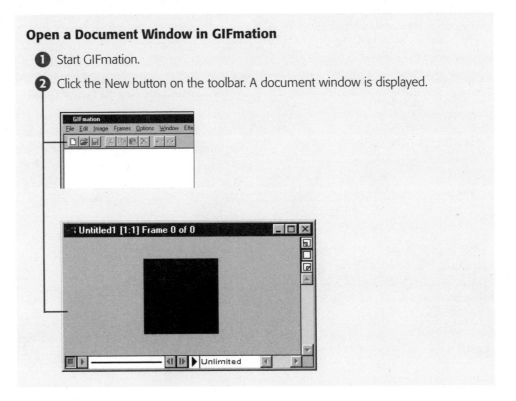

Researching ad dimensions and file size requirements. To avoid any surprises before you launch an ad campaign, research the ad dimensions and files size requirements before you design an ad. Zapa Digital's Microsite software includes a membership in the Zapa Digital SiteLocator. The SiteLocator searches a database of sites by geographic location or by URL. After locating the sites that match your search requirement, the SiteLocator displays site descriptions, rates, contact information, maximum file size, and the banner ad size requirement (www.zapadigital.com).

Set the Animation Size

1 From the Options menu, choose Logical Size.

2 In the Width field, type *500*. Type *65* in the Height field, and then click OK.

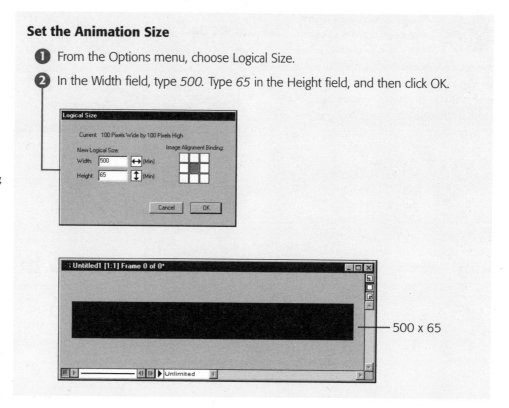

500 x 65

Setting the Browser Background Color

In traditional animation, a foreground image moves over a stationary background. If the background is a Web page, you should set the browser background color in GIFmation to match the browser background color on your Web site.

Green animation background (www.webtv.net)

Black Web page background

Animated Banner Ad

Logical screen size vs. image size. The logical screen size is defined as the area reserved for the GIF file by the viewing application. Individual images that make up a GIF animation can be as large as the logical screen size, but not larger.

Coloring Web Graphics.2 Lynda Weinman and Bruce Heavin's *Coloring Web Graphics.2*, published by New Riders Publishing, is an excellent text that teaches how to create optimal color graphics for Web pages.

Set the Background Color

① Choose Show Background from the Window menu.

② Drag the R, G, and B sliders all the way to the left to set the background color to black.

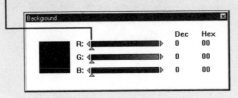

Adding Frames to the Animation

You can import up to 12 images at a time by holding down the Shift key when you select the images to be imported, but the images may not be imported in the order you want. To ensure the proper importing order, you should import images one at a time. As you import each image into the animation, you will see it added to the Frames palette.

Import Images

① To open the Frames palette, choose Show Frame Info from the Window menu.

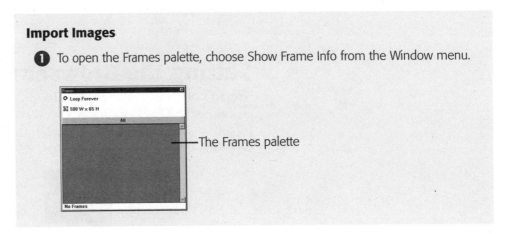

The Frames palette

Incentives to click.
Netcentives, BonusMail, and MotivationNet have launched incentive programs that reward users who visit Web sites, click on banners, participate in market research surveys, or buy something on line. The rewards are points or credits for users who sign up or agree to participate.

Import Images *(continued)*

2 Choose Import from the File menu and then choose GIF from the Import submenu.

3 Double-click 01_alien.gif. This file and the other GIF files for the animation are available for downloading at mspress.microsoft.com/mspress/products/1576. The first frame is a blank black screen, which appears in the document window. It also appears as Frame 1 on the Frames palette.

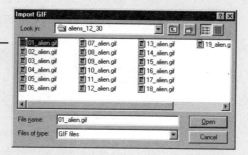

4 Continue to import in sequential order all the frames.

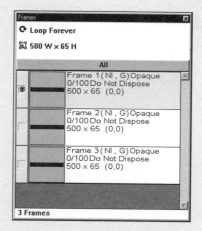

Reducing the number of colors in images. To reduce the number of colors in GIF animation frames, GIF-mation's Reduce Bit Depth command can be used to reduce the number of colors in a selected frame or frames. To reduce the number of colors in other Web graphics, DeBabelizer by Equilibrium Software is a specialized color management tool that has powerful controls for optimizing palette sizes. Adobe Photo-shop also has features that allow an artist to create custom-sized palettes. GIF Wizard at Raspberry Hill is an online tool that can be used to reduce the number of colors in a GIF image located anywhere on the Web or on your local hard disk (www.raspberryhill.com/gifwizard.html).

Stepping Through the Animation

At this stage, you should check the order of the frames you have imported by stepping through the animation in the document window. As you step through the frames, an eye icon appears next to each frame on the Frames palette.

Preview Your Animation

Step through the animation by clicking the Step Forward button.

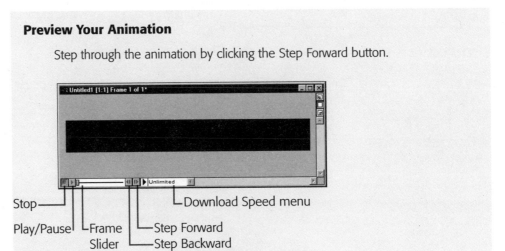

Using the Frames Palette

The Frames palette, pictured on the opposite page, lets you select a frame for an adjustment. It also provides an excellent tool that you can use to track the adjustments you have made because it provides a capsule summary of the setting for each frame. You will be learning about these settings in this chapter.

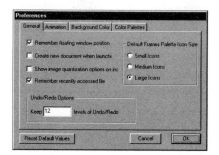

Changing the size of the Frames palette icons.

The size of the icons on the Frames palette can be made smaller or larger for ease of use while you are working in GIFmation. Choose Preferences from the File menu. On the right side of the General tab of the Preferences dialog box, select Small Icons, Medium Icons, or Large Icons and click OK. The size of the icons will change in response to your selection.

The Frames Palette

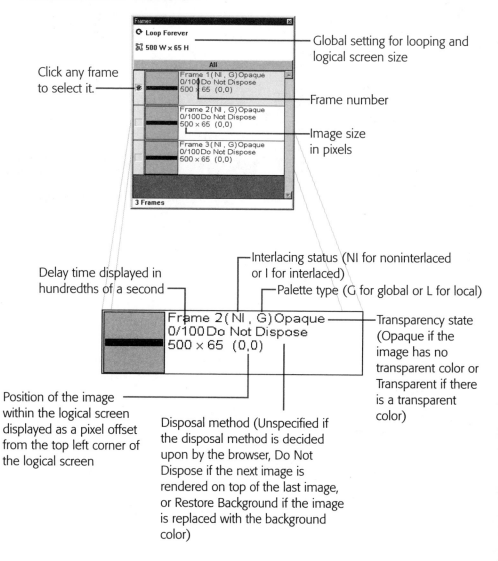

Click any frame to select it.

Global setting for looping and logical screen size

Frame number

Image size in pixels

Delay time displayed in hundredths of a second

Interlacing status (NI for noninterlaced or I for interlaced)

Palette type (G for global or L for local)

Frame 2 (NI , G) Opaque
0/100 Do Not Dispose
500 × 65 (0,0)

Transparency state (Opaque if the image has no transparent color or Transparent if there is a transparent color)

Position of the image within the logical screen displayed as a pixel offset from the top left corner of the logical screen

Disposal method (Unspecified if the disposal method is decided upon by the browser, Do Not Dispose if the next image is rendered on top of the last image, or Restore Background if the image is replaced with the background color)

Animated Banner Ad

GIFmation document-ation. The documentation for GIFmation 2.0 is available on line at nergal.boxtopsoft. com/GIFmation/Documentation/ index.html. The documentation is also available for offline review from the GIFmation ftp site at ftp://ftp.boxtopsoft. com/pub/GMDOCS.EXE.

Adjusting the Frames in the Animation

Each of the frames imported is a full 500 by 65 pixels in size. As the animation plays, each frame is redrawn on top of the previous frame.

To limit the total number of pixels in each animation and keep the file size to a minimum, you can use onion skinning to visualize each frame and crop the next image so that it is just large enough to cover the image preceding it. You'll learn how to use GIFmation's onion skinning feature in "Cropping with Onion Skinning," later in this chapter.

Delay time, measured in hundredths of a second, refers to the amount of time a frame will remain visible before it is replaced by the next frame.

Setting the Disposal Method

In Curtis Eberhardt's animation, the alien ship moves from the left side of the animation to the right. This two-dimensional movement is simulated with a series of spaceship images, each of which is a little farther to the right. For the animation to work, the previous spaceships must disappear from view. The removal of previous animation frames is called the disposal method and it is performed by the browser, which responds to the disposal method setting in the animation file. Although the Restore To Background disposal method setting would seem like the appropriate choice for this animation, it is not supported by all browsers. To account for this, you should always choose Do Not Dispose and learn to hide the previous image with background pixels.

	Animation Settings for the Animation's Frames				
Frame	Cropped Size	Position	Delay	Transparency	Disposal Method
1	500 x 65	0, 0	20/100	Opaque	Do Not Dispose
2	243 x 27	0, 0	200/100	Opaque	Do Not Dispose
3	245 x 29	2, 0	20/100	Opaque	Do Not Dispose
4	105 x 52	63, 3	20/100	Opaque	Do Not Dispose
5	154 x 56	76, 0	20/100	Opaque	Do Not Dispose
6	125 x 64	0, 0	20/100	Opaque	Do Not Dispose
7	317 x 63	114, 2	200/100	Opaque	Do Not Dispose
8	313 x 63	199, 3	20/100	Opaque	Do Not Dispose
9	186 x 64	320, 4	20/100	Opaque	Do Not Dispose
10	175 x 61	280, 5	20/100	Opaque	Do Not Dispose
11	137 x 60	172, 32	20/100	Opaque	Do Not Dispose
12	413 x 58	348, 4	200/100	Opaque	Do Not Dispose
13	437 x 56	349, 2	20/100	Opaque	Do Not Dispose
14	100 x 61	337, 0	20/100	Opaque	Do Not Dispose
15	111 x 65	362, 1	20/100	Opaque	Do Not Dispose
16	110 x 64	368, 8	20/100	Opaque	Do Not Dispose
17	85 x 63	371, 8	20/100	Opaque	Do Not Dispose
18	62 x 58	353, 21	20/100	Opaque	Do Not Dispose
19	139 x 57	359, 6	200/100	Opaque	Do Not Dispose

GIFmation's Dropper tool. Setting the background of an image to transparent will create a silhouette because the background of another frame will show through. The Dropper tool allows you to set the transparency color for the image that is currently visible in the document window.

Set the Disposal Method

1 From the Edit menu, choose Select All.

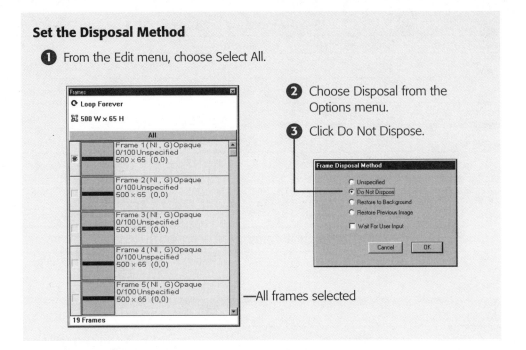

2 Choose Disposal from the Options menu.

3 Click Do Not Dispose.

—All frames selected

Cropping with Onion Skinning

The term "onion skinning" comes from the onion-skin paper used by traditional cartoon animators. Translucent paper allows them to see a sequence of frames. Animators draw successive new frames using the previous frames as reference. The onion skinning feature in GIFmation can be used to position frames and space the action between frames. Onion skinning can also be used to crop each new frame in your animation—providing just enough background pixels to cover the previous image.

Now you can begin cropping images to reduce the size of successive frames, which reduces the file size of the animation in turn. The three onion skinning controls in the upper right corner of the document window include (from top to bottom) Onion Skin Next, No Onion Skinning, and Onion Skin Previous.

GIFmation's onion skinning controls. Onion skinning is an advanced feature that provides a visual aid for positioning and aligning the images in an animation. The three onion skinning controls at the upper right corner of the document window include Onion Skin Next, No Onion Skinning, and Onion Skin Previous.

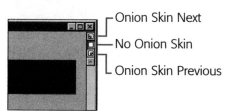

— Onion Skin Next
— No Onion Skin
— Onion Skin Previous

When Onion Skin Next is on, the next image is visible through the current image. When Onion Skin Previous is on, the previous image is visible through the current image. When No Onion Skinning is on, the current image is opaque.

Open the Toolbar

1 Choose Show Toolbar from the Windows menu. The Toolbar palette appears.

Onion Skin and Crop

1 Click the "visible" button next to the second frame on the Frames palette. The eye icon appears next to the second frame and the second frame becomes visible in the document window.

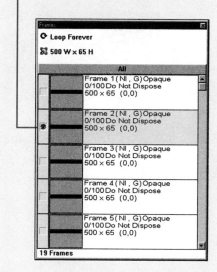

Animated Banner Ad

CNET.com A keyword search for "banner ad" on news.com will yield several dozen articles on topics such as Net advertising, online ad revenues, tracking, and e-mail ads. CNET's news.com site offers a custom search of the cnet database of current and past news stories. Search by keyword, subject, or a combination of these criteria. The site also offers a free subscription to an e-mail summary of important headlines and stories. A weekend edition offers a summary of news from the previous week (www.news.com).

Onion Skin and Crop *(continued)*

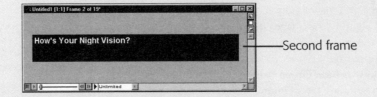

—Second frame

2 Click the Crop tool on the Toolbar.

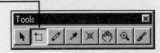

3 Draw a crop box tightly around the text and finish the crop by clicking inside the box. The new cropped size appears on the Frames palette.

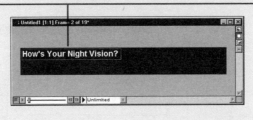

243 x 27 is the cropped size.

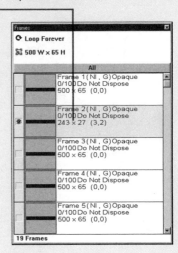

GIFmation's eye icon on the Frames palette. The current visible frame is denoted by an eye icon on the Frames palette. Only one frame can be visible in the document window at any given time. Each frame has a "visible" button to the left of the frame on the Frames palette. Click in this space and the eye icon will appear. This causes the frame to become visible in the document window.

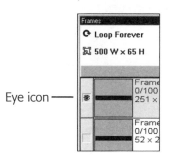

Eye icon

Onion Skin and Crop *(continued)*

4 Bring the third frame to the document window by clicking the "visible" button next to the frame in the Frames palette.

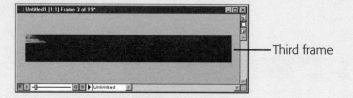

Third frame

5 Click the Onion Skin Previous button and leave it turned on while you crop the rest of the frames. The previous frame shows through the third frame.

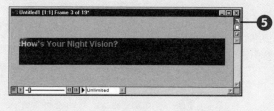

6 With the Crop tool, draw a crop box tightly around the text and cover the graphic at the upper left corner that now shows through. Finish the crop by clicking inside the box. The new cropped size appears on the Frames palette.

Removing transparency.
Setting a color to transparent in the document window is not a permanent change. To remove the transparency, select the frame and select Remove Transparency from the Options menu.

Power Design's design and tech tips. Power Design is a new media and online advertising firm whose Internet 201 site offers tips and tutorials on GIF animation, file formats, and compression. Although their tutorial uses GIFBuilder for the Macintosh, the information presented is equally valuable for the PC (www.powerdesign.com/201/animate1.html).

Onion Skin and Crop *(continued)*

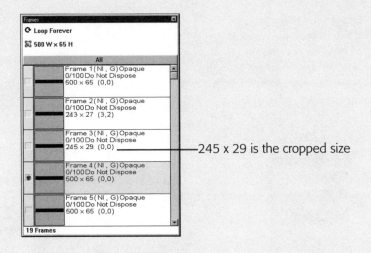

245 x 29 is the cropped size

7 Bring the fourth frame to the document window by clicking the "visible" button next to the frame on the Frames palette.

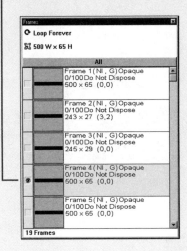

Keyword search on the Red Herring site. A keyword search for "banner ad" on the Red Herring site will yield links to this technology magazine's archive of articles describing the latest trends in Web advertising (www.herring. com).

Onion Skin and Crop *(continued)*

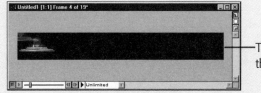

The third frame shows through the fourth frame

8 Draw a crop box around the graphic and click inside the box.

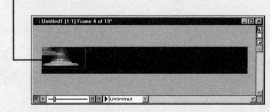

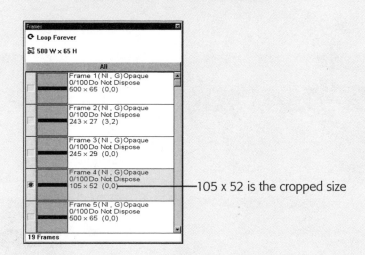

105 x 52 is the cropped size

Onion Skin and Crop *(continued)*

Crop for frame 5

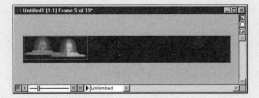

Crop for the frame 9

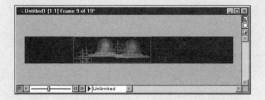

Crop for frame 6

Crop for the frame 10

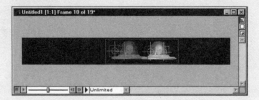

Crop for frame 7

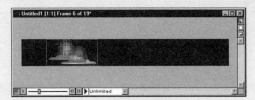

Crop for the frame 11

Crop for frame 8

Crop for the frame 12

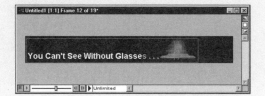

Onion Skin and Crop *(continued)*

Crop for frame 13

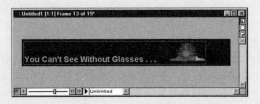

Crop for frame 17

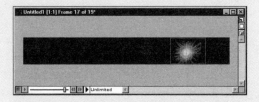

Crop for frame 14

Crop for frame 18

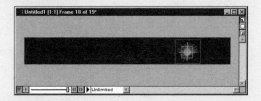

Crop for frame 15

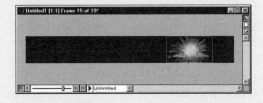

Crop for frame 19

Crop for frame 16

Animated Banner Ad

Web Review. *Web Review* is *Web Techniques* magazine's online sister publication, produced by Songline Studios. Sign up for the *Web Review* e-mail discussion list and receive a once-a-week mailing that includes answers and tips from professional Web designers and new media artists (www.webreview. com).

Reducing File Size with Transparent Backgrounds

The crops you made in the previous section provided enough background pixels to hide the previous image for each frame. Remember, cover-up pixels are required because you selected the Do Not Dispose disposal method that is reliable in all browsers. In this section, you will experiment with transparent backgrounds on all but the first frame. The first frame will provide the animation background that will show through the following transparent frames.

The Web sites where you place your ads may require very small file sizes. Using transparent areas in your frames will keep the number of color pixels to a minimum and keep the file size small.

In traditional animation, the frames that make up the animation are called "in-betweens." This term refers to the frames between the first and last frame of the animation. In this section, you'll set the background of the "in-betweens" and the last frame to transparent and leave the background of the first frame opaque.

You'll need to prepare the in-between frames and the last frame using the Layers palette in Photoshop. You'll need to visualize each previous frame using the Layers palette and paint opaque background pixels to hide spaceship images or type that shows through. Again, this is required because the Do Not Dispose setting is best for viewing in all browser software. When you prepare your frames, make the background in each frame except the first frame 100 percent magenta and paint black pixels over each previous spaceship or line of type. After you have the frames prepared, import them into GIFmation by following the steps described in this chapter.

———— 100% magenta as the background color

———— Black pixels cover the previous image

BoxTop's PhotoGIF plug-in for Photoshop.

BoxTop Software became well known for high-quality software when their PhotoGIF plug-in was first released in May 1995. PhotoGIF is an award-winning Web graphics production tool that has evolved into more than one plug-in:

PhotoGIF 3.0 is a Microsoft Windows 95, Microsoft Windows NT, and Macintosh plug-in for Adobe Photoshop 3.0 or greater.

PhotoGIF Filter 1.0 is a Windows 95, Windows NT, and Macintosh plug-in for applications supporting the Adobe Photoshop 2.5 API filter.

Set the Magenta Backgrounds to Transparent

1 Select an in-between frame on the Frames palette.

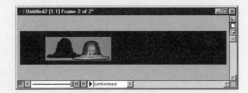

2 Choose the Dropper tool.

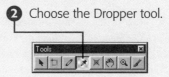

3 Click the magenta background in the document window. Most of the magenta pixels disappear. You can remove the remaining magenta pixels in the image by using the Edge tool, which is discussed in the next section.

4 Repeat steps 2 and 3 and set the magenta backgrounds on the remaining in-between frames to transparent.

Clean Up Your Animation

1 Select an in-between frame on the Frames palette.

GIFmation's Edge tool.
When you set the background of a GIF to transparent, a fringe around the image sometimes appears. The fringe is produced by anti-aliasing around the edge of the image. Anti-aliasing is the blending of colors in pixels that make up an edge to remove jaggies, or small stairsteps visible along rounded edges. The Edge tool is designed to clean up the edges of your image's transparency. To use the tool, drag the tool along the edge of the image.

Clean Up Your Animation *(continued)*

2 Select the Edge tool, designed for cleaning up edges.

3 Drag the Edge tool along the edge of your image in the document window to paint with transparency. The remaining magenta pixels disappear.

Changing the Frame Settings

After you complete image editing your animation, you can adjust the animation's settings before saving it.

Set the Delay Time

The default value for delay time is zero. You will need to slow the image frames in the animation to 20/100ths of a second and slow the text frames to 50/100ths of a second. Although you can set these values in a GIF animation tool, they are really approximations, because browsers all work differently when the animation is displayed.

GIFmation's Selection tool and the Position/Set Position dialog box. If you need to reposition an image in any of your frames, use the Selection tool or use offset coordinates in the Position dialog box found on the Options menu. Either method will cause a change in the horizontal and vertical offset of the image, measured in pixels from the upper left corner of the document window and displayed in the Frames palette. The Selection tool allows you to select an image within an animation and drag it to a new location.

Set the Delay Time *(continued)*

1 Select the first frame on the Frames palette.

2 Choose Delay Time from the Options menu. The Interframe Delay dialog box appears.

3 Click the button next to the empty text field, type *20* in the field, and click OK. The Frames palette displays the delay time and a browser compatibility warning icon appears at the top of the Frames palette.

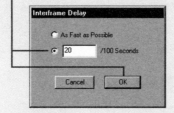

4 Double-click the browser compatibility warning icon to read the warning.

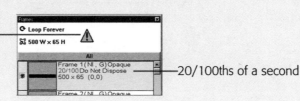

—20/100ths of a second

Optimizing existing GIF animation with GIF-mation and PhotoGIF.

Look for Travis Anton's article about the *Web Techniques* magazine GIF animation contest on BoxTop Software's Web site, www.boxtopsoft.com. The article describes the steps used to trim bytes from an animation and it displays three versions of a penguin animation from the contest. Anton's 4423-byte version broke a previous small-file record.

Set the Delay Time *(continued)*

5 Click OK after you've read the message warning of an incompatibility with delay time in the Cyberdog browser.

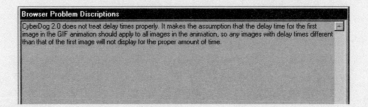

6 Right-click the second frame in the Frames palette.

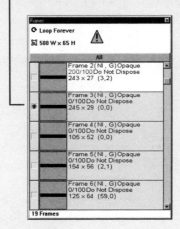

7 Select Delay Time from the shortcut menu. The Interframe Delay dialog box appears again.

GIFmation's Alpha Brush tool. The Alpha Brush tool allows you to paint with transparency. For example, you may discover a few pixels are not needed to cover the previous image. To set a small number of pixels to transparent, you can zoom in and paint with transparency.

Set the Delay Time *(continued)*

8 Type *200* in the empty text field to delay the frame by 2 seconds.

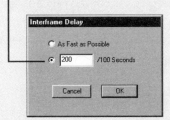

9 Use the chart on page 147 to set the delay time for the remaining frames.

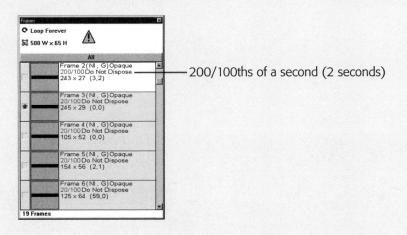

200/100ths of a second (2 seconds)

Animated Banner Ad

Browser compatibility warning icon. When a browser compatibility warning icon appears in the Frames palette, the settings you have chosen will not work as expected. When clicked, the browser compatibility warning icon will show a dialog box that displays information about what settings are incompatible and a description of the projected browser behavior.

Set Looping

1 Choose Looping from the Options menu to set how many times the animation repeats. The Looping dialog box appears.

2 Click the Loop button, type *1* in the text field, and then click OK. The Looping value is displayed in the upper left corner of the Frames palette and a browser compatibility warning icon is displayed.

3 Click the browser compatibility warning icon. The message warns of an incompatibility in the CyberDog 2.0 and Netscape 2.02 Mac browsers, which ignore looping settings.

Browser Problem Discriptions

CyberDog 2.0 ignores the looping value set in the Netscape Application Extension block, which controls looping, and all animations will loop infinitely, although slightly different behavior is exhibited in animations that do not contain the Netscape Application Extension block. In those animation delay times will also be ignored and all frames will be played with an interframe delay of approximately 10/100ths of a second.

The loop value is ignored by Netscape 2.0.2 Mac. All animations will loop infinitely in Netscape 2.0.2 Mac if the Netscape Application Extension Block is present in the GIF file. If this is not present, animations will play to the end then stop.

Bit depth. Bit depth is defined as the number of bits used to make up a color pixel. For print graphics, the objective is to increase bit depth, and for Web graphics, the objective is to reduce the bit depth. By reducing the bit depth in an image, you reduce the number of colors and the file size. You'll be surprised how lower bit depths will still yield acceptable color. Ideally, you should experiment with smaller bit depths until you reach the point where you're not satisfied with the color in your images.

Reduce the Bit Depth

1 From the Edit menu, choose Select All.

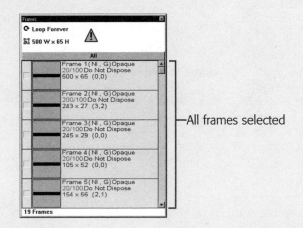

—All frames selected

2 Choose Palette from the Options menu, and choose Reduce Bit Depth from the Palette submenu. The Reduce Bit Depth dialog box appears.

3 Click 7-bit: 128 Colors, and then click OK.

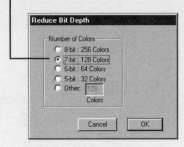

Animated Banner Ad

GIFmation's upcoming features. BoxTop Software has an aggressive upgrade plan for GIFmation. Planned for the future are effects plug-ins, contextual menus on the Frames palette, a pencil tool, and multiple undos.

GIFmation's 8-bit super palette. The GIF graphic file format is an 8-bit, 256-color format originally defined in 1987 by CompuServe for the CompuServe online service. All images, regardless of their palette size, have an 8-bit super palette applied when they are imported into GIFmation. This super palette optimizes the color in the images, providing superior image quality.

Saving and Testing the Animation

GIFmation's Export Optimized command helps you save the smallest possible file. Banner ads should be as close to 20K as possible or even smaller. To test the animation, you will build a small HTML file in WordPad and open the .htm document in Microsoft Internet Explorer.

Save the Animation

1 From the File menu, choose Export Optimized.

2 Click the button labeled Smallest File, Most Lossy, and click OK.

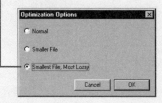

3 Name the animation "Alien.gif" and click Save.

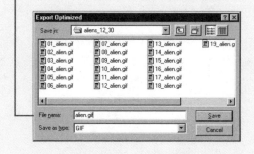

Selecting frames. To select a frame, click the frame in the Frames palette. To select multiple frames in sequence, select the beginning frame, hold down the Shift key, and click the last frame. To select multiple frames not in sequence, select the first frame, hold down the Ctrl and Alt keys, and click to select the additional frames.

 Deselecting frames. To shorten a sequential selection of frames or to remove a single frame from a selection of multiple frames, hold down the Ctrl and Alt keys, and click the last frames in the sequence. To deselect all frames, use the Deselect All command on the Edit menu.

Save the Animation *(continued)*

4 Check the GIF animation file size on your hard disk.

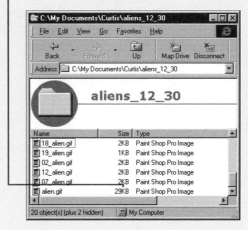

Create an HTML Document to Test the Animation

1 Start Microsoft WordPad.

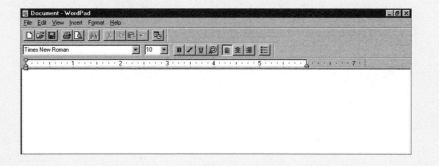

GIFmation's Hand tool.
The Hand tool allows you to move the current view in the document window when the entire image will not fit within the window.

GIFmation's Zoom tool.
The Zoom tool allows you to increase or decrease the magnification level in the document window. Clicking with the Zoom tool increases the magnification and Shift-clicking decreases the magnification.

Create an HTML Document to Test the Animation *(continued)*

2 Type the text shown.

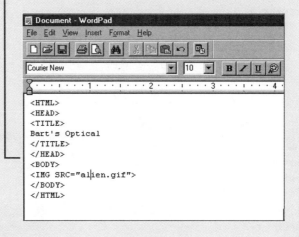

3 From the File menu, choose Save. The Save As dialog box appears.

4 Navigate to the folder in which you saved the animation, select Text Document from the Save As Type drop-down menu, name the HTML document "alien.htm," and click Save.

GIF animation and browser compatibility.
Many browsers support GIF animation, but there are differing levels of support. For example, the delay between images may vary from browser to browser even though the delay time has been set. Tools for creating GIF animations have more support for the GIF specification than browsers do. As a result, it is possible to create animations that behave differently in different browsers.

Open the HTML Document in Internet Explorer

1 Start Internet Explorer. You don't have to connect to the Internet first.

2 From the File menu, choose Open.

3 Click Browse.

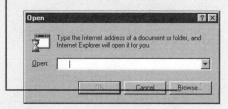

4 Navigate to the folder containing the Alien.htm document.

5 Double-click Alien.htm.

Animation preferences.
When you select Preferences from the File menu, a Preferences palette with tabs for General, Animation, Background Color, and Color Palettes is displayed. These tabbed pages contain settings for nearly all the settings in GIFmation, allowing you to customize to fit your work habits. For example you may want to set 20/100ths for the default delay time and Do Not Dispose for the disposal method.

Interlacing. An interlaced image is a low-resolution image that gradually fills in with pixels as the image is downloaded. Although the GIF file format includes support for interlacing, it is not recommended for GIF animations.

Open the HTML Document in Internet Explorer *(contined)*

6 Click OK on the Open dialog box, which displays the path to Alien.htm.

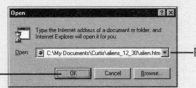

—Path to Alien.htm document.

The animation plays automatically in Internet Explorer.

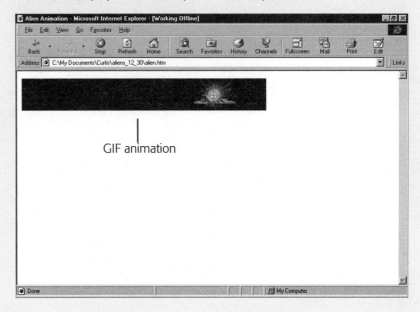

GIF animation

PART 3

Providing Customer Service

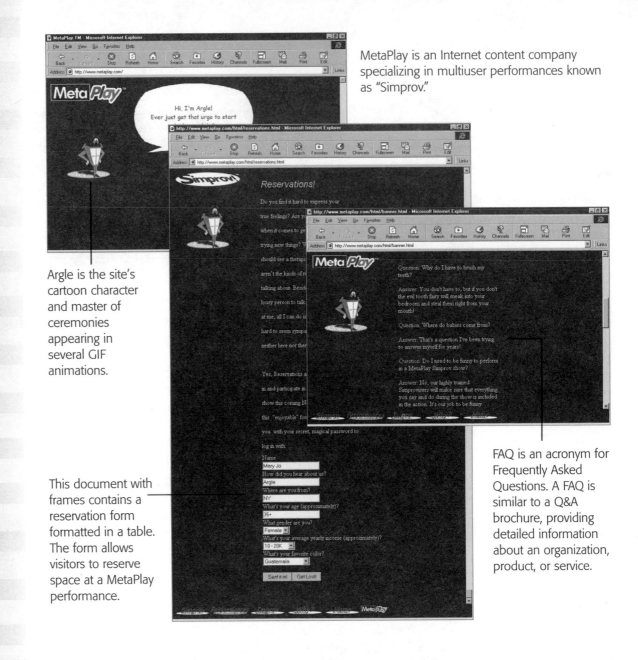

MetaPlay is an Internet content company specializing in multiuser performances known as "Simprov."

Argle is the site's cartoon character and master of ceremonies appearing in several GIF animations.

This document with frames contains a reservation form formatted in a table. The form allows visitors to reserve space at a MetaPlay performance.

FAQ is an acronym for Frequently Asked Questions. A FAQ is similar to a Q&A brochure, providing detailed information about an organization, product, or service.

FAQs, Registration Forms, and Questionnaires

Mom's Truck Stop.
Anyone can attend a MetaPlay Simprov show, an online improvisational comedy performance that takes place in a virtual diner called "Mom's Truck Stop." The multiuser performances are limited to the first 10 people who reserve a virtual space in the virtual diner. The main characters at Mom's are always the same, and visitors are invited to play a secondary character in an improv performance each Sunday night. For reservations and details on how to participate using the Pueblo browser or a Telnet client, visit www. metaplay.com.

Y ou can use FAQs, registration forms, and questionnaires to provide customer service 24 hours a day, seven days a week—an option that would be either too expensive or impossible to provide with a staff of employees. FAQs (Frequently Asked Questions) help customers troubleshoot problems. Online registration forms offer a convenient customer-centric service that's always available, and questionnaires measure customer satisfaction.

The MetaPlay Web site (www.metaplay.com), shown in this chapter, has a humorous FAQ and a reservation form for virtual improvisational comedy shows that MetaPlay calls "Simprov." Using the Pueblo browser, which is enhanced with sound and images, or a Telnet client, ten people participate over the Internet in a chat experience.

This chapter demonstrates how you can use Microsoft FrontPage to set up a FAQ that can provide information about a product or service, in this case the Simprov shows. It also shows how to create a form within a frame document that you can provide to visitors for registering for an event or a service or for providing responses to a questionnaire.

Titling the MetaPlay frameset document. The title of the MetaPlay frameset document should be descriptive because it will be picked up by search engines. Frames are separate HTML pages that make up a single page. The separate HTML pages are held together by a frameset document. Titling and making an adjustment to a frameset page to attract search engines will not be enough unless you also alter the content between the Noframes tags. These changes are covered in this chapter.

FAQ Layout

The number of questions on FAQ pages will determine their format. A short list can be formatted as straight text or a two-column table. If the list has many questions, group the questions according to topics and create subheads. To make the words "Question" and "Answer" stand out, you can give them a different color or make them bold.

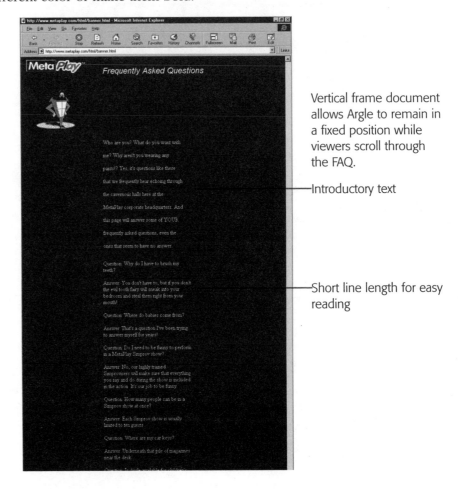

Vertical frame document allows Argle to remain in a fixed position while viewers scroll through the FAQ.

Introductory text

Short line length for easy reading

Custom form handler options. A Web page form provides fields for a user to type data into text boxes, select from multiple-choice radio buttons, or choose options from drop-down menus. These responses must be routed from the Web page to some destination on the Internet. The easest way to route form data is to send data as a text file to an e-mail address. More advanced methods require script development by programmers. The development interface options for programmers that are supported by FrontPage 98 include:

ISAPI Internet Server Application Programming Interface, developed by Process Software and Microsoft.

NSAPI Netscape Server Application Programming Interface, developed by Netscape.

CGI Common Gateway Interface, a popular interface for extending a Web server's functionality using executable programs or scripts stored on a Web server. CGI scripts execute in response to Web browser requests.

ASP Active Server Page, a method first available on the Microsoft Internet Information Server 3.0 for creating programs that run on a Web server.

Registration Form and Questionnaire Layout

Registration forms and questionnaires both use HTML form fields to gather data from Web visitors, and drop-down menus and radio buttons to minimize visitors' work in filling them out. You can see examples of form fields and drop-down menus in the figure below. These elements, along with radio buttons, will be demonstrated in this chapter.

The MetaPlay ticket reservation form uses the same frame layout that is used on the rest of the MetaPlay site. Although you don't need to create a form within a frame, you are limited to a single form per page in HTML.

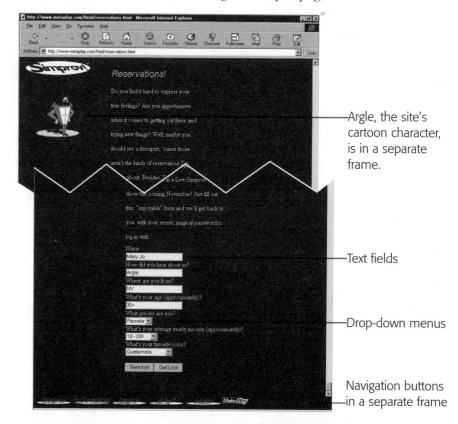

Argle, the site's cartoon character, is in a separate frame.

Text fields

Drop-down menus

Navigation buttons in a separate frame

Setting Up a Frame Document

Before setting up the FAQ document, you will create a frame document in FrontPage to learn how frames are created. Frames are created with templates, and you will modify a frame template so that it resembles the MetaPlay page.

A three-frame document actually consists of four documents: one document for each of the frames and a fourth document called a frameset, which holds the frame documents together. The fourth document won't be apparent until you save the set.

Create a MetaPlay Web

1. Start FrontPage.

2. Choose Create A New FrontPage Web, and then click OK.

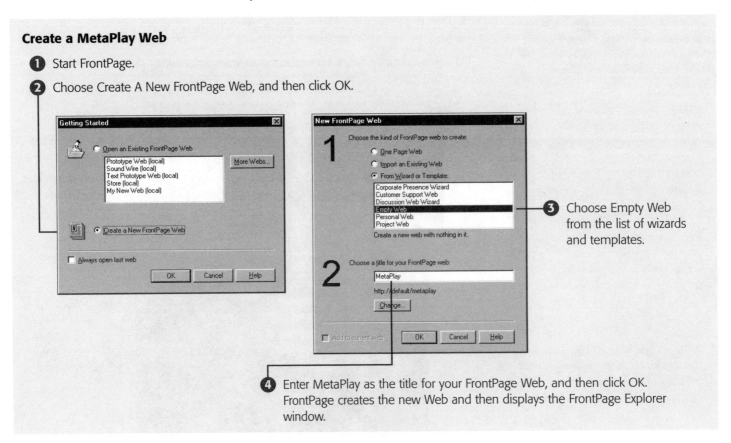

3. Choose Empty Web from the list of wizards and templates.

4. Enter MetaPlay as the title for your FrontPage Web, and then click OK. FrontPage creates the new Web and then displays the FrontPage Explorer window.

Storytelling in 3-D.

Seeking to attract Hollywood and advertisers, VRML evangelists Mark Pesce and Jan Mallis have launched a VRML animation shop called blitcom (www.blitcom.net). They've produced a series of five two-minute webisodes, or episodes performed on the Web, starring Bliss.Com. Bliss is a young, digitally aware avatar weighing 202K and 1350 polygons. Bliss.Com's voice and movement were created with Ascension's motion-capture suite and Protozoa's real-time animation software.

Create Pages for the MetaPlay Web

1 Click the New Page button on the toolbar. A Home Page icon appears in the FrontPage Explorer window.

2 Click the New Page button again.

3 Click No in the dialog box that asks if you want FrontPage to create navigation bars linking your pages together. (You'll create a graphical navigation bar.) A second page labeled "New Page 1" appears below the Home Page.

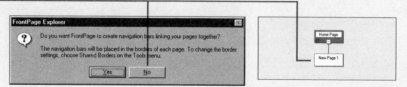

4 With the Home Page icon still selected, click the New Page button four more times. Four new pages will be created.

5 Click the first default name, labeled "New Page 1," pause, and then click again. The selected text will be highlighted.

6 Type *Simprov* and press Enter to rename "New Page 1."

Artnetweb's virtual classrooms. Artnetweb, a nonprofit educational organization in New York City, has launched Web-based graphics and programming classes for artists with Internet connections. Instruction is provided through threaded discussions with teachers, who are also linked virtually (www.artnetweb.org).

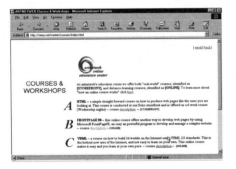

Create Pages for the MetaPlay Web (continued)

7 Repeat these steps and name the other default pages "Performances," "Improv," "Why?" and "MetaPlay."

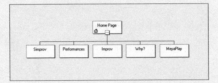

8 Double-click the MetaPlay page icon to open the page in the FrontPage Editor.

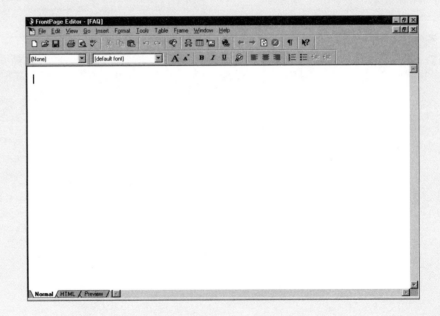

Insert a Frames Page

1 From the Frame menu in the FrontPage Editor, choose New Frames Page. The New dialog box appears.

2 Click Header, Footer And Contents and click OK. A page with four frames is displayed, and the Header frame at the top is selected.

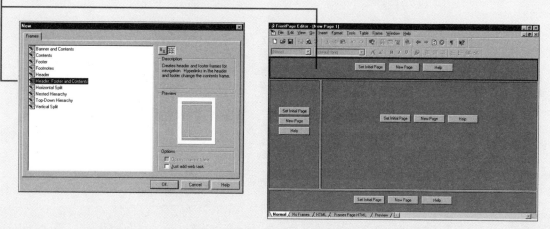

3 Because you don't need a header frame for this design, leave the header frame selected and choose Delete Frame from the Frame menu. The header frame is deleted.

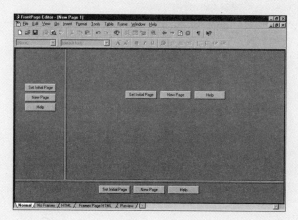

Text box validation rules. You can set up text box validation rules for one-line text boxes or scrolling text box fields. Rules can limit the type of data a user can enter in a form. For example, you can allow text fields to contain only letters, digits, white space, and specially defined characters. You can also allow numeric fields to contain only numbers, commas, periods, and decimals. You can define data length and a data value using less than, greater than, less than or equal to, greater than or equal to, and equal to or not equal to a data value limit. An example of a text box validation rule for a field containing numbers might be "field must be greater than 100."

Add Images to the Left Frame

1 Click the New Page button in the left frame. The background of the left frame changes to the default white color of the FrontPage Editor.

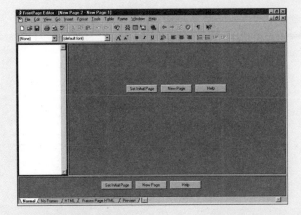

2 Drag the border between the left and right frame to increase the width of the left frame. Line up the border under the word "Format" on the FrontPage menu.

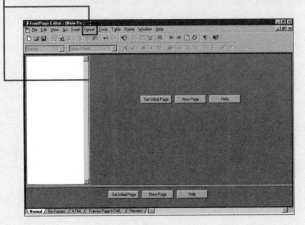

Add Images to the Left Frame *(continued)*

3 Click the left frame and then choose Image from the Insert menu. The Image dialog box appears.

4 Click the Select A File On Your Computer button. The Select A File dialog box appears.

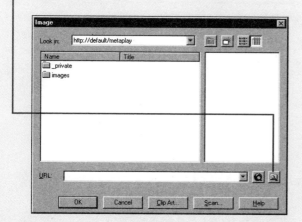

5 Click the file named "Simlogosm.gif," and then click OK. You can download this file and the other files for this chapter from this book's Web page at mspress.microsoft. com/mspress/products/1576. The Simprov logo appears in the left frame.

6 Press Enter and repeat steps 4 and 5, but insert a file named "Argleblinkanim.gif." The Argle image appears in the left frame.

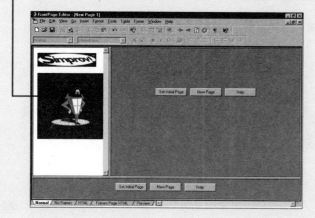

Live Picture's press room. Live Picture uses a frame document to display press releases. When a press release is loaded in a browser window, there's a supplementary set of text links displayed in a left column, which provide access to a company backgrounder, evaluator guides, and graphics.

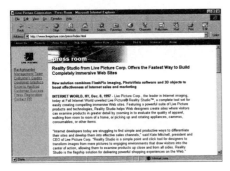

Add Text to the Right Frame

1 Click the New Page button in the right frame.

2 Type *Frequently Asked Questions* into the right frame.

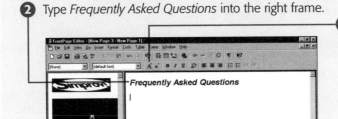

3 Select the text and click the Increase Text Size button on the toolbar three times. Also assign Arial, Bold, and Italic to the text.

Add a Table to the Right Frame

1 Press the End key on the keyboard to move the cursor to the end of the line and then press Enter five times to move the cursor down the page.

2 Choose Insert Table from the Table menu, and on the Insert Table dialog box, change the number of rows and columns to 1 each, set the table width to 340 pixels, and click OK.

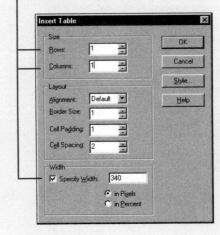

What is a URL? A URL is often referred to as an Internet address. The URL, or Uniform Resource Locator, is a standard method for locating resources on the Internet. Resources are usually files that can exist on any machine and can be served via several different methods. The most common URLs are Hypertext Transfer Protocol (HTTP), File Transfer Protocol (FTP), Gopher, and News and Electronic Mail Protocol (Mailto). Others include Telnet, Wide Area Information Search (WAIS), Host-Specific Filename (File), Usenet News Using NNTP Access (NNTP), and Prospero Directory Service (Prospero).

The Internet Engineering Task Force. The specifications for URLs were defined in 1990 by the Internet Engineering Task Force of the World Wide Web Global Information Initiative. The documents that describe the work accomplished by the task force are archived at Ohio State University (www.cis.ohio-state.edu/hypertext/information/rfc.html).

Add a Table to the Right Frame *(continued)*

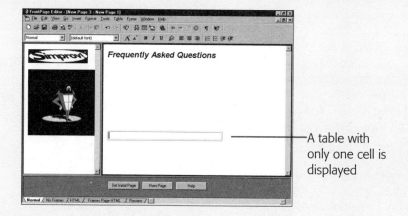

—A table with only one cell is displayed

③ From the Insert menu, choose File.

④ Choose Word 97 (*.doc) from the Files Of Type drop-down list. Double-click the file named Questions.doc. The table is filled with text. The "Questions.doc" file is available on the book's Web page at mspress.microsoft.com/mspress/products/1576.

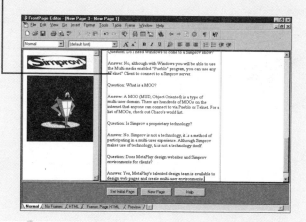

Web files for Mungo Park expeditions. Microsoft Expedia's Mungo Park Web site chronicles expeditions to exotic places, where there is often no cellular or land line telephone service. Within hours of each expedition, text, pictures, and sound files are published on the Mungo Park site. Files are uploaded to Redmond, Washington, from anywhere in the world with a lightweight personal satellite telephone that's about the size of a notebook.

The Mungo Park field teams use Kodak digital cameras, Toshiba notebook computers, DAT sound recorders, and a portable satellite phone from Magellan Systems. For details, see "Behind the Scenes: How We Bring You Mungo Park" (www.mungopark.com).

Add a Table to the Right Frame *(continued)*

5 Delete any extra space at the top of the table.

6 From the Table menu, choose Table Properties.

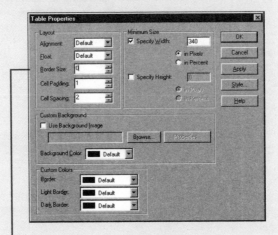

7 Enter 0 in the Border Size field and click OK. The table border is now displayed as a faint dotted line, which will not appear in a browser window.

> Question: Why do I have to brush my teeth?
>
> Answer: You don't have to, but if you don't the evil tooth fairy will sneak into your bedroom and steal them right from your mouth!
>
> Question: Where do babies come from?
>
> Answer: That's a question I've been trying to answer myself for years!

Troubleshooting a URL.
Have you ever typed a URL in the Address field in your browser and discovered the page you're looking for is not returned? URLs are case-sensitive so review what you've typed carefully to check for typing errors. If you've carefully typed a URL and you're still getting an error message, try truncating the URL to stop just after the top-level domain (the part of the domain name after the period). The home page should be returned, and you can look there for navigation links to the page you're looking for.

Address [icon] http://www.microsoft.com/gallery/files/images/default.htm

Address [icon] http://www.microsoft.com

Add a Table to the Right Frame *(continued)*

8 Select the text in the table and click the Text Color button on the toolbar.

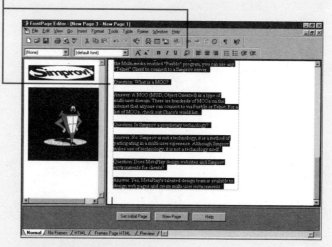

9 Click the red chip, and then click OK. Use the same steps to change "Frequently Asked Questions" to yellow.

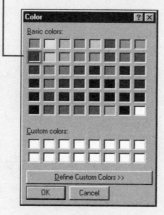

Hypertext Transfer Protocol (HTTP). HTTP is the most common URL scheme on the World Wide Web. A URL's syntax is the order in which the components are arranged. Although it is unlikely you'll ever encounter some URL types, knowing that other forms exist will help you troubleshoot problems. The syntax for HTTP is:

http://<host>:<port>/<path>?
<searchpart>

where

host is the Internet address of the WWW server.

port (usually omitted) is the port number to connect to; it defaults to 80.

path is the directory path to a particular file, usually a home page document. The path may contain a pound sign (#), which can be used to point to a named anchor or a specific section identified by a name tag.

searchpart is a component of the URL used to pass information to a server, such as a CGI script.

Example: http://www.microsoft.com/deskapps/office/guide.html#word

Change the Background Color of the Right Frame

1 From the Format menu, choose Background. The Page Properties dialog box appears.

2 Choose Black from the Background drop-down list and then click OK. The background becomes black.

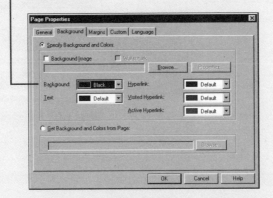

3 Repeat these steps to make the background of the left frame black, too.

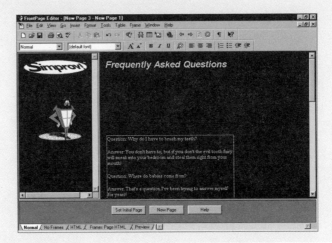

File Transfer Protocol (FTP). FTP is a popular URL scheme for transferring files over the Internet. The syntax is:

ftp://<user>:<password>@<host>:
<port>/<cwd1>/<cwd2>/.../
<cwdN><name>;type=<typecode>

where

user is an optional user name.

password is an optional password. If present, the password is followed by an @ sign, which must be encoded with the escape sequence %40.

port (usually omitted) refers to the port number to connect to; it defaults to 80.

cwd1...N is an optional series of change directory commands used to move to a particular directory. FTP client programs assume a Web server is UNIX-compatible and attempt to retrieve a file with path/filename.

name is a file name.

type=typecode (usually omitted) is an optional reference to a transmission method (ASCII or binary).

Example: ftp://ftp.mcafee.com/pub

Color the Question and Answer Text

1 Select the question text but leave the word "Question" unselected. Set the selected text to white.

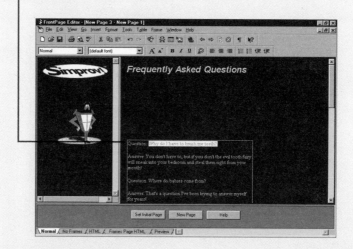

2 Continue selecting text, except for the words "Question" and "Answer," and set the remaining text to white.

Fill the Bottom Frame with a Navigation Bar

1 Click the New Page button in the bottom frame.

2 Choose Insert from the Table menu. The Insert Table dialog box appears.

Gopher Protocol (Gopher). The Gopher protocol is a simple text protocol that originated at universities. It's an infosystem that is similar to HTTP. In a Gopher system, however, documents are not linked to other pages and do not lead anywhere. Menus lead to other documents but provide limited information about links. The syntax is:

gopher://<host>:<port>/<gopher-path>

where

host is the Internet address of the server.

port is the port number to connect to. The default gopher port is 70.

gopher-path is made up of a complex string consisting of a gopher type-code and a gopher selector string. Details are available at www13.w3.org/Addressing/URL/4_1_Gopher+.html.

Fill the Bottom Frame with a Navigation Bar *(continued)*

3 Set the table size to 1 row and 6 columns, set the width to 560 pixels, and click OK. A table with six cells appears in the bottom frame.

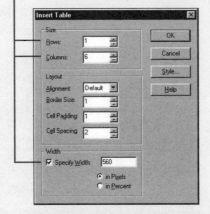

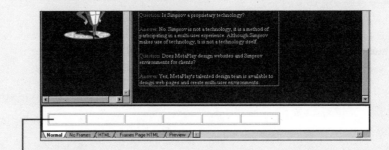

4 Click the leftmost cell and choose Image from the Insert menu. The Image dialog box appears.

5 Click the Select A File On Your Computer button. The Select File dialog box appears.

Electronic Mail (Mailto) Protocol. Unlike other URL schemes, which identify files on the Internet, the Mailto URL, used in a link, identifies an e-mail address. If a Web browser can handle mail, a Mailto URL will display a mail form with the address filled out. The Mailto URL used in HTML for a form will route form data to an e-mail address. The syntax is:

mailto:<account@site>

where

account@site is an e-mail address.

Examples:

<a href="mailto:mjfahey@interport. net"> mjfahey@interport.net</a>

or

<form method=post action="mailto: mjfahey@interport.net">

Fill the Bottom Frame with a Navigation Bar *(continued)*

6 Double-click Simlogotiny.gif and then click OK. A Simprov button logo appears in the first cell.

7 Drag the border between the first and second cell to make the first cell fit the Simprov logo.

8 Repeat steps 4–6 but add the following images to the remaining cells: Performances.gif, Improv.gif, Why.gif, and Home.gif. These files are available on this book's Web page at mspress.microsoft.com/mspress/products/1576.

Finish the Bottom Frame and Turn Off the Scrollbars

1 Set the background color of the bottom frame to black.

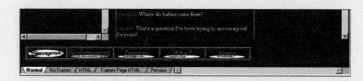

2 Turn off the table border.

3 Click inside the right frame. A blue line appears around the edge.

4 Choose Frame Properties from the Frame menu. The Frame Properties dialog box appears.

⑤ Name the frame "Right," deselect Resizable In Browser, and click OK.

⑥ Click inside the left frame and choose Frame Properties from the Frame menu. The Frame Properties dialog box appears.

⑦ Type *Left* into the Name field, deselect Resizable In Browser, select Never from the Show Scrollbars drop-down menu, and click OK.

⑧ Click inside the bottom frame and select Frame Properties from the Frame menu. On the Frame Properties dialog box, name the frame "Bottom."

⑨ Notice that FrontPage has preselected the settings you selected for the left frame. Click OK to accept these settings. The scrollbars become invisible.

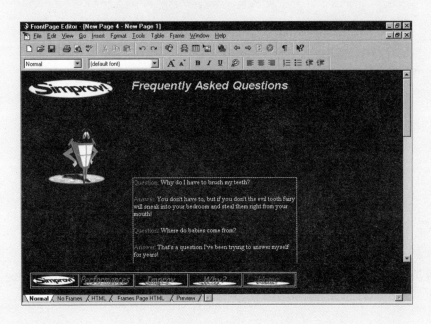

Host-Specific Filename Protocol (File). The file URL is used to retrieve files on a local host computer.

The syntax is:

file://path/file

or

file:///localhost/path

where

localhost is the local host computer.

path/file is the directory path to the file. The path is assumed to originate at the root or top-level directory.

Example: file:///HD/Desktop/ web%20site_vrml/aug.htm

Note: Some browsers will insert three slashes after "file," and all browsers will substitute "%20" for spaces in directory names or file names.

Saving the Frames Document

When you save the frames document, you really save four different documents. The Save As dialog box displays a page diagram to show you exactly which component of the frames document you are saving. The first document is the frameset that keeps the others together.

Save the Document

1 Choose Save All from the File menu. The Save As dialog box appears, and a large, blue highlighted line appears around the entire document thumbnail.

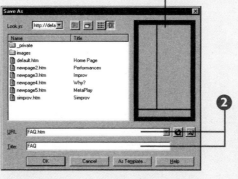

2 Enter *FAQ.htm* in the URL field and *FAQ* in the Title field, and then click OK. You have now saved the frameset document. The left frame becomes highlighted in the dialog box.

3 Type *left_frame.htm* in the URL field and *left frame* in the Title field. Click OK. The Save Embedded Files dialog box appears.

Save the Document *(continued)*

4 Click OK. In the Save As dialog box, the right frame is highlighted.

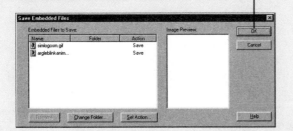

5 Type *right_frame.htm* in the URL field and *right frame* in the Title field, and click OK. The bottom frame is highlighted.

6 Type *bottom_frame.htm* in the URL field and *bottom frame* in the Title field, and then click OK. The Save Embedded dialog box appears again.

7 Click OK to save the graphics files for the page.

The trailing slash on a URL. The trailing slash on a URL requests an index of a directory from an HTTP server. The server will either return an index.html document in the directory, if it exists, or construct an HTML document listing all the files in the directory.

Creating an Image Map

To learn how to create an image map, a graphic with an embedded link, you will create a hotspot on Argle, MetaPlay's cartoon character. The hyperlink in the image will jump to a page describing the Argle character. In this case, you will designate the right frame as that page. Web page designers often put a table of contents in the left frame so viewers can click its entries to reach content in the right frame.

Create a Hotspot

1 Click the Argle image. The toolbar along the bottom of the FrontPage window becomes available.

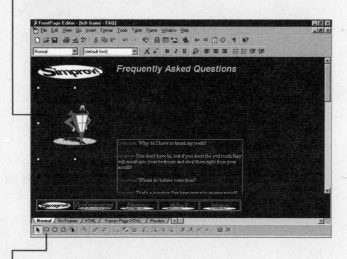

2 Click the Rectangle button on the toolbar.

File names, case sensitivity, and special characters. UNIX considers Filename.html and filename.html to be two different documents. Because of this distinction, it is a good idea to use lower case letters in all of your file names. UNIX also prohibits the use of slashes in filenames; a–z, 0–9, the underscore character, hyphen, and period are all safe characters to use in file names.

Create a Hotspot *(continued)*

③ Drag a rectangle over the Argle image from the upper-left corner of the image to the lower-right corner. When you release the mouse button, the Create Hyperlink dialog box appears.

④ Select the document named "Argle.htm."

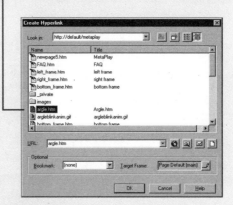

⑤ Click the button next to the Target Frame field. The Target Frame dialog box appears.

How do viewers scan Web pages? Market Research specialists at New York's Poppe Tyson, an interactive advertising agency, have learned that viewers scan a Web page from left to right and then down. This pattern is very different from the "Z" direction pattern that's typical when readers scan a regular, printed page.

BrowserWatch. Founded and maintained by Dave Garaffa, BrowserWatch is Mecklermedia's information site for providing browser developments, plug-ins, and ActiveX controls (browserwatch. internet.com).

Create a Hotspot *(continued)*

6 Click the right frame and then click OK.

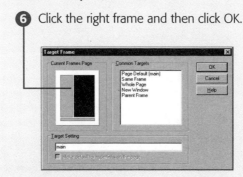

Adjusting the HTML for Search Engine Robots

Chapter 6 described adjustments you can make to your HTML in Microsoft Word to attract the attention of search engine robots, such as adjusting Meta tags and the content of the frameset page. In this chapter, you will make similar adjustments to the HTML on your page using FrontPage.

Copy the Right Frame HTML to the Frameset Document

It's the right frame that holds all the text for the FAQ. If you paste the content from the right frame into Noframe tags inside the frameset document, the FAQ will be indexed by search engine robots. The Noframe tags are designed to tell frames-capable browsers to ignore all information within the beginning and ending Noframe tags. Frames-challenged browsers will see the information, and so will search engine robots.

**Mecklermedia's
E-Commerce Guide.**
The E-Commerce Guide on
the Mecklermedia site provides a
comprehensive list of links to hundreds
of sites that are devoted to the electronic
commerce industry. The site also includes
links to information about online
commerce regulations, research groups,
and newsgroups (e-com.internet.com).

Copy the Right Frame HTML to the Frameset Document *(continued)*

① Click the HTML tab at the bottom of the FrontPage window. The HTML is
displayed.

② In the HTML, select the text starting with the <body> tag and ending with the
</body> tag.

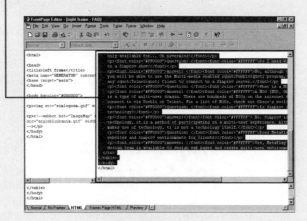

③ From the Edit
menu, choose
Copy.

④ Click the Frameset
document's HTML
tab.

⑤ Select the HTML text starting with <body> and ending with </body>.

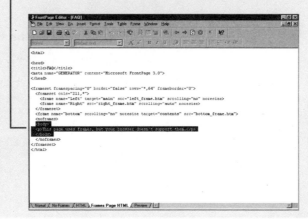

Assigning color to hypertext links. Most browsers use bright blue as the color for a hypertext link and a duller, lighter shade for visited links. If you decide to change the color of hypertext links, use a color that provides a strong contrast with the background. Use a lower contrast shade of the same color for visited links.

Copy the Right Frame HTML to the Frameset Document *(continued)*

6 From the Edit menu, choose Paste. The HTML from the right frame replaces the selected text.

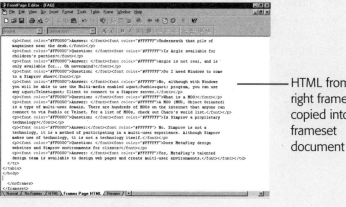

HTML from the right frame copied into the frameset document

Adjust the Contents of the Meta Tags and Title

1 In the frameset document, select <meta name = "GENERATOR" content= "Microsoft FrontPage 3.0">. For more information about Meta tags, see "Attracting Search Engine Spiders," page 118.

```
<html>

<head>
<title>FAQ</title>
<meta name="GENERATOR" content="Microsoft FrontPage 3.0">
</head>
```

2 From the Edit menu, choose Copy.

Mecklermedia's Web Developer.com. Web Developer.com contains content designed for Web developers. New sections include Java Boutique, Search Engine Watch, and Webreference. Sign up for a free weekly newsletter that will keep you informed about changing content (wwwwebdeveloper.com).

Adjust the Contents of the Meta Tags and Title *(continued)*

③ Create a blank line underneath this text and paste two copies of the Meta tag text.

```
<html>

<head>
<title>FAQ</title>
<meta name="GENERATOR" content="Microsoft FrontPage 3.0">
<meta name="GENERATOR" content="Microsoft FrontPage 3.0">
<meta name="GENERATOR" content="Microsoft FrontPage 3.0">|
</head>
```

④ Select the word "FAQ" inside the Title tags and type *MetaPlay: an Internet Content Company; FAQ Page*

⑤ Edit the two new META tags that you've added to read:

<meta name="DESCRIPTION" content="An Internet content company specializing in multi-user performances known as Simprov">

<meta name="KEYWORDS" content="IMPROV, SIMPROV, MUD, MOO, VRML DESIGN, Multi-user performances, 3D Design">

```
<html>

<head>
<title>MetaPlay: an Internet Content Company; FAQ Page|</title>
<meta name="GENERATOR" content="Microsoft FrontPage 3.0">
<meta name="DESCRIPTION"
content="An Internet content company specializing in multi-user performances known as Simprov">
<meta name="KEYWORDS"
content="IMPROV, SIMPROV, MUD, MOO, VRML DESIGN, Multi-user performances, 3D Design">
</head>
```

Free virtual greeting cards. Hallmark, Blue Mountain Arts, NEC Systems Laboratory, Disney, and Greet Street have discovered an enormous demand for free electronic greeting cards, which include interactive art and multimedia enhancements.

Although most cards are for consumers, Greet Street hopes to expand its line into business marketing. It is planning human resource announcements and sales correspondence for 1998.

www.hallmarkconnections.com

www.bluemountain.com

www.auraline.com

www.family.com

www.disneyblast.com

www.greetst.com

Resave the Frameset Document

Choose Save from the File menu to resave the frameset document.

Creating a Form

You can use the MetaPlay frames layout that you've completed to create a page for the MetaPlay registration form. The form is designed to allow people to reserve tickets to MetaPlay events. FrontPage 98 will automatically add Submit and Reset buttons when you add the first form field. To keep the fields together, you will build a one-cell table to hold the form.

Routing Form Data

You'll need to plan ahead and create a strategy for receiving form data before you design a form. The simplest method is to route the data to an e-mail address using a Mailto. The data will be delivered as an e-mail text file attachment and can be read with a text editor such as Word, WordPad, or Notepad. With this scheme, each submission is handled separately, and data you can cut and paste into a database.

The other routing alternative is to use a script that sends the data to an e-mail address. CGI scripts to route form data are so popular that many are available on the Web for free. Matt's Script Archive at www.worldwidemart.com/scripts/ offers a mail form CGI script that works well. This technique assumes that you are able to run CGI scripts on the Web server you're using. Contact your Internet Service Provider and inquire about whether you have access to the server's CGI directory or whether you can run CGI scripts in your directory. Access might be included with a commercial account, but it is not always included with a personal account.

Live Picture's Image Server software for e-commerce. Live Picture's suite of server software provides customer image archiving solutions for e-commerce. The Internet Imaging Protocol (IIP) enables a plug-in, Java applet, or ActiveX component to request image data from a Web server, allowing only specific data to be transferred across the Internet. When images are stored as FlashPix files, detail in clothing, furniture, or manufactured goods gets progressively better as viewers zoom in (www. livepicture.com). For information on the FlashPix plug-in, see the tip on the opposite page.

Add Introductory Text

1 Follow the directions starting on page 177 to set up a frames document. Add the text "Reservations!" to the top of the page, and use the Insert Table command to build a one-cell table in the right frame that is 340 pixels wide.

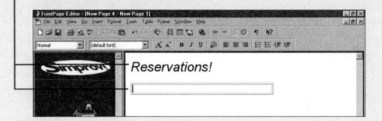

2 Import a document named "True_feelings.doc" into the table. This document and the other files required for this exercise are available on the book's Web page at mspress.microsoft.com/mspress/products/1576.

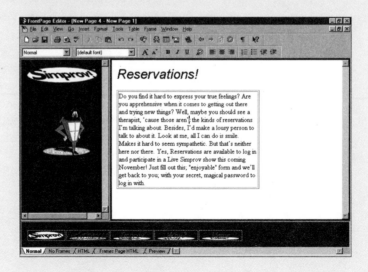

Live Picture's FlashPix plug-in for Photoshop and Image Composer. Live Picture's FlashPix Plug-In for Photoshop also works with Microsoft Image Composer. Together, Live·Picture's FlashPix and Internet Imaging Protocol cause pictures to become progressively more detailed as you zoom in. This combination of tools is ideal for stock photographers, catalogers, and museums. The FlashPix plug-in is available as a free download at www. livepicture.com/download/index.html.

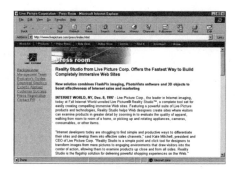

Add Introductory Text *(continued)*

3 Position the cursor at the end of each line and press Enter to add blank lines.

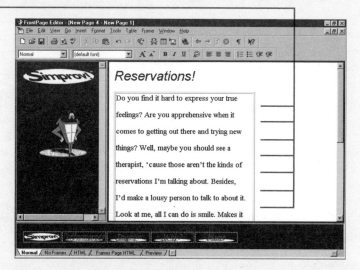

4 Right-click the table, choose Table Properties from the shortcut menu, and change the border size to 0. The border disappears.

Create a Table for the Form

1 Click in the space beneath the table.

2 Press the Enter key.

3 From the Table menu, choose Insert Table. The Insert Table dialog box opens.

Zapa Digital's banner ad site locator. Zapa Digital's Site Locator is an online database of advertising-supported Web sites organized by geographic location. For $99.95, customers can access the Online Ad Wizard, a private Web site with rate cards and ad placement information. For an online demo, visit www.zapamicrosites.com.

Customizing one-line text boxes. One-line text boxes provide fields for users to type data into forms. The width of a text box can be adjusted to accommodate the text that you anticipate users will enter. Change the width of a one-line text box by dragging on a size handle or by typing a number in the Width In Characters field in the Text Box Properties dialog box.

Create a Table for the Form *(continued)*

4 Set the table size to 1 row and 1 column, and set the width to 340 pixels. A one-cell table is displayed.

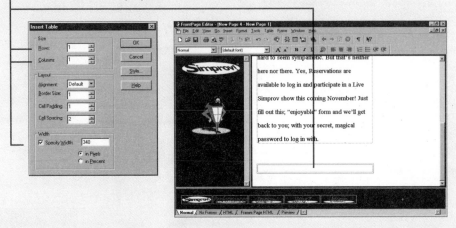

Create One-Line Text Boxes

1 Click inside the table, choose Form Field from the Insert menu, and then choose One-Line Text Box from the Form Field submenu. A text box and a pair of buttons appear.

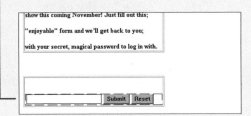

Color guides. Are you faced with the job of selecting a combination of colors for your Web pages? Color guides are books that help graphic designers visualize color combinations and choose color for typography and images. Color choices can determine whether page elements project, recede, harmonize, or clash. Although the following guides, written by Dale Russell, and published by North Light Books in 1990, are designed for print, the color swatches are helpful for visualizing color combinations for Web pages:

Colorworks1: The RedBook

Colorworks2: The BlueBook

Colorworks3: The YellowBook

Colorworks4: The PastelBook

Create One-Line Text Boxes *(continued)*

2 Click the line above the text box and press the Backspace key. This will close up the extra space.

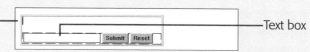 Text box

3 Click in front of the text box to insert the cursor.

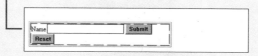

4 Type *Name* and then press Shift+Enter.

5 Press the right arrow key on the keyboard to move the cursor to the right of the text box, and then press Shift+Enter.

6 Type *How did you hear about us?* and then press Shift+Enter to insert a line break.

The shape-shifting nature of forms. Forms look different from browser to browser and from platform to platform. For example, text boxes created on a PC will look shorter on Macintosh browsers. Be sure to check the appearance of a page with a form on other platforms before

Create One-Line Text Boxes *(continued)*

7 From the Insert menu, choose Form Field, and then select One-Line Text Box from the Form Field submenu. A second text box is inserted.

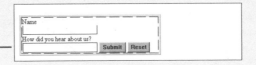

8 Insert two more text boxes. Above the first, type *Where are you from?* and above the second, type *What's your age (approximately)?*

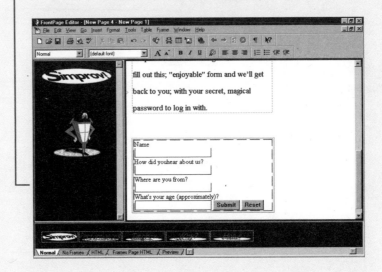

you publish the site.

Stock Objects. Stock Objects, a division of Rhizome Internet L.L.C., is a one-stop shop for images, animations, Java applets, 3-D models, and Shockwave animations. Modeled after a stock photography library, the site (www.stockobjects.com) is available to Web developers 24 hours a day, anywhere in the world. The site has a keyword search engine, and objects can be purchased online. Artists who are interested in selling objects online at Stock Objects can upload art. Rhizome will provide a royalty agreement for

Create Drop-Down Menus

1 Press Shift+Enter to create a new line.

2 Type *What gender are you?* and press Shift+Enter.

3 From the Insert menu, choose Form Field, and then choose Drop-Down Menu from the Form Field submenu.

4 Insert two more drop-down menus. Above the first, type *What's your average yearly income (approximately)?* and above the second, type *What's your favorite color?*

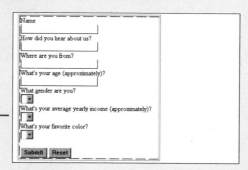

contributors.

Exchanging files with a client in cyberspace. The Web server space that comes with a personal Internet account can be used as an FTP site to transfer files back and forth to your client. Use it to drop off files any time of the day or night. You'll need to give your client your user ID and password. Create folders on the Web server named *To ClientName* and *From ClientName*. WS_FTP Pro, described on page 210, is a useful tool for uploading files.

Configure the Drop-Down Menus

1 Double-click the first text box. The Text Box Properties dialog box appears.

2 Type *Name* in the Name field, and then click OK.

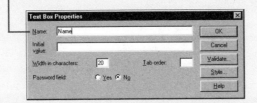

3 Double-click each of the other text boxes and type *Hear*, *From*, and *Age* in each of the Name fields on the Text Box Properties dialog box.

4 Double-click the first drop-down menu. The Drop-Down Menu Properties dialog box appears.

Configure the Drop-Down Menus *(continued)*

⑤ Type *Gender* into the Name field and click Click Add.

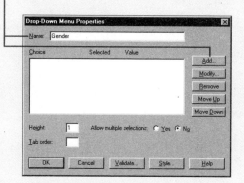

⑥ Type *Neuter* into the Choice field and click OK.

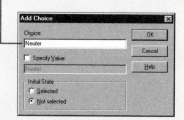

⑦ Click the Add button again to add *Male*, *Female,* and *Other* to the list of choices. The choices you've added appear on the drop-down menu.

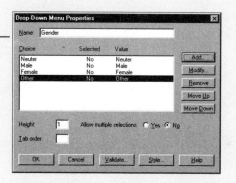

⑧ Double-click the second drop-down menu and add the following choices:

Student

10-20K

20-30K

30-40K

40-50K

50-100K

100-200K

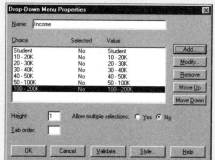

The FrontPage task list.
If more than one person is working on your FrontPage Web, you can use the task list to communicate among the members of the Web team. It's designed to record the actions necessary to complete a FrontPage Web. To create a task, choose Add Task from the Edit menu in the FrontPage Editor window. In the dialog box, type a task name and the name of the Web team member who will be assigned the task, select a priority level, and type a description.

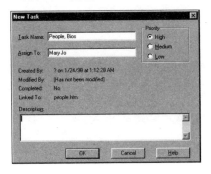

Configure the Drop-Down Menus *(continued)*

9 Double-click the third drop-down menu and add the following choices:

Red

Yellow

Guatemala

Abraham Lincoln

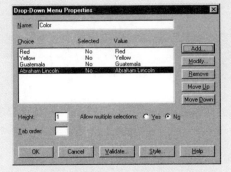

Configure the Submit Button

1 Click the space to the right of the third drop-down menu and press Shift+Enter. This creates a blank line between the last drop-down menu and the two buttons.

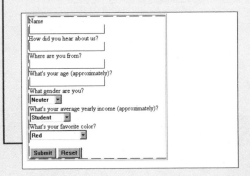

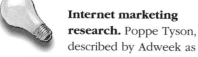

Internet marketing research. Poppe Tyson, described by Adweek as one of the "highest flying" new media shops, has spun off Decision Tree, a research and strategic communications company specializing in online research. Among the services offered are traditional focus groups, one-on-one interviews, telephone polling, in-depth interviews, and live online round table discussions. Decision Tree clients include IBM, Johnson & Johnson, Lycos, Bristol-Myers Squibb, Mellon Bank, National Easter Seals Foundation, Kaplan Educational Centers, Polygram, and Dow Chemical.

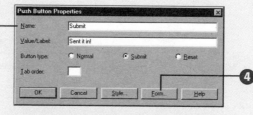

Configure the Submit Button *(continued)*

2 Double-click the Submit button. The Push Button Properties dialog box appears.

3 Type *Submit* in the Name field and *Send it in!* in the Value/Label field.

4 Click Form. The Form Properties dialog box appears.

5 Click the Send To Other button.

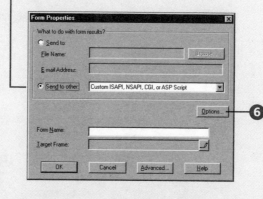

6 Click Options. The Options For Custom Form Handler dialog box opens.

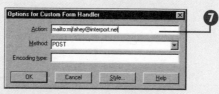

7 In the Action field, type *mailto:* followed by your e-mail address in this format: *youremail@yourdomain*, and then click OK.

8 Click OK to close the Form Properties dialog box, and then click OK to close the Push Button Properties dialog box.

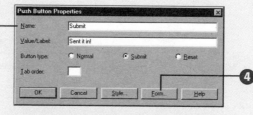

FAQs and Forms

Avoiding "Click Here" text links. Although "Click Here" is considered acceptable in banner ads, it is not considered good form as a text link on a Web page. It is more appropriate to embed hyperlinks in related keywords that occur in your text.

The Alt attribute for Internet shell account users. UNIX shell accounts are text-based Internet accounts that are economical and popular on university campuses. Many users prefer text to graphics because of the speed of display. In fact, some people who browse the Web with Internet Explorer or Netscape also turn off images for faster downloading.

For shell account users, there are numerous text-based tools that do not display graphics. Examples include Lynx for Web browsing, Elm or Pine for e-mail, and Tin for Usenet news.

Configure the Reset Button and Finish the Form

1 In the right frame, double-click the Reset button. The Push Button Properties dialog box appears.

2 Type *Reset* in the Name field and *Get Lost!* in the Value/Label field, and then click OK. The Reset button is renamed.

3 Choose Background from the Format menu and set the background color to black on the Page Properties dialog box.

4 Choose Table Properties from the Table menu and set the border size to 0 on the Table Properties dialog box. The table border is removed.

5 Select the text on the form and set its color to white by clicking the Text Color button on the Format toolbar and selecting the color white on the Color dialog box.

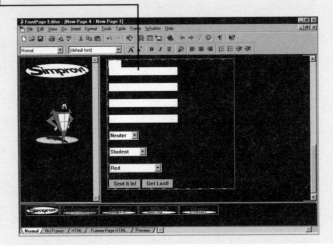

The Alt attribute in image tags. To accommodate UNIX shell account users and viewers who turn off their graphics, use an Alt attribute in image tags. Alt refers to alternate text or a descriptive line of text that will appear in a text browser in place of an image. As you roll your mouse over an image in Internet Explorer, this alternate text is displayed as boxed text. A descriptive line of text will appear in a text browser in place of the image.

In FrontPage, click an image in the FrontPage Editor window. An image toolbar is displayed at the bottom of the screen. Click the Text button in this toolbar (Note: The Text button will not be available if the image is a GIF animation). Type a description in the rectangular area that is displayed. The added text will be displayed only in text-based Web browsers and in browsers that have images turned off.

Save the Form Document

1 Choose Save All from the File menu.

2 Save the form document in the dialog boxes that are displayed.

Preview the Form in a Browser Window

1 From the File menu, choose Preview In Browser.

2 In the Preview In Browser dialog box, select a browser and click OK. Your form page will be displayed in the browser.

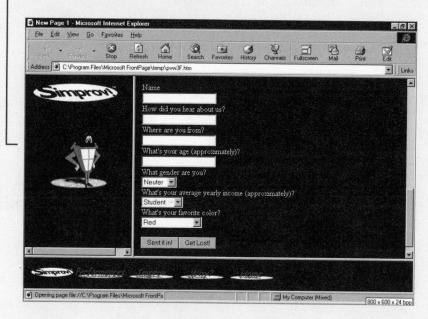

Publishing and Testing the Form on the Web

To test the form document, you will need to publish it on a Web server. You can use WS_FTP Pro to copy the four frame documents to a Web server. A demo copy of WS_FTP Pro can be obtained at www.ipswitch.com. Although you can use the Microsoft Web Publishing Wizard to copy your documents to a server, if you've created any other pages when you create your form, the wizard will copy all your pages to your Web, and not just the form.

Move the Frame Documents to a Web Server

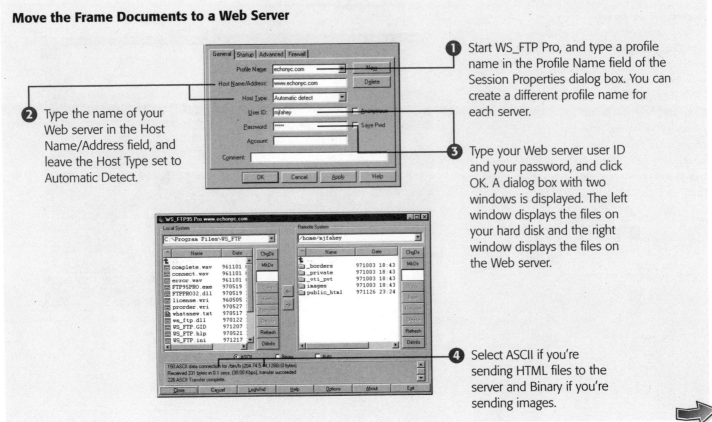

❶ Start WS_FTP Pro, and type a profile name in the Profile Name field of the Session Properties dialog box. You can create a different profile name for each server.

❷ Type the name of your Web server in the Host Name/Address field, and leave the Host Type set to Automatic Detect.

❸ Type your Web server user ID and your password, and click OK. A dialog box with two windows is displayed. The left window displays the files on your hard disk and the right window displays the files on the Web server.

❹ Select ASCII if you're sending HTML files to the server and Binary if you're sending images.

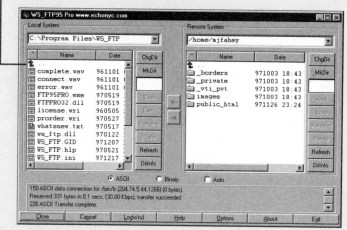

Java navigation. Visit Hasbro Interactive's Frogger site to see an innovative example of Java navigation. The "Frogtroller" is created with a Java applet that gets preloaded before you view the site. It's a purple mushroom that sits in the lower left corner of the screen, allowing you to roam through screen modules that explain new enhancements in Hasbro's Frogger CD-ROM game. The Frogger site at www.frogger.com was created by a new media creative team at Poppe Tyson Interactive.

Move the Frame Documents to a Web Server *(continued)*

⑤ Double-click the Public_html folder to open it. If you want, you can then click the MkDir button to create a folder inside the Public_html folder.

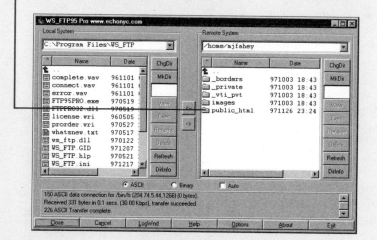

⑥ Click the up arrow to move up the directory tree on your hard disk.

Software factory for the financial industry.

Transaction Information System's new FLITE lab is a software factory dedicated to building mostly Web-based electronic commerce solutions for the financial industry (www.flitelab.com). There are approximately 20 member firms, including Digital Equipment Corporation, Foote, Cone and Belding, IBM, Lotus Development Corporation, Reuters, Sybase, and Visa. Amid stone gargoyles and stained glass, in a space that was once the New York Lawyers' Club on top of the historic United States Realty building in downtown Manhattan, the technology staff uses the FLITE lab facility for jointly developing interactive products with FLITE engineers.

Move the Frame Documents to a Web Server *(continued)*

7 Locate the folder labeled "Webshare" and double-click it. Double-click the Wwwroot folder within the Webshare folder, and double-click the Metaplay folder within the Wwwroot folder.

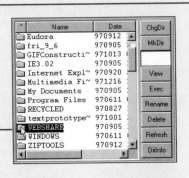

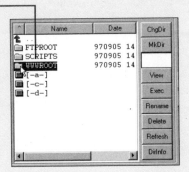

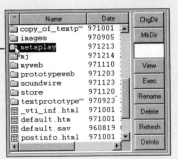

8 Select each of the four frame documents you created in the Metaplay folder and click the right arrow button. The documents are copied to the Web server.

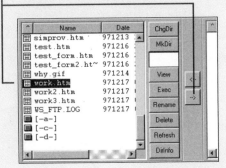

Do you have a story idea for a Web publication? Editor-in-chief Mike Floyd of *Web Techniques* magazine welcomes story ideas. He recommends an e-mail pitch describing a story idea followed by a paper proposal. Floyd looks forward to proposals from developers who have hands-on experience with technology and want to write about it.

Testing the Form

Once your form is on the Web, you can try filling it out and sending it to the e-mail address you configured in the Mailto. The data will be sent to your e-mail box as an attachment that can be opened in Word.

Test the Form

1 Start Internet Explorer.

2 Navigate to the form document on your Web server.

3 Fill out the form and click Send It In!

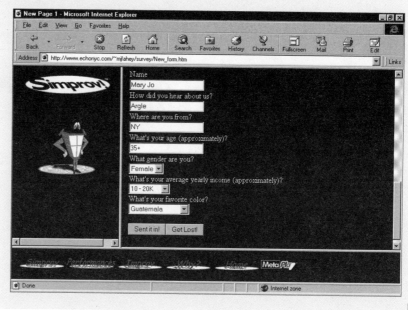

Free e-mail: How does it work? If you can access the Web, you can have a free e-mail account. It's advertiser-supported and it's an efficient solution for people who have e-mail at work, mobile professionals, students, teachers, and those who don't own computers. You can access an Internet computer at libraries, cafes, airports, and universities. Register with a free e-mail site such as HotMail (www.hotmail.com) and send and receive e-mail whenever you log on. E-mail is entirely private. You can send and receive e-mail attachments, and develop your own e-mail address book.

Test the Form *(continued)*

④ Click OK in the Internet Explorer dialog box that warns that the form is being submitted using e-mail.

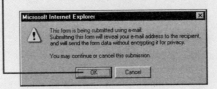

⑤ In your e-mail program, retrieve your e-mail and then open the form data e-mail message.

⑥ Double-click the attachment. The Open Attachment Warning dialog box appears.

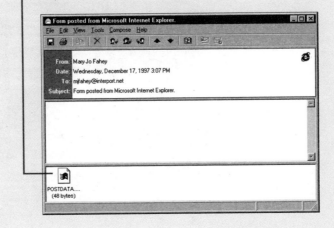

What is POP e-mail?

POP is an acronym for Post Office Protocol. Protocol is another word for signalling, and POP protocol allows users to download and read mail. Most mail sent and received over an Internet connection uses POP. In a shared environment that is not password-protected, such as a school computer lab, POP is not a popular option, because mail must be downloaded to be read. IMAP, or Internet Message Access Protocol, is more desirable for shared computer labs because messages can be read, managed, and deleted without having to be downloaded.

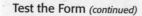
Test the Form *(continued)*

7 Click Save It To Disk, and then click OK.

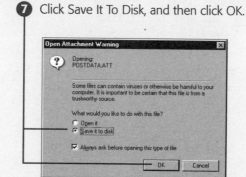

The document opens in Word. Data from the form's fields are separated with & (ampersand) characters.

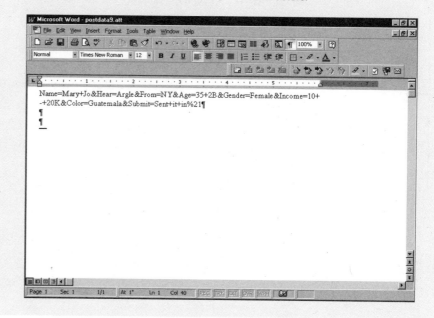

Radio buttons. Radio buttons used on a form can either be selected or unselected. A selected radio button has a black, filled-in appearance.

Creating a Questionnaire

Round radio buttons are a good choice for online questionnaires, surveys, or evaluations forms. They allow a user to select one option from among a group of options.

The following Computer Workstation Feature Importance Ratings form is not related to the MetaPlay site. It's a fictitious, abbreviated form that provides an example of how to create radio buttons for your multiple-choice-style questionnaires or surveys.

Create a Table

❶ On a new page in the FrontPage Editor, choose Insert Table from the Table menu. The Insert Table dialog box appears.

❷ Type *2* in the field labeled Rows, *1* in the field labeled Columns, and *480* in the field labeled Specify Width. Click OK. A table with two cells appears

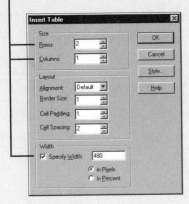

❸ Type *Computer Workstation Feature Importance Ratings* in the top cell.

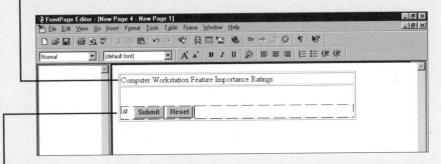

❹ Press Tab to move the lower cell.

❺ From the Insert menu, choose Form Field, and then choose Radio Button from the Form Field submenu. A radio button and two push buttons are inserted.

Navigation bars: Text, buttons, or an image map? Use a navigation bar on every page of your site. Although you cannot link to every section or every page, the navigation bar can contain links to essential pages. Include a link to your home page in case visitors want to start over. Navigation bars can be created with text, button graphics, or an image map. Many sites provide a text and graphic version to accommodate text-only browsers or people who browse with images turned off.

If you create navigation buttons, create a one-row table to hold the buttons in place. An image map is a single graphic with embedded links. The procedures for creating an image map are covered in this chapter.

Add Radio Buttons

1 Click the space above the radio button and press the Backspace key on the keyboard. This closes up the space around the radio button.

2 Insert the cursor in front of the radio button, type *Monitor*, and press Shift+Enter to insert a line break.

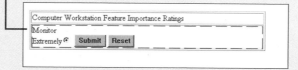

3 Type *Extremely Important*, and then press the right arrow key to move the cursor to the right of the radio button.

4 Type *Neutral.*

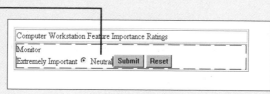

VRML banner ads or "spanners." At the Fall Internet World held in New York City, Cosmo Software, a subsidiary of Silicon Graphics, discovered a favorable response to VRML banner ads called "spanners" or spinning banners. "Spanners" is a term that was invented at the show to describe VRML animated banner ads. VRML 2.0 offers 3-D animation, and files are much smaller than comparable animations created with GIF images.

Add Radio Buttons *(continued)*

5 From the Insert menu, choose Form Field, and then choose Radio Button from the Form Field submenu. A new radio button appears.

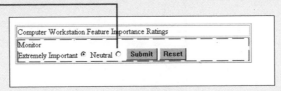

6 Type *Marginally Important.*

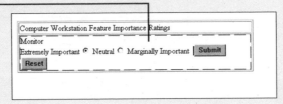

7 Insert another radio button and press Enter.

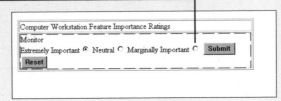

If I use FrontPage to create my Web, does my ISP need FrontPage server extensions? FrontPage server extensions are a set of programs and scripts that support Web sites created in FrontPage and extend the functionality of a Web server. Some FrontPage components, such as the Registrations Form Handler, the Save Results Form Handler, and the FrontPage Discussion Form Handler, won't work without FrontPage server extensions.

If your ISP does not have FrontPage server extensions, they are available for the Microsoft Internet Information Server and other popular Microsoft Windows and UNIX Web servers.

If your ISP does not have the Microsoft Server extensions, most of the FrontPage Web page components will still work. Forms handling is one component that won't work. The procedure for routing form data in this chapter demonstrates how to use a Mailto URL to route form data to an e-mail address instead of relying on a FrontPage server extension. CGI scripts in the public domain are also an alternative.

Add More Radio Buttons

1 Type *CD-ROM Speed*, and press Shift+Enter.

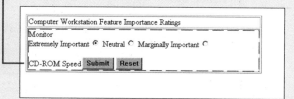

2 Select the line of text that contains the radio buttons and click the Copy button on the FrontPage toolbar.

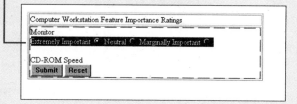

3 Move the cursor to the start of the line that contains the Submit and Reset buttons and click the Paste button. The text appears.

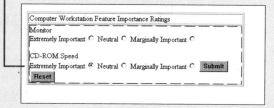

4 Press Enter.

If I add HTML tags to my Web, is there a way to test my page? WebTech's Validation Service lets developers test their HTML syntax (www.webtechs.com/html-val-svc/).

HTML-on-the-fly. The process of creating pages dynamically from components stored in databases is referred to as "HTML-on-the-fly." The newest trend in Web development is the harnessing of database technology to create a unique experience for Web viewers. Viewer preferences and Web viewing patterns are recorded in a database. Custom Web pages are generated dynamically and tailored to individual users.

Add More Radio Buttons *(continued)*

5 Repeat these steps to create additional sets of radio buttons for Keyboard, Speakers, and CPU Speed.

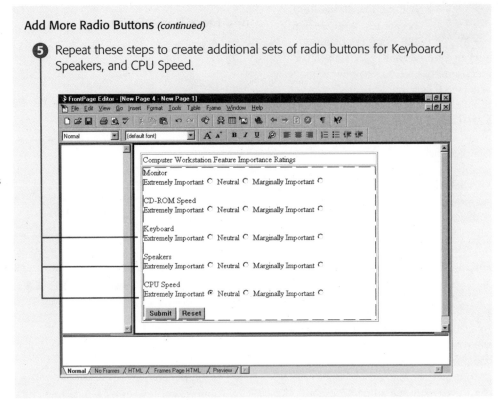

Configuring the Questionnaire Form

You'll want the radio buttons in each row to belong to a group so that when one is selected, the others cannot be selected. For each row, you'll invent a group name that corresponds to a workstation feature and enter it in the Radio Button Properties dialog box for each button. You will also set the initial state of each of the buttons; in each of the rows, Extremely Important will be on, and Neutral and Marginally Important will be off.

Yahoo's press releases.
Yahoo doesn't send its electronic news releases. Instead, it has created an area on its site called Information Center, which contains a link to a list of press releases called "Find Out What Yahoo Has Been Up To."

Configure the Form

1 Double-click the first radio button. The Radio Button Properties dialog box opens.

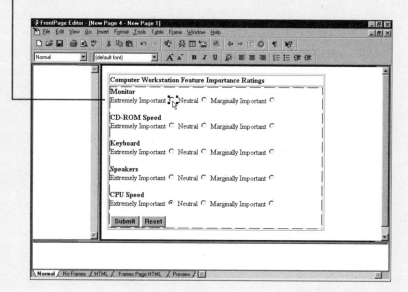

2 Type *Monitor* in the Group Name field and *Extremely* in the Value field and click OK. The first radio button is assigned to the new group named "Monitor."

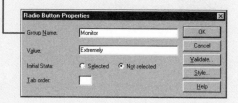

Internet World trade shows. Mecklermedia, the company that publishes *Internet World*, *Web Week*, *Web Developer*, and *Internet Shopper*, also produces domestic and international Internet World trade show events. For a list of trade show events in Singapore, Toronto, Abu Dhabi, Los Angeles, Tel Aviv, Buenos Aires, Oslo, Lisbon, London, Bogotá, São Paulo, Berlin, Mexico CIty, Chicago, Hong Kong, Sydney, Tokyo, Paris, Kuala Lumpur, Rio de Janiero, New York, Manila, Santiago, Stockholm and Caracas, visit events.internet.com.

Configure the Form *(continued)*

3 Double-click the second radio button in the first row. Type *Monitor* in the Group Name field and *Neutral* in the Value field and click OK.

4 Double-click the third radio button in the first row. Type *Monitor* in the Group Name field and *Marginally* in the Value field and click OK.

5 Continue to configure the Radio Buttons, naming the groups "CD," "Keyboard," "Speakers," and "CPU." Type *Extremely* as the value for the first radio button in each row, *Neutral* as the value for the second radio button, and *Marginally* as the value for the third button in each row.

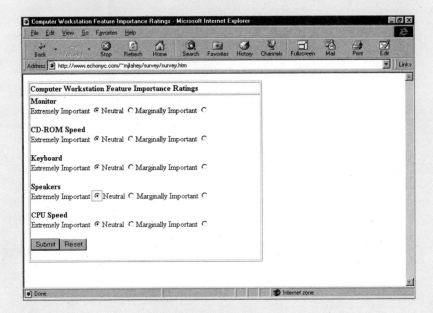

The completed questionnaire form.

TeleAdapt Online.
TeleAdapt Online is a resource for international modem connectivity. The Traveler's Help Desk contains FAQs on connecting in hotels, offices, and pay phones, as well as advice on traveling with a laptop and a modem. A hotel database planned for the site will give essential information concerning modem connectivity in hotels (www.teleadapt.com).

3-D GIF animation.
Although most GIF animations are two dimensional, a 3-D animation can be built from stills generated in 3-D animation software. Mind of the Machine, a digital studio specializing in 2-D and 3-D graphics for multimedia, has built a small 3-D GIF animation at the following address: www.mindofthemachine.com.

Configure the Form *(continued)*

When the form data is delivered through e-mail, each group name will be followed by an equal sign and the value the respondent filled in.

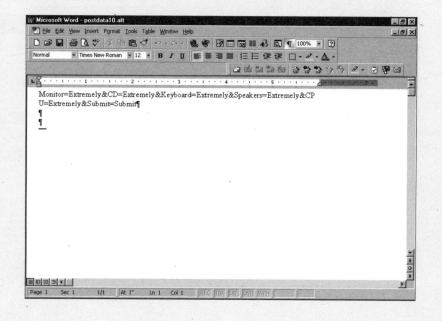

Page banners, which appear to be images, are table cells with a background color.

Tables provide an invisible page grid for a three-column newsletter.

Hyperlinks jump to additional newsletter pages and the table of contents.

Browser window:

C:\My Documents\John\News.html - Microsoft Internet Explorer - [Working Offline]

File   Edit   View   Go   Favorites   Help

Back   Forward   Stop   Refresh   Home   Search   Favorites   History   Channels   Fullscreen   Mail

Address C:\My Documents\John\News.html   Links

alt.coffee

News

A newsletter for those who enjoy coffee, computers and comfy chairs

Fall, 1997

Table of Contents

Calendar of Events

Every Monday ... Two sets beginning at 9:00pm. NO COVER! Donations accepted.

Sept. 1: Cuong Vu - Jim Black, Curtis Hasselbring, Chris Speed, Stomu Takeishi, Cuong Vu

Sept. 8: John Hollenbeck's Claudia Quintet - Drew Gress, John Hollenbeck, Matt Moran, Ted Reichman, Chris Speed

Sept. 15: Jim Black, Matt Moran, Andrea Parkins, Cuong Vu

Sept. 22: Peshko featuring sami da (from Toronto!) - Adam Good, Matt Moran, Jeff Fine;

A Day in the Life of a Coffee Entrepreneur

Ever wonder what it's like to be a coffee barista? What makes people passionate about a brew? What makes cafe regulars loyal to an establishment where they sip in the a.m.? The afternoon or late into the evening?

The neighborhood coffee movement is rumored to have started in San Francisco--the city that also started the newer hybrid coffee establishment - the wired cafe. In New York's East Village, the alt.coffee approach to the neighborhood coffee retailing is an enigmatic style that has made the cafe a citywide phenomenon.

The Bar
The up-close-to-what's-happening stools that line the coffee bar at alt.coffee are right in the center of the klatch. The seat at the end of the counter belongs to a PC station. Owners John, Melissa and Nick have all learned how to carry on required cafe business on this machine while simultaneously carrying on a conversation. Its their style - never let a guest feel abandoned. Each of these baristas is ever-vigilante of nuances or signs that there's a request from a cafe patron. Most customers hover near the cafe's pastry display while their coffee is prepared. Those that slip into the barstools are the cafe regulars -- Paula, the psychologist and Peter, the screenwriter to name just a few.

The Comfy Chairs
alt.coffee's advertised comfy chairs that line the cafe are what push the atmosphere boundary into the realm of home away from home. Although there have been times when owner/barista

TOC *Continued on page 2*

Above: Still image from the alt.coffee panorama available on the Cafe's site.
Foreground: Café guest and owner Melissa Caruso at the alt.coffee bar. Center Right: Owner John Scott behind the bar.

Having Company Over? ... the alt.coffee Guide to Coffee Pots

Sophisticated coffee drinkers may be interested in a comprehensive list of coffeepots used around the world. This varied mix of vessels add dimension to the American specialty coffee movement:

Flip-Drip - a double percolating coffeepot invented by a French tinsmith. Composed of two metal cylinders with a filter basket between. In Italy, the Flip Drip is called a Napoletana Macchinetta and in France the Café Filtre.

Plunger Pot - Also called the French Press. This cylindrical

TOC *Continued on page 2*

Done   My Computer

A Newsletter

The alt.coffee newsletter in this chapter is a close approximation of a four-color print version developed by Internet café owners John Scott, Melissa Caruso, and Nick Bodor. The market-oriented publication they have created provides them with ongoing visibility and contact with their customers. Because alt.coffee (www.altdotcoffee.com) is a wired café, the newsletter reaches an audience who enjoys lots of coffee and fast computers.

In this chapter, you will use both Microsoft Word and Microsoft Image Composer to develop the first page of the newsletter. You can find the completed newsletter at mspress.microsoft.com/mspress/products/1576.

Newsletter Page Design

The page elements you'll need for the alt.coffee newsletter include:

> A three-column page grid set up with Word's versatile Table tool.

> Page rules and a tinted sidebar created by adding color to table cell backgrounds.

> Initial caps at the start of articles to help readers find the beginning of text.

> Subheads that break longer articles into smaller pieces. The subheads will be set with a bold, sans serif typeface. A single line space above each subhead will make article sections stand out.

Serif vs. sans serif.
Typefaces fall into two categories: serif and sans serif. Serifs are small counterstrokes at the ends of letterforms. Nicknamed "little feet," serifs are said to create a resting place for the eye. As a result, body type is often set in a serif face. "Sans" is French for "without." Hence, sans serif means without serifs.

S   S

Serif   Sans serif

> A color for table cell backgrounds selected from the palette of 216 browser-safe colors found in Image Composer's Web palette.

> Article page jumps that contain hyperlink text as a navigation aid.

> Newsletter photos sized to fit inside a single column for minimal downloading. Photo heights can vary, but widths fit inside a column grid.

> A Table of Contents (TOC) button at the end of each article containing a hyperlink to page 1.

Formatting Large Amounts of Information

Newsletters, manuals, and other multiple-page documents require a formatted page structure to hold and organize large amounts of text. For long documents, use HTML text as much as possible and keep images to a minimum.

You can use the conventions in this chapter to format any type of multi-page document.

Working with a Grid

An invisible grid created with Word's Table tool provides an underlying structure for your newsletter. Grids make multiple-page documents feel organized and look unified. Sometimes the grid structure is obvious. At other times, when type, borders, pictures, and other images run across more than a single column, it is not.

For best results, consider developing a preliminary page layout in a page layout software program, such as Microsoft Publisher or Adobe PageMaker, before you test a Web page layout in Word or FrontPage. Designers who create

alt.coffee art. If you want to create the alt.coffee newsletter in this chapter, you'll find the art and text files for it at mspress.microsoft.com/mspress/products/1576.

a paper comp (a comp is a sample of the proposed appearance of the finished work) in advance discover the following benefits:

> The text layout in Word helps you judge the text layout in HTML.

> A paper comp helps visualize table cell requirements for the page.

> A paper comp can be used to show an approximate layout to your Web team or client.

Sample Layouts

In print, grids with more than four columns are thought to be the most versatile. Although this may be true from a design standpoint, large, complex grids are a little too much for HTML editors at this time. For best results, use a two, three, or four-column grid on a Web page. The alt.coffee newsletter in this chapter uses the first of the three-column grid examples:

Examples of a Two-Column Grid:

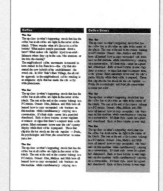

Examples of a Three-Column Grid:

Variations, Three-Column Grid:

Examples of a Four-Column Grid:

How You Will Create the Newsletter

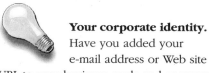

Your corporate identity. Have you added your e-mail address or Web site URL to your business cards and company letterhead?

You will start the alt.coffee newsletter by reducing Word's default margin settings to create more space, and then create a page-sized, three-column grid with the Table tool. After saving the page as a Word document, you will merge certain cells inside the table to accommodate headlines and to create a skeleton document with headline text. If necessary, you can delete extra rows before proceeding to copy body text from a second Word document.

After you paste the body text into the table, you will save the document as HTML and test it in a browser window. Finishing touches you will make include adding a dark brown shade or custom color to the cell backgrounds that contain headlines, applying white to the headline text to reverse the type, and creating nonbreaking spaces to word pairs that should stay together. You will also add table of contents text, hyperlinks to page jumps, and button graphics that link to the table of contents. The last thing you will do for each page is turn off the table border, which serves as a useful guide while you are building the newsletter, but which can be distracting to the viewer.

Your domain name on the Internet. Domain names offer a way to promote your online presence. On the Internet, they are the language equivalents of an address or telephone number. Behind the scenes, the name translates to a number called the IP (Internet Protocol) address on the Internet, but people use your domain name to reach you.

The portion of the domain name after the period is called the top-level domain (TLD). TLDs categorize the name according to purpose. The TLDs currently in use include:

.com (commercial)
.org (organization)
.edu (educational institution)
.net (network)
.gov (government)
.mil (military)

Getting Organized

Before you begin working in Word, you'll need to:

> Develop a page grid in advance using your favorite page layout software. This will approximate how copy fits into each article.

> Create one or more folders on your system to store HTML documents, art files, and any other files that you plan to transfer to a Web server. Ideally, the folder structure you create will be identical to the folder structure on the Web server, so the hyperlinks will work the same way in both places.

> Prepare images for your Web page in advance using Image Composer, and save your art files in GIF or JPEG format.

> Acquire software to copy your files to a Web server. For example, the Microsoft Web Publishing Wizard can be used to copy files to an Internet Service Provider (ISP), a Microsoft Internet Information Server (IIS) or an intranet server on a local area network (LAN).

Creating a Page Grid Using the Table Tool

Page layout programs will create space between columns automatically. For the alt.coffee newsletter, however, you will need to create gutters using narrow columns. Create a three-column grid using a five-column table. You'll make the second and fourth columns narrow to act as gutters. If you've created a paper comp for your newsletter, use a pencil to sketch columns and rows over your page elements to estimate how many rows and columns you'll need. If you've miscalculated, you can always add or delete rows and columns later.

Web market research samples. Forrester Research, specializing in Web market research data, publishes sample reports of market research findings online at www.forrester.com. Jupiter Communications, an online market research firm, publishes similar sample reports at www.jup.com.

Begin the project by reducing the margins in a Word document from 1.25 inches to 1 inch. This will give you more room in which to create the table.

Create a Page and Adjust the Page Margins

1 Start Word.

2 Choose Page Setup from the File menu.

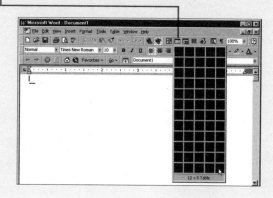

3 Set the Left and Right margins to 1 inch and click OK.

Create a Page-Size Grid

1 Create a table that is five columns wide and twelve rows high using the Insert Table button on the Word toolbar.

Newsletter

Digital money. Merchants who are interested in setting up shop on the Internet should watch the development of the micropayment, a digital substitute for real currency. Micropayments are designed for small ticket items of $.01 to $10.00. Traditional credit cards are not designed to handle such small transactions. Participating firms who are providing micropayment technology include:

First Virtual (www.fv.com)
Digital (www.millicent.digital.com)
CyberCash (www.cybercash.com)
Microsoft (www.microsoft.com)

CyberCash and Microsoft both refer to a virtual debit card as a wallet. Wallet holders fill a wallet with a payment by check or traditional credit card. After money is transferred into a wallet, the wallet holder has purchasing power with thousands of merchants on the Web.

CyberCash has provided its Cyber-Coin payment module for Microsoft's new Wallet software, which is distributed with Internet Explorer 4.0 and future versions of Windows. The Wallet software is also available for Netscape Navigator 3.0 users. (www.microsoft.com/commerce/callet/local/plginst.htm)

Create a Page-Size Grid *(continued)*

An empty table containing five columns of equal width is displayed.

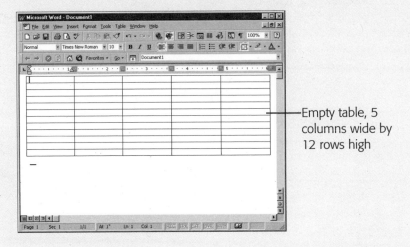

Empty table, 5 columns wide by 12 rows high

Select and Center the Table

1 Click any cell in the table.

2 Choose Select Table from the Table menu. The table you select becomes highlighted.

3 Click the Center button on Word's Formatting toolbar to center the table on the page.

New proposed top-level domains. The part of the domain name after the period, the "com" in microsoft.com, for example, is called the top-level domain. Because domain name registration has soared, many companies have had difficulty finding a suitable domain name. To solve this problem, members of a United Nations agency called the World Intellectual Property Organization (WIPO) have proposed new top-level domain names in seven categories:

.firm   for businesses or firms

.store   for businesses offering goods for purchase

.web   for entities emphasizing Web activities

.arts   for entertainment and cultural entities

.rec   for recreation and entertainment entities

.info   for entities providing information services

.nom   for individuals

Adjust the Width of the Table Columns

1 Click anywhere in the first column.

2 Choose Select Column from the Table menu. The column is highlighted to indicate that it is selected.

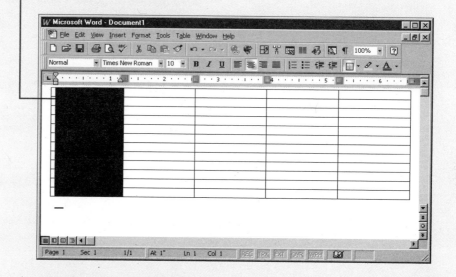

3 Choose Cell Height And Width from the Table menu.

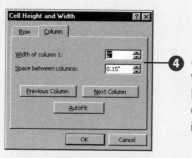

4 On the Column tab of the Cell Height And Width dialog box, type 2 in the field labeled Width Of Column 1, and then click OK. The width of the first column is increased.

Collecting marketing data from server logs. Your Internet Service Provider's Web server produces server log files, which record visitor domain names and other marketing data. Ask your provider for a monthly copy of the log file and ask to be shown how to identify hits and visitor domain names.

Adjust the Width of the Table Columns *(continued)*

⑤ Repeat steps 1 through 4, but make the second and fourth columns 0.19 inches wide and make the third and fifth columns 2 inches wide.

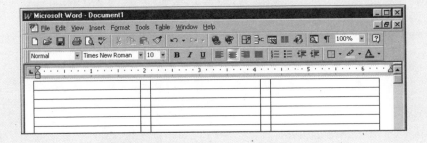

Saving the Page As a Word Document

Although you can save pages.as HTML files in Word, you'll want to save a copy of your newsletter page as a Word document first. When you've completed the page, you can save the file as an HTML document.

Save Your Page

❶ Choose Save As from the File menu.

❷ In the Save As dialog box, select a folder and enter a name for the Word document, and then click Save.

Finding computer trade shows in your area.
Computer trade shows are an important source of marketing contacts, even if you're not in technology. CMPnet's Tech Calendar contains an online listing of 2000 worldwide computer-related events. Visit www.techweb.com/calendar and type in your city. The search engine will list the events in your area.

Merging Cells to Accommodate Newsletter Headlines

The Merge Cells and Split Cells commands in Word are two powerful commands that a designer can use to make a table act as an invisible grid. In this example, you merge table cells to provide space for alt.coffee headings that run across two columns.

Merge Two Cells for Heading Text

1 Select the third, fourth, and fifth columns in the top row.

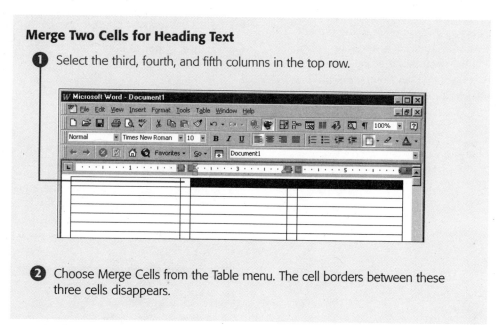

2 Choose Merge Cells from the Table menu. The cell borders between these three cells disappears.

Gathering computer information from user groups. User groups are an important source of information about new technology and local trade shows. There are thousands of user groups all over the world devoted to every hardware platform, operating system, and application. Most groups hold monthly meetings that are open to the public.

Yahoo's Internet user group pages will help you locate groups in your area (www.yahoo.com/Computers-and-Internet/Internet/User-Group).

Add Heading Text to Merged Cells

1 Type *News* in the merged cells.

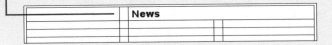

2 Select the text and choose Arial Black from the Font drop-down menu.

3 Choose 14 points from the Font Size drop-down menu.

Add Logo Art

1 Click inside the top cell in column 1.

2 From the Insert menu, choose Picture, and then, from the secondary menu, choose From File.

3 In the Insert dialog box, locate the art file "Logo.gif" and click Insert. You can download the logo art file from the book's Web site at mspress.microsoft.com/mspress/products/1576. The cell automatically expands to allow the logo art to fit. Notice that the cell containing the word "News" has also expanded in height.

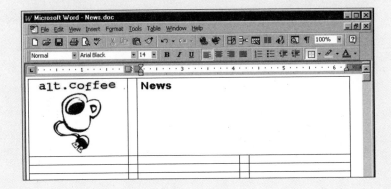

Ornamenting newsletters with charts, graphs, and tables. Use charts, graphs, and tables in your newsletter to make data visually interesting. You can summarize detailed information about trends or products in your industry with tables that will provide readers with quick summaries that are easy to read. Don't assume your customers already know details about your business.

What you consider to be very basic information may be news to your readers. For example, the alt.coffee table contains a list of coffee grinds that is likely to have at least one or two pieces of information that are news to even the most sophisticated coffee drinkers.

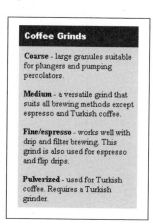

Coffee Grinds

Coarse - large granules suitable for plungers and pumping percolators.

Medium - a versatile grind that suits all brewing methods except espresso and Turkish coffee.

Fine/espresso - works well with drip and filter brewing. This grind is also used for espresso and flip drips.

Pulverized - used for Turkish coffee. Requires a Turkish grinder.

Split Cells to Shorten the Height of the Heading Cell

You can split the cell that contains the word News to make it look a bit less clunky.

1 Click inside the cell containing the word News.

2 Choose Split Cells from the Table menu.

3 In the Split Cells dialog box, type *1* in the field labeled Columns and type *2* in the field labeled Rows. Don't worry about the Merge Cells Before Split option. The cell containing the word "News" will be split into two rows.

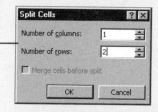

4 Click in the cell with the word "News" and reselect Split Cells from the Table menu.

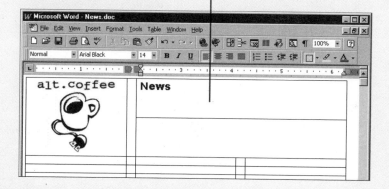

5 Repeat steps 2 and 3 to split this cell into two more rows. The row height of the heading cell will be reduced.

Putting your staff on the Web. Can the art directors, graphic designers, copywriters, and account staff at your firm access the Web? If your company has built a Web site, it is essential that the entire company become familiar with the content.

Add Headlines to Create a Page Skeleton

Enter the headline text as shown below to create a page skeleton.

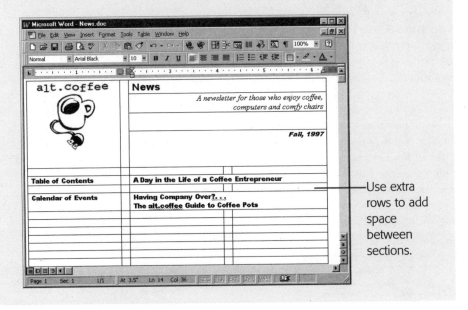

Use extra rows to add space between sections.

Delete Extra Rows

1 Select unused rows. The rows are highlighted to show that they are selected.

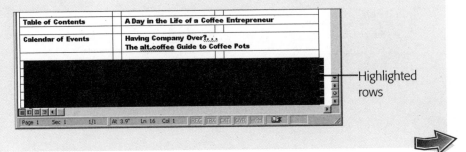

Highlighted rows

Organizing newsletter content. Newsletters should be organized around a theme. Examples include promotional newsletters to sell products or services and informational newsletters for employees or subscribers. The arrangement of newsletter copy and the choice of typography are important for readability and comprehension. Short paragraphs are more effective than long, verbose articles. Serif typefaces, such as Garamond and Times Roman, work best as body text. Sans serif typefaces, such as Arial and Franklin Gothic, are appropriate for headlines.

Delete Extra Rows *(continued)*

2 Choose Delete Cells from the Table menu.

3 In the Delete Cells dialog box, select Delete Entire Row, and click OK. The rows you selected will disappear.

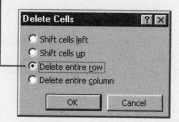

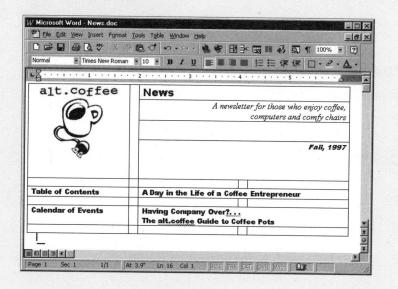

Placing classified ads on the Web. The latest trend in online marketing and advertising is classified advertising for real estate, automobiles, employment, and personals. This $17-billion market, which has been dominated by local newspapers, will soon see competition from services such as:

Microsoft Sidewalk: www.sidewalk.com

CitySearch: www.citysearch.com

Digital City on AOL: www.digitalcity.com

Yahoo: www.yahoo.com

Classifieds2000: www.classifieds2000.com

Vicinity: www.vicinity.com

CNET's Snap Online: www.snap.com

Adding Body Text

You will need to copy the body text for the alt.coffee newsletter from a second Word document. You can also gradually add text to fill the columns by by copying a few lines at a time.

Copy Body Text From a Second Word Document

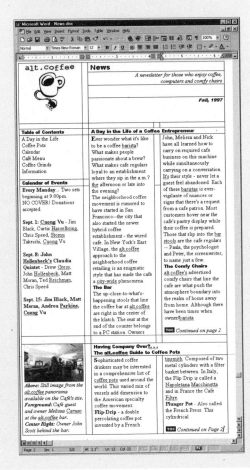

❶ Open the file containing the body text in a second Word document on your computer. You can download this file from the book's Web page at mspress.microsoft.com/mspress/products/1576.

❷ Alternate between the newsletter and the second Word document to copy text into the remaining empty table cells on your page.

Saving a Copy as HTML

When you save your newsletter page as HTML, the appearance of the document will change slightly. However, the page grid you've created with Word's powerful Table feature maintains its integrity.

Save Your Document as HTML

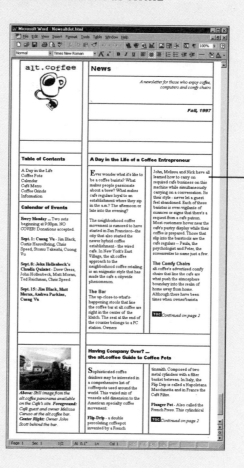

Choose Save As HTML from the File menu.

When the document is saved as HTML, the row height will change slightly. You'll work with visible table borders until the document is completed.

The text in the HTML document may have line breaks that are different from those in the Word file. As a result, you may need to copy and paste more text.

Newsletter

Checking your document in a browser window. You'll discover that the line breaks in your newsletter will change when you save the document as HTML. They will change again when you view the document in a browser window. Check the appearance of your document in a browser window shortly after you start to copy text. It's the line breaks in the browser window that count; use them as your guide.

Testing Your Document in a Browser Window

You'll want to test the appearance of your newsletter in a browser window to determine how the Word tables adapt to HTML.

View the Page in a Browser Window

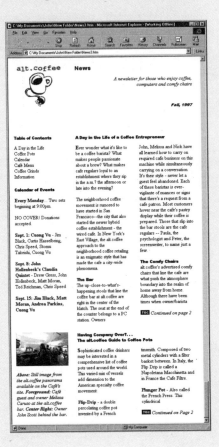

Choose Web Page Preview from the File menu. The page will be displayed in the Internet Explorer browser window.

Selecting a Custom Color For Headline Cells

Now that you have added body text to your newsletter, you can begin to add finishing touches to the page. You should start by adding dark brown to the background of the headline cells and white to the headline type so that the type is reversed.

Although Word has a command to add color to cell backgrounds, there is no dark brown shade. You will need to add custom color information to the HTML source in Word 97, and you will use Image Composer to help find the dark brown shade. For the best results, you'll want to select a browser-safe shade from Image Composer's 216 browser-safe colors. Browser-safe means the shade will look consistent in browsers on any platforms.

The Web color palette in Image Composer can help you select a browser-safe color. Although Image Composer displays colors numerically, you'll need a hexadecimal triplet to add to the HTML Table tags in the HTML source in Word. You can convert RGB color information to a hexadecimal triplet using Best Business Solution's Color Editor tool on the Web.

Select a Browser-Safe Color in Image Composer

1 Start Image Composer.

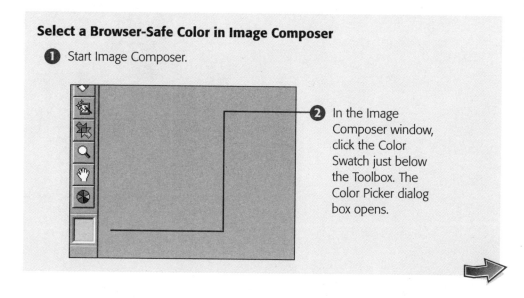

2 In the Image Composer window, click the Color Swatch just below the Toolbox. The Color Picker dialog box opens.

Public Relations links on the Web. The Public Relations Society of America maintains a Web site for the Capitol National Chapter in Washington, D.C. Go to www.prsa-ncc.org/pr-sites. html for links to local chapters, publication relations links, and the PRSA newsletter.

BPI Web publications. BPI, publisher of entertainment, advertising, marketing, media, art, design, and photography magazines, maintains a helpful online directory to the company's Web publications (www.billboard-online.com/mast.urls.htm).

Select a Browser-Safe Shade in Image Composer *(continued)*

3 On the Custom Palette tab of the Color Picker dialog box, select Web (Solid) from the Color Palette drop-down menu and then click a dark brown shade.

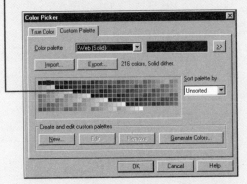

4 Click the True Color tab and note that the shade you have selected is displayed and the color's RGB numbers are displayed in the fields labeled Red, Green, and Blue.

5 Copy down the numbers you see displayed, and then click OK. In this example, a dark brown shade for the alt.coffee newsletter has these values:

Red	102
Green	0
Blue	0

Newspaper links. The Associated Press Managing Editors Association maintains a searchable online database of U.S. and Canadian editors whose newspapers are members of the Associated Press (www.apme.com).

Visiting the Web to Find a Hexadecimal Triplet

Best Business Solutions, in Houston, Texas, has an online tool you can use to convert RGB data to the hexadecimal triplet you'll need to add to Word's HTML.

Convert RGB Data to a Hexadecimal Value

❶ Visit www.bbsinc.com/bbs-cgi-bin/colorEditor.cgi. Make sure to type the capital letter "E" in "colorEditor.cgi"

❷ Scroll to the base of the online Color Editor and click the check box labeled Input RGB value (0-255).

> BlueViolet
> Brown
> CadetBlue
> CadetBlue1
>
> *Default*
>
> ☑ **Input RGB value (0-255)**
> R: 102 G: 0 B: 0
>
> *Default*
>
> Test it now

❸ Type the Red, Green, and Blue values you copied down from the Image Composer Color Picker dialog box into the fields labeled R, G, and B.

❹ Click the Test It Now button. The background color of the Color Editor Web page changes to the color you are testing.

❺ Look for the converted hexadecimal triplet information above the Color Editor table. It will be displayed in a <body> tag. In this example, the dark brown color is displayed as:

```
<body bgcolor="#660000">
```

Newsletter

Using the Web to locate newsroom contacts in major cities. Cities such as Denver, Boston, Baltimore, Dallas, Houston, Kansas City, Cincinnati, Fort Worth, Indianapolis, Knoxville, Cleveland, Detroit, Honolulu, and many others are considered major markets. Newspapers in these cities with online editions often list contacts such as city editor, assistant news editor, editorial page editor, and sports editor. Some newspapers even list the e-mail addresses of newsroom contacts.

Fort Lauderdale's Sun-Sentinel page at www.sunsentinel.com/SunServe/edit-dir.htm includes e-mail links to news editors, for example.

Convert RGB Data to a Hexadecimal Value *(continued)*

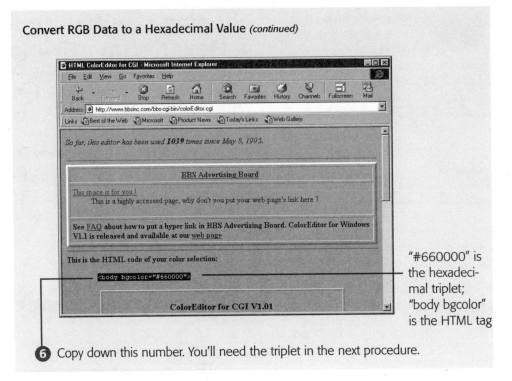

"#660000" is the hexadecimal triplet; "body bgcolor" is the HTML tag

6 Copy down this number. You'll need the triplet in the next procedure.

Editing the HTML in the Word Document

To add the dark brown to the background of the headline cell in the Word table and to make the text white, you'll need to edit the HTML in the Word document.

If you do not want to edit HTML, click inside a cell (on a page that has been saved as HTML), choose Cell Properties from the Table drop-down menu, and select a shade from the Background drop-down list in the Cell Properties dialog box.

Reverse type. White type on a black background is called reverse or knock-out type. The effect is dramatic because the eye is used to seeing dark type on a light background. As a result, many designers feel that reverse type should be limited to small amounts of copy.

View and Edit Your HTML

1 Choose HTML Source from the View menu. The HTML page view opens.

2 Look for the newsletter heading text in the HTML. In this example, it is the word "News."

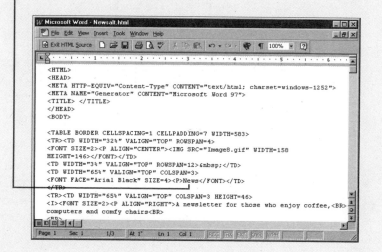

3 Follow the text to the left of the word "News" and look for COLSPAN=3. Click to insert the cursor between the 3 in COLSPAN=3 and the right angle bracket, add a space, and then type *BGCOLOR="660000"*

```
TOP" ROWSPAN=12> </TD>
"TOP" COLSPAN=3>
" SIZE=4><P>News</FONT></TD

IGN="TOP" COLSPAN=3 HEIGHT=
N="RIGHT">A newsletter for
```

```
TOP" ROWSPAN=12> </TD>
"TOP" COLSPAN=3 BGCOLOR="660000">
" SIZE=4><P>News</FONT></TD>

IGN="TOP" COLSPAN=3 HEIGHT=46>
N="RIGHT">A newsletter for those wh
```

Web marketing newsletter. Public relations specialist Ralph Wilson publishes a free Web marketing newsletter at www.wilsonweb.com.

View and Edit Your HTML *(continued)*

4 Click to insert the cursor to the left of the "N" in "News" and type:

<FONT COLOR="ffffff">

```
PAN=12> </TD>
SPAN=3 BGCOLOR="660000">
<P>News</FONT></TD>

 COLSPAN=3 HEIGHT=46>
>A newsletter for those w
```

```
PAN=12> </TD>
SPAN=3 BGCOLOR="660000">
<P><FONT COLOR="ffffff">News</FONT>

 COLSPAN=3 HEIGHT=46>
>A newsletter for those who enjoy co
```

5 Click to the right of the "s" in "News" and type: *</FONT>*

6 Click the Save button on the toolbar.

7 Click Exit The HTML Source. You will return to the newsletter page. The cell containing the heading banner type will be brown and the text will be white.

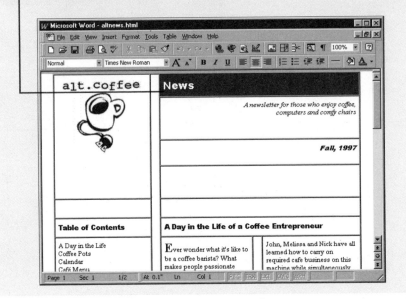

Directory of online magazines. The eZines magazine database contains a searchable directory of online magazines at www.dominis.com/Zines/query.shtml.

Viewing Your Page As a Thumbnail

Word's Print Preview command is useful for seeing a thumbnail of your page. The default page size is letter-sized.

Use Print Preview to See a Page Miniature

Choose Print Preview from the File menu. A miniature page view is displayed.

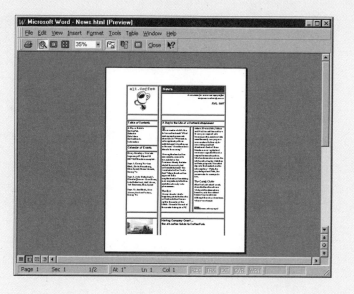

Completing and Testing Your Page

Continue to add color to cell backgrounds and to the text within cells. Although your changes will be displayed in the Word window, you will want to test your page in a browser window.

Previewing pages larger than letter size. If your page is larger than letter size, choose Page Setup from the File pull-down menu and choose Legal, A4, B4, or Custom from the Paper Size drop-down menu on the Page Setup dialog box. Enter page dimensions in inches in the fields labeled Width and Height if you selected Custom from the Paper Size drop-down menu.

Creating Additional Newsletter Pages

Use Word's Table tool to build a similar three-column grid for the other pages of your newsletter. You may want to view the completed newsletter at mspress.microsoft.com/mspress/products/1576.

Use the top cells as a page header containing the publication name and page number

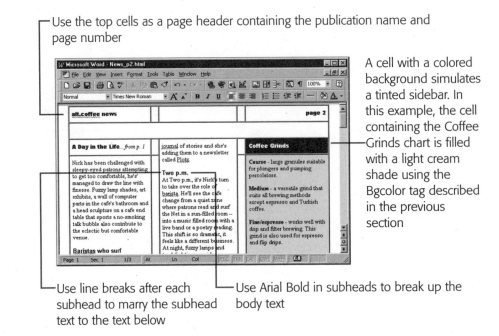

A cell with a colored background simulates a tinted sidebar. In this example, the cell containing the Coffee Grinds chart is filled with a light cream shade using the Bgcolor tag described in the previous section

Use line breaks after each subhead to marry the subhead text to the text below

Use Arial Bold in subheads to break up the body text

Adding Special Characters to Text

Word's Symbol and Special Character palettes will help you add non-keyboard characters to your text. Most of the characters in Word's Symbol palette are available in HTML except for special spaces and hyphens (en space, em space, optional hyphen, and a nonbreaking hyphen).

GRIT's live audio review show. GRIT (Gould Resources Internet Tele-communications), at www.grit.net, is an Internet audio Web review station broadcasting 24 hours a day, seven days a week via RealAudio and Microsoft NetShow. GRIT's live audio shows review Web sites relating to entertainment, music, sports, games, and politics. The site also maintains a directory of Web sites. Listings are free but they must be kept up-to-date.

This section demonstrates how to add a nonbreaking space to the words "New York." The nonbreaking space will prevent Word from breaking the line or the page between "New" and "York." Similar steps can be used to add any of the special characters from Word's Symbol and Special Character palettes. The table below shows examples of text that should stay together.

Word Pairs	
Word Pair	**Example**
Month and day of the month	A nonbreaking space between "June" and "21" in "June 21, 1997"
Number and street in an address	A nonbreaking space between "2400" and "Sheridan" in "2400 Sheridan Drive"
Proper names and company names in addresses	A nonbreaking space between "New" and "York" in New York
Numbers and units in anything measurable	A nonbreaking space between "page" and "80" in "page 80."

Add a Nonbreaking Space to "New York"

❶ Locate the words "New York," click the space between "New" and "York," and delete the existing space.

❷ Choose Symbols from the Insert menu.

❸ In the Symbols dialog box, click the Special Characters tab.

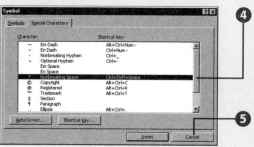

❹ Select Nonbreaking Space from the list of special characters and click Insert. A nonbreaking space will be added between "New" and "York."

❺ Click Cancel to close the dialog box.

Streaming sound on the Web. Since April 1995, more than 10 million RealAudio Players have been distributed. Thousands of RealAudio servers deliver over 45,000 hours of audio content per week. For more information, visit www. real.com.

State-of-the-art music hubs. Music industry Web sites are state of the art. Sony Music, Warner Brothers, Geffen/ DGC, Atlantic, and Capitol are examples of music hubs. Visit www.sony.com, www.music.warner.com, geffen.com, www.atlantic-records.com, and www. hollywoodandvine.com.

Adding Hyperlinks

Hyperlinks to bookmarks in a Word document provide page jumps to newsletter pages or to the newsletter table of contents. In HTML, bookmarks are called named locations.

Add a Bookmark to the Table of Contents Text

❶ Select the words "Table of Contents."

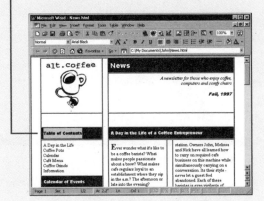

❷ Choose Bookmark from the Insert menu.

❸ Type *TOC* and click Close.

Add Bookmarks to Article Subheads

❶ Use the steps in the previous section to add bookmarks to your article subheads.

❷ Create bookmarks on the other pages of your newsletter if your articles jump to those pages.

News radio on the Web.
CNET Radio broadcasts news three times a day from www.news.com. Host Brian Cooley is the director of CNET Radio and can be reached at brianc@cnet.com.

Add Hyperlinks to Table of Contents Items or Jumps

1 Select an article title or page jump text.

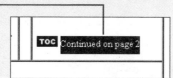

2 Choose Hyperlink from the Insert menu. The Insert Hyperlink dialog box appears.

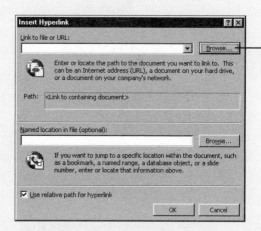

3 Click the Browse button to the right of the field labeled Link To File Or URL. The Link To File dialog box appears.

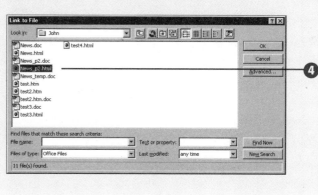

4 Locate the newsletter page that you want to be the destination of the link and click OK.

Newsletter

Free classifieds at Yahoo.
Online classifieds are free at Yahoo. For an overview of the classified service, visit classifieds.yahoo.com/info/overview.html.

Add Hyperlinks to Table of Contents Items or Jumps *(continued)*

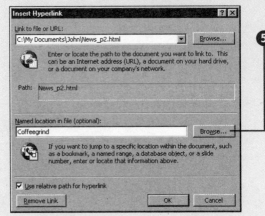

5 In the Insert Hyperlink dialog box, click the Browse button to the right of the field labeled Named Location In The File. The Bookmark dialog box appears.

6 Select the named location from the list of bookmarks and click OK. The hyperlink text will gain an underline indicating that it is a link.

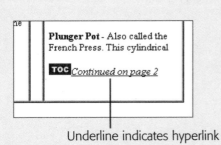

Underline indicates hyperlink

Listing your event at a Microsoft Sidewalk site.
List an event on any of the regional Microsoft Sidewalk sites by clicking the Submit Event button. Microsoft Sidewalk sites include:

Boston: www.boston.sidewalk.com
San Francisco: www.sanfrancisco. sidewalk.com
Seattle: www.seattle.sidewalk.com
Denver: www.denver.sidewalk.com
Sydney: www.sydney.sidewalk.com
Houston: www.houston.sidewalk.com
New York: www.newyork. sidewalk.com
Twin Cities: www.twincities. sidewalk.com

Add Hyperlinks to Table of Contents Button Graphics

1 Select a button graphic on the page that is designed to link to the table of contents.

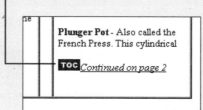

2 Follow the steps in the previous section to add a hyperlink to the button graphic.

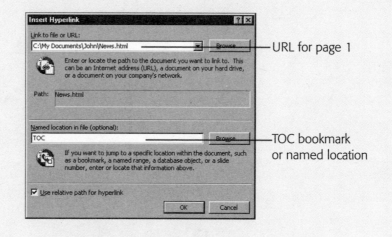

— URL for page 1

— TOC bookmark or named location

Turning Off the Table Border

After you've completed the pages of your newsletter, you will want to turn off the table border. Although borders provide grid lines during newsletter construction, table borders are distracting to readers and should be turned off. Set the table border value to zero in your HTML and the border will disappear.

Finding free real estate on the Web. Are you without a home on the Web? Sites that have become famous for providing free online real estate to Web netizens include:

Geocities: www.geocities.com

MarketNet: mkn.co.uk

NiteHawk: www.nitehawk.com

Phrantic: www.phrantic.com

Edit the HTML in Your Document to Turn Off the Table Border

1 Choose HTML Source from the View menu. The HTML page view appears.

2 Locate TABLE BORDER CELLSPACING=1

3 After the word "BORDER" add "=0" to set the border size to 0 (zero).

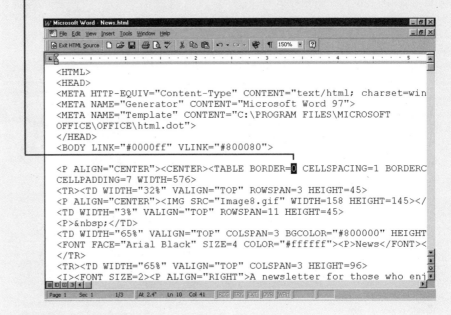

4 Save the file.

Cosponsoring a newsletter. If an online newsletter seems like too much of a commitment, consider collaborating with another company whose product or service complements your own.

Edit the HTML in Your Document to Turn Off the Table Border (continued)

5 Click the Exit HTML Source button on the Toolbar. The newsletter appears on the screen. The table border is no longer in view.

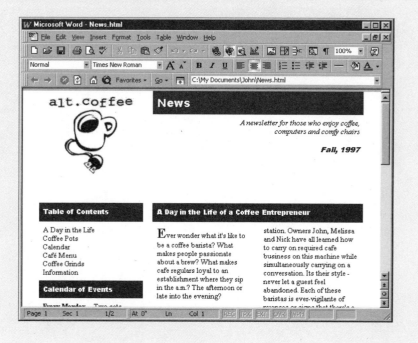

PART 4

Direct Marketing

A single-page
Starbase C3
satellite store-
front page

Larry Rosenthal of Cube
Productions sells Starship
Datakits in several locations
on the Internet. His
Microsoft and CyberCash
Wallet transactions are
handled by Sound Wire,
Inc., a CyberCash broker.

This storefront page can be
located anywhere. Thumbnails
of starships are arranged in a
catalog format. The coin
graphics below each spaceship
link to the Sound Wire server
and initiate a wallet transaction
and download of a Cube
Productions product to a
customer's system.

A Storefront
with a Catalog

O nline commerce has caught the attention of traditional retailers, catalogers, and a new category of businessperson called an online-only merchant. Online-only merchants might sell hard goods or digital products such as software, games, information, or artwork. They may use traditional payment systems such as MasterCard, Visa, and American Express, or newer micropayment technology developed for small-ticket items.

This chapter is a step-by-step introduction to online-only digital sales with micropayment technology. The Web page that you will build with Microsoft FrontPage and Microsoft Image Composer to sell digital products is called a storefront with a catalog. Because digital products are downloaded immediately when they are purchased, an order form is not required. A customer's name and address are not collected because there is no need to ship a product by conventional means. In fact, there are so few steps required that this chapter suggests that digital artists, musicians, animators, game programmers, 3-D designers, and writers can set up their own single-page storefronts.

The Starbase C3 Site

The Starbase C3 storefront page that is described in this chapter is a smaller, single-page version of the Cube Productions Web site created by Larry Rosenthal (www.cube3.com/starbase). Rosenthal is an entertainment designer and a 3-D

Complementary 3-D chat. Larry Rosenthal's Starbase C3 Web site is an example of how a 3-D chat environment can complement a retail storefront. Visitors buy inexpensive, digital space-ship parts, build their own ships, and use the ships as avatars in the VRML3D chat zone called the Flight Deck. Larry has used Blaxxun's VRML Community Platform 3.0 to create the 3-D chat area. This tool enables developers to create their own 3-D multiuser communities.

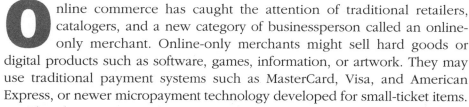

Microsoft Wallet add-on to Internet Explorer 4.0. Microsoft Wallet software is available as a Microsoft Internet Explorer 4.0 add-on and can be downloaded from the Microsoft Web site at www.microsoft.com. A version of the wallet software is also available for Netscape Navigator and will be shipped with future versions of Windows.

world builder who sells digital spaceship models through CyberCash and Microsoft Wallet payments.

Wallet software is a virtual debit card that customers fill with a check or traditional credit card. After money has been transferred into a wallet, the customer has purchasing power with thousands of wallet merchants who have recently set up storefronts on the Web.

Instead of setting up his own server to conduct transactions, Rosenthal worked with Sound Wire owner Joe Maissel (joe@soundwire.com), an electronic commerce specialist who brokers CyberCash transaction processing to other merchants. Because CyberCash recently provided their CyberCoin Payment Module for Microsoft's wallet software, Microsoft Wallet can be used to purchase goods from CyberCash merchants.

How Do Merchants Sell Digital Goods and Get Paid?

Maissel operates a commerce server and provides merchants with software that they can use to upload digital products to his server. Merchants maintain their own storefronts all over the Internet. On their sites, they place button links that initiate secure sales and downloads of digital product from Maissel's server. Each merchant who works with Maissel gets a merchant wallet. The dollar value inside a merchant's wallet increases each time a product is sold. Transactions are handled with no up-front cost to the merchant. When goods are sold, the merchant owes Maissel a percentage of the sale. As the wallet grows, merchants may transfer money into a checking account to pay Maissel.

Direct marketing over the Internet. Selling products and services directly to consumers or businesses is called direct marketing. Prior to the electronic commerce initiative on the Internet, direct marketing was accomplished through telephone sales, catalogs, business reply cards, and television.

Internet usage estimates by the year 2000. The growth rate of the Internet is enormous. Projections of household Internet usage by the year 2000 illustrate the potential for Internet commerce.

Country	Households with Internet Access
United States	36 million
Europe	20 million
Japan	12 million

The Storefront Page Layout

Rosenthal planned Starbase C3 graphics to fit within a screen that is 640 by 480. His layout is a simple, centered format that uses line breaks to separate the graphics.

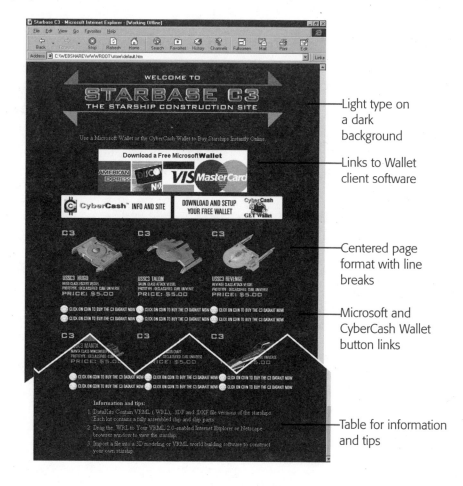

—Light type on a dark background

—Links to Wallet client software

—Centered page format with line breaks

—Microsoft and CyberCash Wallet button links

—Table for information and tips

Storefront with a Catalog

Moving sprites in Image Composer. Use the arrow keys on your keyboard to position sprites in Image Composer.

Cutting-edge customer service. The leading virus protection software manufacturers have devised unique customer service applications on the Web. McAfee and Symantec both provide new virus definitions and software updates on their Web sites. McAfee uses BackWeb Push technology to automatically download product updates to registered users.

Symantec's Live Update feature is similar, but the download doesn't happen automatically. You must remember to click a button that logs you on to the Symantec Web site. Both companies have a try-before-you-buy offer. McAfee's VirusScan Security Suite (VSS) is $49 and Norton AntiVirus is $69.95. (www. mcafee.com and www.symantec.com).

Creating the Storefront

You will start the Starbase C3 storefront project with an Image Composer project, assembling a Microsoft Wallet banner from separate credit card images. Image Composer's sprite technology allows you to import the credit card graphics separately and combine them into a horizontal banner graphic.

After the Microsoft Wallet banner is complete, you will start a new Web site in FrontPage 98 and create the single-page storefront using the graphics on the Starbase Web page.

Getting Organized

Before you start using FrontPage to create your own storefront, you'll need to:

> Obtain the link information that you'll add to the Microsoft and CyberCash coin links.

> Prepare images for the Web page in advance, using Image Composer or another image editor, and save the files in GIF or JPG format.

Designing a Microsoft Wallet Banner in Image Composer

In Image Composer, you will combine text and images to create a banner for the storefront page.

Coin wallet hyperlinks.
The two coin graphics beneath each Starship contain links to CGI programs on Maissel's server. One initiates a Microsoft Wallet transaction and the other initiates a CyberCash Wallet transaction.

Open a New Document

1 Start Image Composer. A workspace containing the Image Composer composition space is displayed.

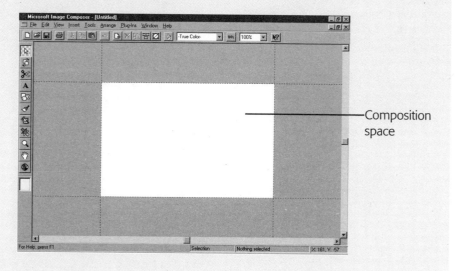

Composition space

2 From the Insert menu, choose From File.

3 Select Amex.bmp and click OK. This file and the other files you'll need for this chapter are available at this book's Web site: mspress.microsoft.com/mspress/products/1576.

Start an in-house corporate Web user group. Companies that have introduced employees to the Internet should consider starting an in-house user group. Hold meetings once a month at lunch time in a company conference room. Invite guest speakers, hold a question and answer session, and demonstrate software. An HTML newsletter and an intranet discussion mailing list both complement monthly user group meetings.

Open a New Document *(continued)*

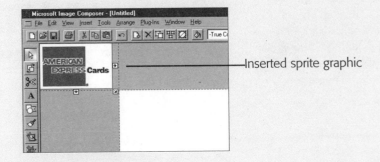

Inserted sprite graphic

④ Use the same technique to insert three other graphics files: Discover.bmp, Visa.bmp, and Master.bmp.

⑤ Move the sprites so that they are side by side.

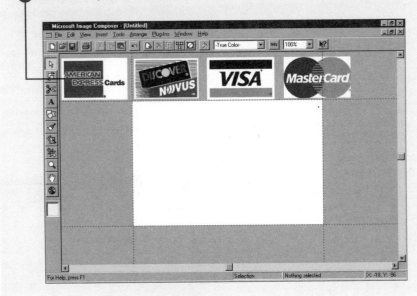

Have you considered starting an Internet mailing list? An Internet mailing list can make your company accessible to your customers. If you like the idea of exchanging e-mail with your customers and you're new to mailing lists, here are some definitions and resources:

Publisher: The person who maintains or manages the list.

Subscriber: The person who participates in the list.

Announce list: E-mail that travels one way from the publisher to subscribers.

Discussion list: E-mail posted by subscribers and sent to everyone on the list.

Liszt Directory: Catalog of 70,000 mailing lists organized by subject (www.liszt.com).

Mailing list host: Internet Service Provider that hosts a mailing list for a fee. To research which ISPs host mailing lists, visit Mecklermedia's resource guide called "The List" (www.thelist.internet.com).

MLM: Mailing List Manager software that handles subscriptions and distributions. The comp.mail.list-admin.software newsgroup is devoted to comparing features of the popular freeware programs for all server platforms.

Save the Document

1 From the File menu, choose Save As. The Save As dialog box appears.

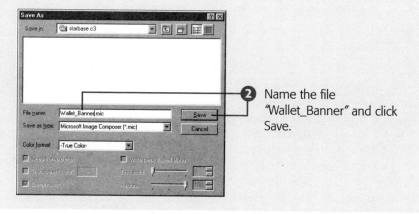

2 Name the file "Wallet_Banner" and click Save.

Resize the Composition Space

Reduce the size of the composition space to an area that is 400 pixels wide and 112 pixels tall.

1 Choose Composition Setup from the File menu and then change the Height and Width entries on the Composition Setup dialog box. Click OK.

Adding background sound to your FrontPage Web. Background sounds that play as a page is loaded in a browser can be an interesting addition to a Web page.

To add a background sound in FrontPage 98, choose Page Properties from the File menu in FrontPage 98. The Page Properties dialog box is displayed. On the General tab of the Page Properties dialog box, click the Browse button next to the Background Sound field and select a WAV, MIDI, AIF, or AU sound for your Web page. The Loop field beneath the Background Sound field allows you to specify the number of times the sound repeats.

Producing Text for the Microsoft Wallet Banner

The text you create for the Microsoft Wallet banner should describe the purpose of the banner, such as "Download a Free Microsoft Wallet."

Preselect Text Formatting and Add Text

1 Click the Text tool on the toolbox, and on the Text palette, choose 12 point, black, Arial text. Click OK.

2 Click the composition space. A text bounding box and a blinking insertion point appear.

3 Type *Download a Free Microsoft.*

4 Deselect the text bounding box by clicking the surrounding workspace.

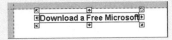

5 Reselect the Text tool and choose 12 point, black, Arial Black text on the Text palette.

6 Click inside the composition space. Another text bounding box and a blinking insertion point appears.

Managing junk e-mail with Microsoft Outlook Express. Microsoft Outlook Express' Inbox Assistant has a sort rule feature that allows you to create a filter to handle e-mail automatically when it arrives. If you're plagued by junk e-mail, create a new rule to automatically delete e-mail forwarded from spammers.

Collecting mail from all your Internet mail accounts. Outlook Express allows you to define multiple e-mail accounts in the same user profile.

Preselect Text Formatting and Add Text *(continued)*

7 Type *Wallet.*

8 Deselect the text bounding box by clicking the surrounding workspace. A set of selection handles appears.

9 Position this new text sprite to the right of the first text.

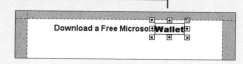

Center the Text Inside the Composition Space

1 Shift-click both text sprites so that they are selected.

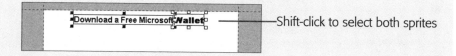

—Shift-click to select both sprites

2 Move the sprites together and center them on the composition space.

Sprite stacking order. If your credit card art stacking order is different from the order shown here, use the Bring To Front or Send To Back Commands on the Arrange menu to alter the stacking order of the individual graphics.

Position the Credit Card Sprites

Drag the credit card sprites into position below the text.

Save the Banner

❶ Choose Save For The Web from the File menu. The Save For The Web Wizard opens.

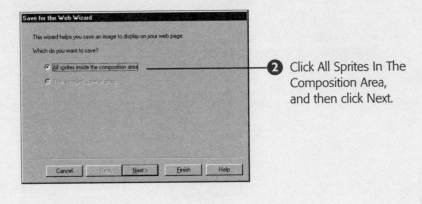

❷ Click All Sprites In The Composition Area, and then click Next.

Save the Banner *(continued)*

❸ Click Fill Them With The Background Color, and then click Next.

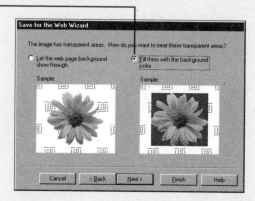

❹ Accept the default white color, and then click Next.

❺ Choose the image labeled JPEG (Best Quality), and then click Next.

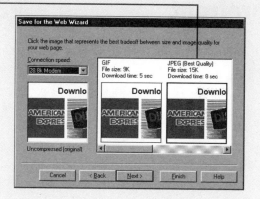

❻ Click Save.

Designing for WebTV.
There are now 150,000 subscribers surfing the Web via a TV, a set-top box, and a phone line. The newest addition to the WebTV product line is a WebTV Plus receiver. It's a $299 box that comes with a 1.1-GB hard drive, a 56K modem, and printer support. A WebTV account costs $19.95 per month and includes up to six individual e-mail accounts—ideal for families who don't own computers.

Realizing that Web via TV is a growing market, a number of entertainment firms are designing Web pages that are optimized for the WebTV interface. You can find design guidelines at www.webtv.net/primetime/preview/design/index.html.

Save the Banner *(continued)*

7 Open the folder in which you want to save the file and then click Save.

Creating the Storefront

When you start FrontPage, the Getting Started dialog box provides a variety of start-up Web sites. You will use the Empty Web because you are creating a single page.

Open a New Web Site

1 Start FrontPage.

2 Create a new, empty FrontPage Web and title it "Starbase."

Cable modems are a reality. Oceanic Cable, a subsidiary of Time Warner Cable, is the first cable operator to launch cable modem services using Microsoft's Commercial Internet System, a Microsoft Windows NT platform designed for ISPs. Using Motorola cable modems, the Oceanic service is available in Oahu, Hawaii.

Digital Equipment Corporation employees working from home in Massachusetts are also using cable modems to telecommute.

VRML animation vs. GIF animation. VRML animation files run longer and the files are often a fraction of the size of GIF animations.

Open a New Web Site *(continued)*

3 Click the New Page button on the FrontPage Explorer toolbar. A Home Page icon appears in the FrontPage Explorer window.

4 Rename the home page "Starbase C3."

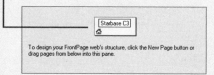

5 Double-click the Starbase C3 page. The FrontPage Editor window opens.

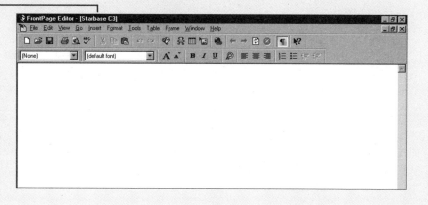

Storefront with a Catalog

Click here. Most people don't know that banner ads are clickable. Always include a call to action in your banner ad copy such as "Click Here."

Free customized news delivery to Outlook Express users. Infobeat, formerly Mercury Mail, has partnered with Microsoft to provide HTML versions of its news to Outlook Express users. Infobeat is a provider of customized e-mail news. For more information, visit www.infobeat.com.

Add the Starbase C3 Graphics

1 From the Insert menu, choose Image. The Image dialog box appears.

2 Click the Select A File On Your Computer button.

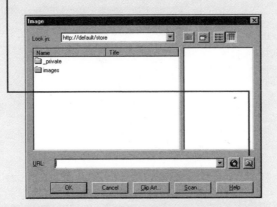

3 Double-click the file named Welcome.jpg. The graphic appears in the FrontPage Editor window.

Add the Starbase C3 Graphics *(continued)*

4 Click the Center button to center the graphic.

5 Click the Show/Hide ¶ button to show nonprinting characters.

6 Press the right arrow key on the keyboard to move the cursor to the right of the graphic.

7 Press Shift+Enter to add a line break after the graphic.

8 Add the files Biglogo.jpg and News.jpg. Add a line break after biglogo.jpg and press Enter after news.jpg.

Line break
Line break
News.jpg

Welcome.jpg   Biglogo.jpg

The Microsoft VRML 2.0 viewer. To add VRML 2.0 viewing capability to your Internet Explorer browser, you'll need to add it to your browser as a separate component. For detailed information about this and other multimedia component add-ons, visit www.microsoft.com/ie/ie40/download/addon.htm.

Add Text and Color the Text

1 With the blinking insertion point centered beneath the News.jpg graphic, type *Use a Microsoft Wallet or the CyberCash Wallet to Buy Starships Instantly Online.*

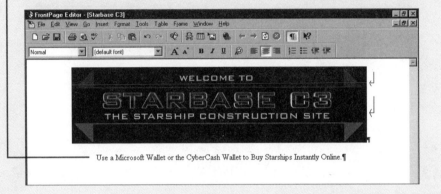

2 Select the text.

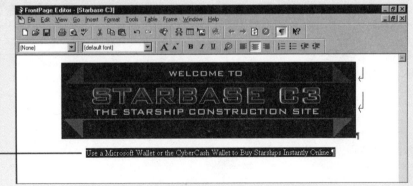

Geek Talk and tips. HotWired's Web Monkey Web site offers Web authoring tutorials, demonstrations, and an advice column called Geek Talk (www.webmonkey.com).

The digital camera market. Digital cameras have become popular with Web developers because there's no need to develop film. First introduced in 1996, digital cameras have become increasingly sophisticated while becoming less and less expensive. While most digital cameras fall into the point-and-shoot category, Olympus has recently introduced a line of digital cameras with features such as interchangeable lenses, manual exposure settings, and higher resolutions.

Add Text and Color the Text *(continued)*

3 Click the Text Color button on the FrontPage Editor toolbar.

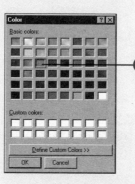

4 Click a green color, and then click OK. The text becomes green.

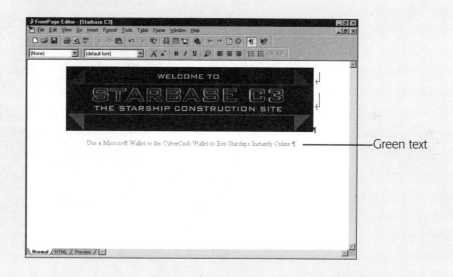

Green text

Storefront with a Catalog

Recruiting over the Internet. There are now more than 600 Internet sites dedicated to jobs and careers. Human resource managers are excited about the cost savings associated with recruiting on the Internet, which is particularly advantageous for recruiters looking for candidates with technical expertise. Although the Internet may not be a good resource for reaching non-technical people, the Web represents a global medium with an exceptionally wide reach.

Add the Remaining Starbase C3 Graphics

Repeat the previous steps to add the following Starbase C3 graphics:

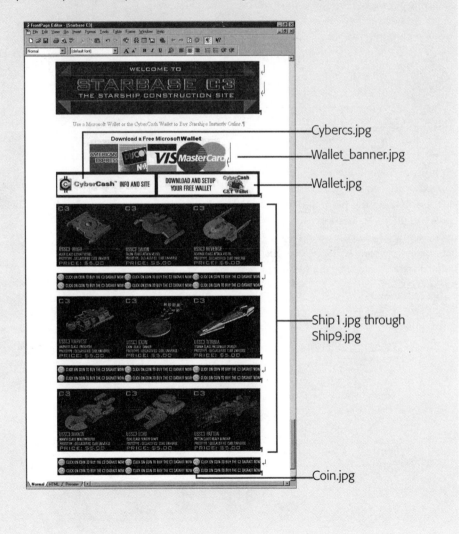

Cybercs.jpg

Wallet_banner.jpg

Wallet.jpg

Ship1.jpg through Ship9.jpg

Coin.jpg

Fare Tracker for Microsoft Expedia customers. Fare Tracker is a free airfare reporting service delivered via e-mail. Subscribers can specify up to three trips to track. Each week, a subscriber will receive an e-mail report showing the best fares for each trip. To subscribe to Fare Tracker:

➊ Visit Expedia at www.expedia. com.

➋ Click Travel Agent on the Expedia navigation bar.

➌ Register as a new user.

➍ Click Fare Tracker to enter trips to track.

Build a Table to Hold Information and Tips

➊ Click the Insert Table button on the toolbar and create a table with two columns and four rows.

➋ Click any cell in the table.

➌ Choose Select Table from the Table menu.

➍ Click the Center button on the FrontPage Editor toolbar to center the table.

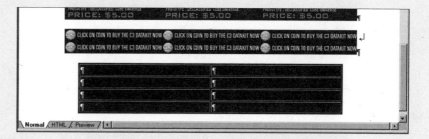

➎ Drag the border between the table columns to the left to make a narrow column and a wide column.

➏ Click the second cell in the first row and type *Information and Tips*.

Storefront with a Catalog

Microsoft's new real estate project. Microsoft's Boardwalk, due to launch in 1998, will introduce home buyers to sellers. The Boardwalk site will partner with multiple listing services throughout the country. The site is expected to complement Sidewalk, Microsoft's local city guide.

Back up your site. Corporate Web sites on the company's Web server are usually backed up by the Management Information Systems (MIS) department. The development site on your hard disk should be protected with a daily backup. Back up your site to another computer on your network or to removable media.

Build a Table to Hold Information and Tips *(continued)*

7 Tab to the first cell in the second row and type *1*.

8 Continue to tab from cell to cell and type the text shown here.

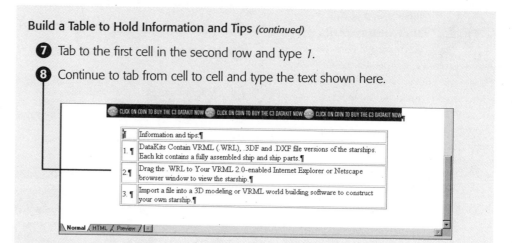

Align Table Text and Add Boldface to the Title

1 Select the text in column one.

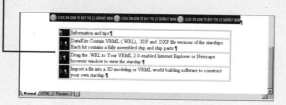

2 Choose Cell Properties from the Table menu.

Adding a vCard link to your contact Web page.

To save your customers the trouble of entering your contact data in an address book, provide them with a link on your contact Web page to a .vcf file. vCards and vCalendars are formats for exchanging personal data on the Internet in the form of electronic business card, and calendar/scheduling information. vCards can also be sent as e-mail attachments. For more information about vCards and vCalendars, visit the Internet Mail Consortium's Web site at www.imc.org/pdi. Also see the tip "How to Create a vCard (.vcf) file in Outlook Express" on the next page.

Download my vCard

Align Table Text and Add Boldface to the Title *(continued)*

3 Choose Right from the Horizontal Alignment drop-down list.

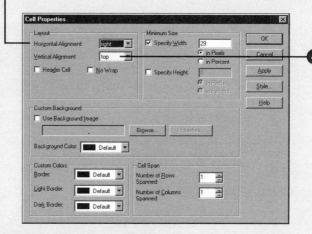

4 Choose Top from the Vertical Alignment drop-down list, and then click OK.

5 Select the text "Information and tips:"

6 Click the Bold button on the FrontPage Editor toolbar. The text will become bold.

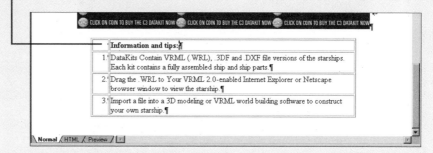

How to create a vCard file (.vcf) in Outlook Express. Creating a vCard file in Outlook Express is easy. Follow these steps:

❶ Create an entry for yourself in the Outlook Express address book.

❷ Select your name from the address book list and select Export/ Business Card from the File menu.

❸ Save the .vcf file on your hard disk.

To add a vCard to a mail message, select Business Card from the Insert menu.

To see a vCard in use, go to www.edventure.com/bios/jerry.html. Jerry Michalski, managing editor of Release 1.0, the monthly newsletter that explores the future of communications and computing technology, has a vCard link on the Release 1.0 Web site. When you view Michalski's biography Web page with Internet Explorer 4.0 and click the vCard link, the file is automatically downloaded and added to Outlook Express.

Remove the Table Border and Color the Text

❶ Choose Select Table from the Table menu.

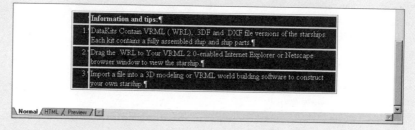

❷ Choose Table Properties from the Table menu.

❸ Type *0* in the Border Size field and click OK. The table border is now displayed as dotted lines, which do not show on a browser page.

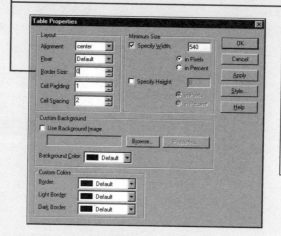

❹ Choose Select Table from the Table menu again.

❺ Color the table text green.

A glossary for your site.
If your site contains special terminology, make it user friendly by building a glossary page. Use the hyperlink-to-a-URL-and-bookmark technique described in Chapters 3 and 8.

Add a Background Color

① Choose Background from the Format menu.

② Choose Black from the Background drop-down menu, and then click OK. The background is displayed as black.

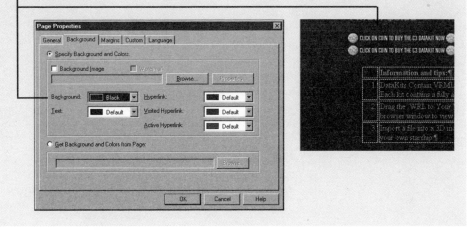

Save the Storefront Page

① From the File menu, choose Save. A Save As dialog box is displayed.

② Type *storefront.htm* to replace "default.htm" in the URL field and then click Save.

Storefront with a Catalog

Streaming audio and video. Streaming technology is an instant download for high-bandwidth multimedia formats such as sound and video. To speed up the development of streaming media, Microsoft, Vivo, Adobe, Intel, and RealNetworks have collaborated on an Active Streaming Format (ASF) specification. Formerly known as Progressive Networks, RealNetworks is a pioneer in the field of streaming software. Microsoft has upgraded its Netshow multimedia streaming software to support RealAudio and RealVideo content.

Save the Storefront Page *(continued)*

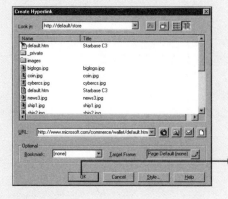

3 In the Save Embedded Files dialog box, click OK.

Add Links to Your Storefront Page

1 Click the Microsoft Wallet banner.

2 Choose Hyperlink from the Insert menu.

3 In the URL field, type *http://www.microsoft.com/commerce/wallet/default.htm.*

Search engine robots.
The title of your Web page is an important element that gets indexed by search engine robots. You may want to add your city name to your Web page title so that it will appear in search engine results.

Add Links to Your Storefront Page *(continued)*

4 Repeat these steps to add hyperlinks to the Starbase C3 graphics. Use the following diagram as a guide.

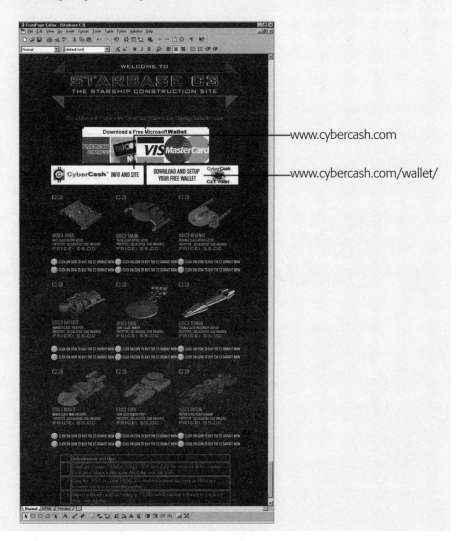

www.cybercash.com

www.cybercash.com/wallet/

Index

em spaces, 250
Empty Web, 6
en spaces, 250
Equilibrium Software, 144
Excite, 104, 120, 127
eZines magazine database, 249

Fact sheets, 28–57
  defined, 28
  layout of, 29
  page elements for, 29
FAQs, 171–223
  layout, 172
Fare Tracker, 279
Fast Company magazine, xiv
FCC, 22
feature articles, 87
File protocol, 189
  example, 189
  syntax, 189
File Transfer Protocol. *See* FTP
files
  AIF, 268
  AU, 268
  exchanging with clients, 204
  GIF, 18
  GIF vs. JPEG, 46
  Image Composer, 16
  importing Word documents into
    FrontPage, 64
  JPEG, 39, 47
  MIC, 16

MIDI, 268
  names for, 192
  saving, 16
  saving as, 125
  transferring to ISP, 7
  transferring with FTP, 33
  transparent GIF, 43
  uploading, 7
  WAV, 268
firewalls, 132
First Virtual, 232
flames, 88
FlashPix plug-in, 198, 199
Fleishman, Glenn, 70
FLITE lab, 212
Floyd, Michael, 87, 213
focus groups, 13
folders, 7
fontpacks, 38
Forer, Kathy, 3
form fields
  drop-down menus, 173
  radio buttons, 173
  text boxes, 173
format marks, 67
forms, 197
  appearance in browsers, 202
  creating drop-down menus in, 203
  custom form handlers, 173
  previewing, 209
  publishing, 210
  questionnaires, 216
  registration, 197

  reset button on, 208
  routing data from, 197
  saving, 209
  submit button on, 206
  testing, 210
  text boxes, 200
Forrester Research, 231
frames, 118. *See also* frameset documents
  adding tables to, 180
  adding text to, 180
  background color of, 178
  defined, 123
  deleting, 177
  inserting images into, 179
  moving documents to a server, 212
  naming, 188
  setting up, 174
  starting a new frames page, 177
Frames palette, 144
  illustrated, 142
frameset documents, 123, 124, 127,
    172, 189, 193
  defined, 117
  publishing, 133
  testing, 130
  titling, 172
free artwork, 42
free classifieds, 254
free e-mail, 214
free Web server space, 256
Freelinks, 113
Frequently Asked Questions. *See* FAQs
fringing, 43

Junod, John A., 89, 130
Jupiter Communications, 231

Kaleidoscope effects, 23
kerning, 37
keyword tag, 118
Kinko's copy centers, 32
knock-out type, 247
Kodak, 102

LAN, 230
last-modified date, 60
Leftmargin tag attribute, 20
Levinson, Jay Conrad, 81
lifestyle marketing, 105
Ligos Software, 5
line breaks, 36, 48, 67, 242, 263
line length, 31
Link To File dialog box, 48
LinkExchange Advertising Network, 114
links, xii, 254. *See also* hyperlinks
    absolute vs. relative, 49
    adding, 10
    adding in Word, 47
    adding to buttons, 24
    assigning colors to, 195
    button, 14
    checking for broken, 17
    clicked, 12
    external, 17

FTP, 33
    in navigation bars, 217
    internal, 17
    Mailto, 50
    storefront, 284
    testing, 3
    testing in FrontPage, 12
    text, 19
    verifying, 17
lists
    adding, 54
    bulleted, 55
    formatting, 54, 70
Liszt Directory, 267
live audio, 251
Live Picture, 102, 180, 198
LMDS. *See* local multipoint distribution
    systems
local area network, 230
local computers, 33
local multipoint distribution systems, 22
logical size, 141, 142
logos, 32
looping, 162
lossless compression, 46
lossy compression, 46
Lycos, 104, 120
Lynx, 54, 208
LZW compression, 46

Macy's, 107

mailing list hosts, 267
Mailing List Manager, 267
Mailto, 181, 197, 207, 219
    examples, 187
    syntax, 187
Mailto links, 50
Maissel, Joe, 262
Mallis, Jan, 175
Management Information Systems, 280
Marino, Paul, 3
Market Focus 3, 109
marketing
    adapting tools to the Web, xiii
    campaigns, xiii
    defined, xi
MarketNet, 256
Marquees, 130
Master Categories list, 106
MasterCard, 261
Matt's Script Archive, 197
McAfee VirusScan Security Suite, 264
Mecklermedia, 193, 194
media, xi
Mercedes-USA, 4
merchant wallet, 262
Mercury Mail, 274
Meta tags, 21, 120, 125, 195, 196
    defined, 21, 118
    description tag, 118
    inserting, 126
    keyword tag, 118
MetaPlay, 171

Radio buttons, 216
Raspberry Hill, 60
RealAudio, 252
RealSpace, 102
RealVideo, 284
recruiting over the Internet, 278
Red Herring, 153
Reduce Bit Depth command, 144
registration forms, 171. *See also* forms
  layout, 173
Release 1.0, 282
remote computers, 33
renting computers, 32
replacing text, 80
repurposing sales materials, 40
Reset button, configuring, 208
Resizable In Browser, 188
reverse type, 247
revision cycles, 16
RGB, 243
Rhizome Internet L.L.C., 203
robots, 117, 124, 133, 285
  blocking, 131
Rosenthal, Larry, 260
round-ups, 87
Rubin, Charles, 81
Rules Wizard dialog box, 99

Sans serif, 225
Save As, 9
Save As dialog box, 18

Save As HTML command, 45
Save Embedded Files dialog box, 24, 189
Save For The Web command, 14, 270
Save For The Web Wizard, 39
Save HTML Document dialog box, 90
Scott, John, 225
Search Engine Watch newsletter, 122
search engines, 21, 116–35, 285
  attracting spiders, 118
  listed, 120
  submitting URLs to, 21
  URL submission forms at, 118
searching. *See* search engines
Sears, 107
Select File dialog box, 23
selection handles, 17
Seller, Don, 120
Send To Back command, 270
serif, 225
Set Position dialog box, 159
Shamson, Alex, 117, 127
shared borders
  and Includes, 77
  defined, 19
  enabling, 20
Shared Borders command, 19
Shockwave animations, 203
Sidewalk, 240, 280
signage, 4
signatures, 98, 226
  adding to e-mail, 98
  creating, 98

  multiple, 98
silhouettes, 43
Silicon Graphics, 218
Simprov, 171
site maps, 3
  illustrated, 5
  importance of, 78
  sketching, 3, 4
Snap Online, 240
soft returns, 48
Softbank Interactive Marketing, 137
Songline Studios, 156
Sony Music, 61, 252
Sound Wire, Inc., 83, 260
spamming, 77
spanners, 218
special characters, 250
spelling, 16
spiders, 117, 125
splash screens, 20, 24, 123
sprites, 32
  aligning, 17
  arranging, 17
  changing the color of, 17
  combining, 4
  defined, 4
  flattening, 16
  moving, 17, 264
  stacking order of, 270
  text, 34
Standard Rate and Data Services, 97
Starbase C3, 28, 53, 260

Window Size command, 13

Wired magazine, 120

word division rules, 56

workspace, 14, 265

World Intellectual Property Organization, 233

World Productions, Inc., 34

World Wide Web Global Information Initiative, 181

WorldChart, xii

WS_FTP Pro, 89, 119, 204, 210

Yahoo, 104, 120, 130, 131, 138, 221, 240

  free classifieds at, 254

Yukon, 120

Zapa Digital

  Microsite, 141

  Site Locator, 141

Mary Jo Fahey

Mary Jo Fahey began her microcomputer career in 1980 selling game software, Microsoft Basic, and Microsoft Word at The Computer Center in midtown Manhattan. After retail computer sales positions at The Computer Store, Future Data, and the IBM Product Center stores, Mary Jo worked as a technical writer and trainer with ComputerKnowledge, a training organization hired to teach classes in the IBM Product Centers nationwide. After providing PC education to over 4,000 people, Mary Jo joined the Information Systems Planning department at Time Inc.

In 1986, Mary Jo formed the Desktop Communications Group, a consortium of independent graphic designers and computer specialists interested in desktop publishing. From 1990 to 1994, Mary Jo provided training and production assistance to graphic designers and art directors at book publishers, advertising agencies, magazine publishers, and graphic design firms.

Mary Jo began teaching computer graphics classes at Pratt Manhattan's School of Professional Studies in 1990 and recently joined the faculty at Cooper Union's Forum Continuing Education Division. She currently teaches at Noble Desktop Publishing, PC Learn, and Open Interactive Media and is the public relations and event planner for the NYVRML Special Interest Group. Her other books include *Web Publisher's Design Guide*, Second Edition, The Coriolis Group, 1995 and 1997, *Web Publisher's 3D and Animation Design Guide,* The Coriolis Group, 1996, and *Macintosh Visiref*, System 7.5 Edition, Que Corporation, 1994. Her articles have appeared in *PC Computing, HomePC, HOW, Marketing Tools, Marketing News,* and Portugal's *@Net* magazines. Mary Jo can be reached at mjfahey@interport.net.

The manuscript for this book was prepared and submitted to Microsoft Press in electronic form. Text files were processed and formatted using Microsoft Word.

Cover Designer and Illustrator   Thomas Draper
Interior Graphic Designer   Kim Eggleston
Compositor   Steve Sagman
Proofreader   Eric Weinberger
Indexer   Audrey Marr

Text composed by Studioserv (www.studioserv.com) in ITC Garamond with display type in Formata. Pages prepared in Adobe PageMaker 6.5 were delivered to the printer as electronic prepress files.

When you have *questions about* Microsoft FrontPage 98,

here's the answer book.

One-Stop Reference

Covers Microsoft FrontPage 98 for Windows 95 and Windows NT 4.0

CD-ROM Included

SELECT EDITION

In-Depth Reference and Inside Tips from the Software Experts

Running Microsoft **FrontPage** 98

Jim Buyens

Microsoft Press

U.S.A.	**$39.99**
U.K.	£37.49 [V.A.T. included]
Canada	$55.99
ISBN	1-57231-645-4

It's packed with everything from quick, clear instructions for new users to comprehensive answers for power users. And it's complete in one volume. With RUNNING MICROSOFT® FRONTPAGE® 98, you'll learn to:

- Create your own Web pages and sites the easy way—unique tools such as FrontPage components make it simple even for beginners.

- Start fast with simple pages and quickly move up to building full-fledged sites.

- Use Microsoft FrontPage 98 to streamline and automate site management chores—especially helpful if you're a Webmaster.

- Spare yourself the usual Web server problems—this is the one book that covers crucial server connection issues.

RUNNING MICROSOFT FRONTPAGE 98 makes information easy to find and understand. The enclosed CD is full of must-have extras, including a searchable version of the book on disc. Get RUNNING MICROSOFT FRONTPAGE 98. And get the authoritative handbook you'll keep by your computer and use every day.

Microsoft Press